Negotiation Essentials *for* Lawyers

Negotiation Essentials *for* Lawyers

EDITORS
ANDREA KUPFER SCHNEIDER
& CHRIS HONEYMAN

AMERICAN BAR ASSOCIATION
Dispute Resolution Section

Printed in the United States of America.

23 22 21 20   5 4 3 2

Library of Congress Cataloging-in-Publication

Names: Schneider, Andrea Kupfer, editor. | Honeyman, Chris, editor.
Title: Negotiation essentials for lawyers / Andrea Kupfer Schneider, Chris Honeyman, Editors.
Description: Chicago : American Bar Association, 2019. | Includes bibliographical references and index.
Identifiers: LCCN 2019019813 (print) | LCCN 2019020205 (ebook) | ISBN 9781641054812 (ebook) | ISBN 9781641054805 (hardcover : alk. paper)
Subjects: LCSH: Dispute resolution (Law)—United States. | Negotiation—United States. | Practice of law—United States. | Attorney and client—United States.
Classification: LCC KF9084 (ebook) | LCC KF9084.N443 2019 (print) | DDC 347.73/9–dc23
LC record available at https://lccn.loc.gov/2019019813

Discounts are available for books ordered in bulk. Special consideration is given to state bars, CLE programs, and other bar-related organizations. Inquire at Book Publishing, ABA Publishing, American Bar Association, 321 N. Clark Street, Chicago, Illinois 60654-7598.

www.shopABA.org

Contents

Acknowledgments

As we write this on Thanksgiving weekend, 2018, we are grateful for the opportunity to write a preface to another book project from the two of us—this is our third book as a team, and the second in two years—and the next step (we won't say culmination) in a learning journey that began about fifteen years ago, when we started to collaborate around the idea of a canon of negotiation.

We have so many people to thank along the way—first and foremost, our authors, who are willing to work on yet another adventure in writing. We are grateful especially for their willingness and enthusiasm to engage with our readers under some very serious space and structural constraints. We are grateful for Andrea's research assistants Rowan Easter, Taylor Hansen, Morgan Henson, Conor McElligot, Dominic Rosso, and Margaret Spring, and her fabulous assistant Carrie Kratochvil, in bringing this project to fruition.

We are thankful that the American Bar Association (ABA) is interested in this book. We particularly thank Gina Brown, Rebecca Price, and Sarah Craig for their enthusiasm and efficiency in shepherding the book from manuscript submission to actual publication in record time, and Sylvia Rebert for her expert and timely copy-editing.

We are also grateful for the underlying work of the publisher of *The Negotiator's Desk Reference (NDR),* DRI Press—and particularly, Sharon Press, Kitty Atkins, and Debra Berghoff, whose terrific work on the *NDR* and whose cooperation with the ABA helped us turn quickly to putting this next project together, and made it easy for both us and our authors to move efficiently.

And we are grateful for each other—for our teamwork and mutual tolerance, for our continued commitment to this field, and for our joint belief that conflict resolution, negotiation skills, and peace-building are increasingly needed in this world. Finally, we are grateful for you, our readers, whose openness and desire to keep learning motivate us to bring the latest and most innovative thinking in negotiation to this audience.

With thanks to all,

Andrea and Chris
November 2018

Part I

Working with Individuals

Section I

Introduction

1

Introduction

Andrea Kupfer Schneider[1] *and Chris Honeyman*[2]

This book has one very specific purpose: to take everything we have learned about negotiation, select only the parts that matter most to attorneys, and then make them as fast and easy as possible for very time-constrained legal practitioners to *apply*.

Simple enough, on the surface. Yet, simplicity was not easy to achieve.

This is our third book on negotiation together, and the second book in two years. We have tried to think clearly about what each project provides for the field. More than fifteen years ago, the idea of

1. **Andrea Kupfer Schneider** is a Professor of Law at Marquette University Law School, where she teaches dispute resolution, negotiation, ethics, and international conflict resolution and is the director of Marquette's nationally ranked dispute resolution program. Andrea has written numerous books, book chapters, and articles on negotiation skills and styles, dispute system design, international conflict, and gender and negotiation. She was given the American Bar Association (ABA) Section of Dispute Resolution Award for Outstanding Scholarly Work for 2017. Andrea received her A.B. *cum laude* from the Woodrow Wilson School of Public & International Affairs at Princeton University and her J.D. *cum laude* from Harvard Law School.
2. **Chris Honeyman** is managing partner of Convenor Conflict Management, a consulting firm based in Washington, DC. He is co-editor of *The Negotiator's Desk Reference* and six other books, and author of more than 100 published articles, book chapters, and monographs. Chris has directed a 30-year series of research and development programs about conflict management (see www.convenor.com/projects). Chris also has served as a consultant to numerous academic and practical conflict resolution programs, held a variety of advisory roles with the ABA, International Mediation Institute (IMI) and other organizations, and served as a mediator and arbitrator and in other neutral capacities in more than 2,000 disputes.

a *canon of negotiation* first intrigued us: What did *everyone* teach about negotiation, in and outside of law school, and why? What did only *some* people teach, based on their field or research area? What did virtually *no one* teach about negotiation, even though it is obviously important? And could it be that the information had not yet been translated into language suited for practitioners?

Our canon of negotiation initiative started with a conference. Based on that, we first organized (and wrote some of) 26 law review articles. We followed this with 80 book chapters in *The Negotiator's Fieldbook*; later, 101 chapters in *The Negotiator's Desk Reference* at the end of 2017, and now, 53 chapters in this book. We have tried to find the best knowledge, theory, and practice out there and to bring it home in ways that the most people possible will find usable.

In our first book in this long-term project, *The Negotiator's Fieldbook* (American Bar Association, 2006), we wrote:

> This book is a working tool that can help you figure out quickly what went wrong in yesterday's meetings, and how to fix it in tomorrow's follow-up. And if you see your needs primarily in those terms, you will be in good company. The wisest and most experienced of negotiators will often admit that at certain critical moments, they simply do not know what to do.

This remains our overarching goal: to be helpful immediately and clearly. Our two earlier books took the view that we can be most helpful by really addressing the complexities and by showing how apparently unrelated things often fit together. That way, those who really need to know things that aren't normally part of their field can find them out, and fast.

Still, we must admit that not everybody needs *everything*. We often are reminded by practicing lawyers and by businesspeople, in particular, that a book of 800 or 1,500 pages might be highly relevant to their needs, but it still might go unread. Even after we and our contributors worked hard to boil down years or decades of study of key negotiation problems into a few thousand words per topic, we have often enough heard the cry, "Just tell me what to *do* in this situation!"

We have long known that our petitioners are not unreasonable in this request. More than twenty years ago, one of us even organized a national project to that end. A direct line can be drawn from the Theory to Practice project (described at www.convenor.com) to this book. This new book is all about making negotiation *work for lawyers*. Every chapter is highly structured to focus on the most *practical* advice you can act on tomorrow.

Each chapter in this book starts with a brief introduction, immediately followed by a standard section, *Why This Concept Might Change Your Thinking*. There, the author explains succinctly why their body of work might be useful specifically *for lawyers*. After that, each chapter has a section called *Action Plan—What You Can Do Differently Tomorrow*. There, each author outlines specific steps a lawyer can take in their next negotiation. This advice is as varied as the topics in the book: the advice might be about a particular piece of preparation, what to say at the table, how to counsel a client, or how to close the deal. But in all cases, we hope you will find the action plan clear, usable, and practical.

Of course, the effort to understand a complicated problem in short order runs a risk of applying a supposed lesson where it *shouldn't* be applied. Our authors have considered this, too. Many authors include a section in their chapters called *Modifiers, Caveats, and No-Go Areas—When This Advice Just Won't Apply*. And then, the chapter wraps up.

In each chapter, we also include a closing section written by the editors designed to show how topics in this book fit together and to provide some hints about what you might want to look at next. We hope that with this consistent chapter organization, you can easily zero in on just what you need.

And note that, in mandating this tight focus for our authors, we firmly declined all requests to include references and supporting explanations in the chapter text. The chapters in this book have only one citation each—on purpose. The chapter's citation is to the contributor's longer chapter in *The Negotiator's Desk Reference*—which in turn contains full citations and references.

If you wonder *why* a contributor gives you a particular piece of practical advice, you will find the answer to that question in *The*

Negotiator's Desk Reference. We have included the full references for each chapter in the public, free version of that chapter at www.ndrweb.com

Our intent is to show a variety of perspectives from different disciplines and forms of practice, among different cultures, and even within the same Western culture, as each author grapples with his or her best advice. This approach is based on the full version of *The Negotiator's Desk Reference.* As we noted in our introduction there:

> Some chapters here are based on empirical research that is truly cutting-edge. Many chapters are based on their authors' far more detailed works or even complete books, and we greatly appreciate their willingness to edit their thoughts into brief pieces. Other chapters are based primarily in stories from the real world. It is our objective to interrelate such practitioners' hard-won wisdom with other chapters, containing scholars' related research and theoretical insights, so that the *next* practitioner to encounter a similar problem has more to go on.

Now, we briefly describe each section of the book.

Part I: Working with Individuals

Section I: Introduction

Section I starts with this introduction and continues with *Learning from Your Negotiations*, an introductory reading that is designed to help readers absorb and implement all the other readings in this book.

Section II: All About You

Section II discusses negotiation style choices, some individual characteristics that might make a difference in negotiations, and understanding your own thinking. Chapter 3 is a thorough analysis of the ways someone's style of negotiation might not mesh with the same person's style of handling conflict—often because of failure to think through the differences between good practices, tactics, and tricks. Chapter 4 demonstrates how hard bargaining really works, in no fewer than 28 varieties.

Chapters 5 and 6 focus on race and gender. Both chapters note how personal differences might play out in negotiations. The chapters also discuss what to do if you want to consider the structural and organizational biases that might perpetuate inequity as a result of negotiations. Chapter 7 is about social intuition—a quality that helps you be aware of yourself, read your counterpart, and attune yourself, so you have the best chance of getting through to your counterpart. We end with Chapter 8, a neuroscience-based explanation of how human beings evolved to be interdependent.

Section III: Making Your Case

Section III is about ensuring that however farsighted and generous you choose to be in a negotiation, your own needs are still met. The section begins with Chapter 9, which is about setting goals—or how to ensure that your aspirations are both high *and* attainable. Chapter 10 discusses six factors that influence whether you will get your way or not (all other things being equal), and then Chapter 11 is on how to distinguish between and work with two kinds of audiences that are responsive to completely different psychological approaches.

We turn next to Chapter 12, which boils down a bestseller into a brief treatment of how each party is likely to formulate (and believe) a completely different story of what is going on. Chapter 13 explains why and how the best salespeople listen far more than they talk—and what questions they ask when they do talk.

But when the story your negotiation counterparts are telling themselves is one that you must challenge, the moves and turns the discussion takes are likely to determine whether you get anywhere in your negotiations—and that is the final subject of this section, in Chapter 14.

Section IV: Strategies of Communication

Section IV addresses the postmodern era of communication and the challenges of listening well. Chapter 15 surveys the confusing panoply of communication options now available and outlines a way to use them more tactically. In Chapter 16, we move to what has probably become the baseline method of ordinary, day-to-day communication, particularly for components of a negotiation that has yet to be framed in complete documents—e-mail.

Two very different groups have specific needs and uses for technology in their negotiations: lawyers and the young. Chapter 17 analyzes lawyers' needs and how technology is changing their practice.

Chapter 18 focuses on the youngest adult generation—such avid users of technology that it is barely possible to pull their attention from it.

Chapters 19 to 21 focus on more than talking. In Chapter 19, the author argues that listening can be used in a disciplined way to avoid either cooperating or competing too much. Chapter 20 demonstrates some key findings from clinical psychology: it focuses on actually *understanding* what you hear, to make you more persuasive.

Yet, listening is not everything. Chapter 21 analyzes nonverbal communication as a whole, it demonstrates how many different forms it can take, and it shows how you can employ nonverbal communication consciously.

Section V: Working with Them

Section V addresses a multitude of concepts around relationships with your negotiation counterpart. Chapter 22 begins with a brief account of how trust and distrust work, and moves on to an analysis of how trust, after it is broken, can be repaired. This, however, is not always possible, and Chapter 23 is a trenchant analysis of what you can do in an environment where trust is impossible.

Trust, of course, is related to reputation. How a reputation is formed and why a trustworthy reputation is important, in far more settings than is commonly believed, are the subjects of Chapter 24. Closely linked to reputation, in turn, is the negotiator's ethical behavior. Chapter 25 moves to an analysis that shows how morals, rules, and law might all treat the same situation, but in vastly different ways. Understanding how they differ can give you a better sense of how your counterpart thinks. This discussion is followed by Chapter 26, which is about how fairness is perceived, particularly with an eye to fair processes and outcomes. Naturally, human beings being what they are, the effort to maintain a good reputation is sometimes going to involve making an apology, which is the subject of Chapter 27. And perhaps, if the apology is effective, forgiveness and reconciliation will follow, as they do in our book, in Chapter 28.

Part II: Complications, Groups, and Firms

Part II of *Negotiation Essentials for Lawyers* is for when things get complicated. Working with groups, firms, different cultures, and more inevitably adds complexity even beyond the challenges of working with individuals, which were the focus of Part I.

Section VI: Complexity and Culture

Section VI starts off Part II by diving straight in to more complicated situations. Chapter 29 addresses whether mental illness might be affecting someone at the bargaining table. The authors lay out information about the surprising frequency of mental illness in our society and the varied ways that we might need to respond to it in a negotiation.

Then, we turn to a triad of chapters about cultural differences, starting with Chapter 30 on how negotiating style integrates with culture—except for when it doesn't. Chapter 31 analyzes how Westerners tend to misread Chinese culture when they negotiate there—and "there," of course, includes the Chinese communities in many American cities. Chapter 32 assesses the often-unfortunate experiences of western or northern negotiators and mediators when they have taken their (implicit, and often unrecognized) cultural codes with them. . . . to an *extremely* different culture.

Chapter 33 combines a classic analysis, of how even a major negotiation in an international setting has some predictable stages in a somewhat predictable process, with an equally classic discussion of timing and ripeness.

Section VII: Context and Other Constraints

Section VII addresses some deliberately varied contexts, each of which poses particular limitations. Chapter 34 describes the common situation in which you, as an individual, must face off with a huge organization that has boiled down all its negotiation moves to a script. (When you read this chapter, you might find that you have more leverage than you think.) This is followed by Chapter 35, which discusses another common setting, arbitration, in which only one side suffers the major constraints—and unless you happen to be a major corporation, this means *you*. In turn, Chapter 36 discusses a very common setting in which the constraints are major for both sides: plea-bargaining.

Some readers might be surprised when we assert that they can also learn negotiation lessons from some seemingly unrelated—not to mention, dangerous—contexts: hostage negotiation and martial arts. Yet, we have three chapters (Chapters 37 to 39) that demonstrate how lessons from hostage negotiation and martial arts really can be adapted into a lawyer's more typical negotiation settings.

Section VIII: Working with Your Client

Working with your client often might be the most challenging part of any negotiation—and four chapters in Section VIII address that particular challenge.

Chapter 40 focuses on how to use psychology to address ethical challenges with your client specifically, and inside their organization. This is followed by Chapter 41, a trenchant analysis of agents' frequent failure to ensure that their clients have given informed consent to the agent's actions. Then in Chapter 42, we turn to the challenge of herding cats—or when your client has a "tribe" behind them that might upend any decision they make. And finally, in Chapter 43, we address the unique circumstances of using an interpreter in negotiations: An interpreter is neither a true neutral nor a client—and he or she needs to be *managed.*

Section IX: Groups and Third Parties

Section IX expands the number of people we must consider as part of the negotiation. Chapter 44 addresses how organizations can improve their overall negotiation performance by managing it strategically, with consistent training, incentives, communication, and support. Chapter 45 analyzes the larger, systematic context in which a negotiation takes place, and shows why lawyers must remain alert to the potential for systemic injustice to be perpetuated by their actions. Chapters 46 and 47 focus on mediation: A general overview of mediation's uses is followed by a chapter analyzing why one mediator is frequently so different from another, and what you might need to watch out for. Mediators, however, are not the only outside people who might become useful in a difficult conflict. Chapter 48 analyzes a whole series of non-neutral (and yet, not classically "agent") roles, under the general heading of *allies* who might be usefully invoked by a party.

Section X: Getting It Done

The final section of the book addresses the strategies that we need to close that deal. Chapter 49 is about ambiguity and how a bit of ambiguity just might be the grease that gets the deal done. Or, one could think about how, for any resolution to be possible, many disputes and other negotiations require a lawyer to adopt more than one kind of role. Chapter 50 explains the dual role of Doberman/Diplomat.

But sometimes, what a situation needs is somebody who will really shake things up. Chapter 51 assesses the possibility that an activist might not (always) create conflict, and instead might sometimes be essential in resolving it. Of course, if the matter is to be truly *resolved*, you'll want the agreement to hold. So, Chapter 52 addresses how to make sure that when you and your counterparts finally do "sign on the dotted line," the results stick.

Finally, we close with Chapter 53, which gives examples of how dispute *prevention* can work—and maybe even reduce the need for many of the strategies discussed in the book—when lawyers actually think about all of this in advance!

Delving Deeper

We should acknowledge that some lawyer readers will quickly absorb a subject of immediate interest and then want more. Some might also ask themselves, "What would this author say about this *other* situation I'm concerned about?" or "I wonder what the setting was for this research, and is there more I should know about that?"

We are happy to say that our publisher agreed with the publisher of *The Negotiator's Desk Reference* that the two books are complementary. At the end of this book, you will find a provision by which the American Bar Association (ABA) and DRI Press have agreed that, as a purchaser of this book, you can buy the full version of *The Negotiator's Desk Reference* in its easy-access and most comprehensive form—the Web edition, with updates—at a healthy discount. We thank both publishers for their mutual courtesy toward our readers.

2

Learning from Your Negotiations

Scott R. Peppet[1] *and Michael L. Moffitt*[2]

Introduction

All of us negotiate all the time: at work, at home, with colleagues, and with friends. We hope we learn from these experiences. Such learning requires high-quality feedback about our negotiation decisions. Unfortunately, we often misconstrue feedback about our negotiations, or even avoid it altogether, shielding ourselves from information that could help us learn. Negotiators can take a few basic steps to increase the odds of learning and improvement. This chapter is based on S.R. PEPPET & M.L. MOFFITT, *Learning How to Learn to Negotiate*, in 1 THE NEGOTIATOR'S DESK REFERENCE 13–31 (Honeyman &

1. **Scott Peppet** is the Getches Wolf Professor of Law at the University of Colorado Law School in Boulder, Colorado, where he has taught since 2000. His work focuses on negotiation and dispute resolution, particularly in the context of family businesses, and on the implications of new technologies for markets and privacy. He is a graduate of Harvard Law School and Cornell University.

2. **Michael Moffitt** is the Philip H. Knight Chair in Law at the University of Oregon School of Law, where he has been a professor since 2001 and served as Dean from 2011 through 2017. He was formerly the Roger D. Fisher Visiting Professor in Negotiation and Conflict Resolution at Harvard Law School, where he also served as the Clinical Supervisor of the Harvard Mediation Program. A graduate of Harvard Law School and Marietta College, he has worked in more than twenty countries on public-sector and private-sector negotiations.

Schneider eds., 2017). The full references in that chapter can be found at www.ndrweb.com/chapter-2--public.html.

Why This Concept Might Change Your Thinking

To improve as a negotiator requires two often-missing things: (1) high-quality information about how you behave when you negotiate, and (2) high-quality inquiry about the implicit mental models that drive that behavior. Under stress (as in a negotiation), we often act inconsistently with our "espoused" plan: we plan to listen to and empathize with the other person, but then we cut them off and argue our own viewpoint; we plan to keep our cool, but we actually seethe with anger; we plan to seek creative, mutually beneficial outcomes, but then we steer the negotiations narrowly toward our existing ideas or toward winning some advantage, etc. These moments offer us a window into our "theories in use": the implicit action strategies that we subconsciously adopt during conflict. It is in the gap between our espoused values and our theories in use where the greatest opportunities for learning often hide. But this gap is visible only with high-quality information (such as video or audio recordings or good feedback from a colleague) about how we've actually behaved—rather than how we wanted to behave or how we *think* we behaved.

Armed with such data, learning then demands high-quality inquiry into those implicit strategies. If you observe yourself avoiding any conflict with your boss, it might be tempting to jump to the conclusion that you should confront her next time. The path to lasting learning, however, comes not from simply trying to reject an unwanted "theory in use," but rather, through a deeper inquiry. *Why* was I avoiding the hard conversation to begin with? What assumptions or beliefs drove that initial choice? Maybe I espouse being collaborative with the other side but often end up quite adversarial. Maybe I speak about the importance of creativity while shutting down ideas that are not my own. Rather than merely scolding ourselves for such patterns, deep inquiry can examine what mental models drive those choices. Many of those models have reasonable and important origins. Part of what makes them sticky is the fact that they came about for reasons other than simple error. If high-quality information reveals how we really act in negotiation, then high-quality inquiry permits us to dig into those patterns to unpack what motivates those implicit action choices.

Action Plan—What You Can Do Differently Tomorrow

In support of the twin goals of high-quality information and high-quality inquiry, consider the following:

Plan to Make Improvement Part of Every Negotiation

Lawyers are busy and the process of learning takes time. But even a very small amount of time spent on feedback and reflection—if spent well—can make an enormous difference:

A focused lunchtime conversation with a colleague immediately following a negotiation.
A few pages of reflective journaling following any important negotiation.
A set of prompting questions built into annual performance reviews.

Normalizing the enterprise of learning can yield important benefits for you and others.

Prepare Ahead to Receive Good Feedback After

If colleagues will be with you during the negotiation, tell them what you are hoping to do and what you are hoping they'll observe. ("I'm working on being more assertive about the numbers. I'll value your perspective on how that goes. In particular, please observe carefully what I do whenever the conversation moves back to the spreadsheet.") Even if colleagues will not be in the room, find someone with whom you will be reviewing afterward, and tell them in advance what you hope to do. ("I think I've been talking too much, in ways that undermine my effectiveness. Once I make the offer this time, I'm going to try to stop and listen, rather than filling the awkward silence.") The fact of articulating the goal to a colleague may increase your awareness and may create an added layer of accountability to yourself.

Collect Data

In many legal contexts, video or audio recording of negotiations may be impossible because of confidentiality and other concerns. This does not mean that you have to give up on capturing high-quality information about your negotiation, however. You might assign a junior colleague or other team member to take detailed notes during a negotiation—not only about the substance of the discussion, but about the specific details of what you said and how the other side responded during heated or difficult moments. Capturing such moments as verbatim as possible allows you to review that quasi-transcript later to mine it for what it can reveal about your skills and approach.

Focus on the Data during Your Feedback

Structure your review or feedback sessions to get the most possible out of each discussion. Use the transcripts or information you've collected from the negotiation to highlight particular moments. Focus on moments when you appear to diverge from your espoused strategy or plan. If each person on your team chooses such an interaction and the team discusses each in turn, you will learn both from exploring your own example and from helping others with theirs.

Engage in High-Quality Inquiry

What could I have done differently that might have led to a better result? Once that better approach is identified, why didn't I do that to begin with—what assumptions, beliefs, or mental models led me to take the less-skillful action initially?

Explore Possible Alternative Approaches with Openness

Not everyone negotiates the way you do. As part of your high-quality inquiry, after identifying the negotiation choices you made, consider what *other* choices might have been possible, including ones that seem counterintuitive. The decisions that feel "natural" or "correct" likely reveal something about your theories in use, and they risk shielding you from seeing that some other approach might have served you better.

Seek to Understand Your Own Decisions before Trying to Change

You made decisions during the negotiations. Maybe you now wish you had done something else. Some people are too defensive; others dismiss their own negotiation decisions too quickly. ("That was a disaster, and I just have to stop caving.") Be kind but critical in examining your decisions. ("Why *didn't* I use most of the arguments I had prepared in advance? Maybe that was tactical, or maybe I was afraid of making them angry. Or, maybe I subconsciously distrusted my preparation. Or . . .") By exploring alternative approaches *and* the unarticulated reasons why you didn't do those things in the first place, you can identify a better action plan for next time *and* the implicit assumptions that may block you.

Find a Learning Community

Implicit in our advice is the assumption that a lawyer has colleagues that negotiate with her *and* who are willing and able to give useful feedback. This isn't always the case. If you can't get others to engage in real learning with you about your negotiations, look to non-work contexts for such feedback. Perhaps you could volunteer as a mediator or with a non-profit and find ways to solicit good negotiation feedback there. Or you may be able to get support and coaching from a friend or family member. Negotiation and conflict can be a rich source for learning if you can find a community to support such efforts.

Modifiers, Caveats, and No-Go Areas—When This Advice Just Won't Apply

Most negotiators actively seek to *avoid* exposing themselves to high-quality information, and seek to *avoid* high-quality inquiry. The reason is simple: most people seem to implicitly value avoiding negative feelings and maintaining unilateral control over their experiences. Learning of the type we advocate here can be provocative. Your ego may take a (temporary?) hit. You may not know where honest feedback conversations are going to lead. You may hear perspectives that challenge how you think. Not everyone can handle this.

Conclusion

Learning to learn to negotiate sounds easy, but in our experience of teaching negotiation to thousands of attorneys and law students, it is anything but. Many lawyers flex the same negotiation muscles over and over, without ever critically examining their strengths and weaknesses. They use the skills they're already comfortable with, getting better at those skills, but neglecting other approaches and capabilities. This underserves their clients and themselves, and it makes them less effective in unfamiliar contexts. If you can seek out and inquire into valid data about how you negotiate, progress is possible. More than that, learning to learn from your negotiations can be intensely rewarding, both professionally and personally.

This Ties in With:
Crampton, Ch. 8, Social Brain; Lee & Shanahan, Ch. 39, Martial Arts

Section II

All About You

Section II discusses negotiation style choices, some individual characteristics that might make a difference in negotiations, and understanding your own thinking. Chapter 3 is a thorough analysis of the ways someone's style of negotiation might not mesh with the same person's style of handling conflict—often because of failure to think through the differences between good practices, tactics, and tricks. Chapter 4 demonstrates how hard bargaining really works, in no fewer than 28 varieties.

Chapters 5 and 6 focus on race and gender. Both chapters note how personal differences might play out in negotiations. The chapters also discuss what to do if you want to consider the structural and organizational biases that might perpetuate inequity as a result of negotiations. Chapter 7 is about social intuition—a quality that helps you be aware of yourself, read your counterpart, and attune yourself, so you have the best chance of getting through to your counterpart. We end with Chapter 8, a neuroscience-based explanation of how human beings evolved to be interdependent.

3

Fashioning an Effective Negotiation Style: Choosing between Good Practices, Tactics, and Tricks (GTT Framework)

Hal Abramson[1]

Introduction

This chapter addresses two longstanding negotiation questions: First, what choices should you make to be effective? This chapter offers a schema for classifying choices based on the benefits and risks of

1. **Hal Abramson,** faculty member and former vice dean at Touro Law Center, New York, teaches, trains, and writes on representing clients in domestic and international mediations, mediations resolving intercultural disputes, and negotiations. His widely used book *Mediation Representation* received the International Institute for Conflict Prevention & Resolution (CPR) Book Award. He has been selected for International Who's Who of Commercial Mediation and has conducted trainings in nineteen countries on six continents. He chaired the American Bar Association (ABA) committee that drafted its mediation representation competition rules, served on the inaugural committee for the International Chamber of Commerce (ICC) global mediation competition, chaired the International Mediation Institute (IMI) task force on certification criteria for intercultural mediators, and served as the first scholar in residence for the International Academy of Mediators (IAM). After his recent visitorship at the U.S. Air Force Academy, he was appointed as Advisor to the Academy's Negotiation and Leadership program.

selecting a good practice, tactic, or trick (GTT). Second, what distinguishes negotiation style, the subject of this chapter, from your natural conflict style? By highlighting the distinction between how you *want* to negotiate (negotiation style) and how you naturally negotiate (conflict style), this chapter offers a way for you to become the negotiator you aspire to be. This chapter is based on H. ABRAMSON, *Fashioning an Effective Negotiation Style: Choosing Between Good Practices, Tactics and Tricks,* in 1 THE NEGOTIATOR'S DESK REFERENCE 59–74 (Honeyman & Schneider eds, 2017). The full references in that chapter can be found at www.ndrweb.com/chapter-5--public.html.

Why This Concept Might Change Your Thinking

Good Practices, Tactics, and Tricks

This chapter offers an answer to a question that occupies every negotiator: what choices should you make to be effective in a fast-paced negotiation process? By viewing your negotiation through the good practices, tactics, and tricks (GTT) lens (or, the GTT Framework), you can quickly answer the question by classifying each choice based on its benefits and risks. Central to the GTT Framework is understanding the differences between good practices, tactics, and tricks. Once you become acquainted with the three categories, you should be able to recognize each one intuitively.

Good practices are risk-free choices, or minimally risky ones, that most negotiation books and courses teach, such as being a good listener and trying to meet both side's interests. *Tactics* are low-risk or moderately risky choices that are conventionally used in negotiations. When discovered by the other side, the choice will not derail the negotiations, although it may mar the negotiation relationship. Common tactics include making an inflated first offer or misrepresenting your bottom line to the other side. *Tricks* are highly risky choices that can be tempting to use due to the potential for a large gain when successful. When discovered, however, they can severely undermine if not destroy the negotiations. Imagine a choice by the other side that would cause you to leave a negotiation or not want to negotiate with the other side, like the other side lying about a material fact or showing up with patently limited settlement authority. These bad-faith choices are tricks.

The utility of this tripartite framework depends on understanding the contours of each category and the opportunities and risks afforded by the choices within each category. The choices you make determine your negotiation style along a continuum, from problem-solving with primarily good practices and possibly a few tactics on one end, to adversarial with primarily tricks and aggressive tactics toward the other end.

Conflict Style

The chapter also considers how your natural *conflict* style, which can be identified by a short, self-administered survey, can influence your negotiation choices and shape your *negotiation* style. Various surveys classify personal conflict styles based on five types: cooperative (problem-solving), competitive, compromiser, accommodator, and avoider. If your conflict style is cooperative or competitive, for instance, you may naturally negotiate according to that style. By distinguishing between your natural conflict style and your negotiation style, you can learn to recognize and overcome what might be a suboptimal *conflict style* by proactively selecting options under the GTT schema to fashion an effective *negotiation style.*

Action Plan—What You Can Do Differently Tomorrow

Good Practices, Tactics, and Tricks

Based on the GTT Framework, you ought to choose good practices, which have been demonstrated to be effective, curtail use of tactics, and avoid using tricks even in the face of irresistible temptations. If tempted to use a trick, the framework provides a pragmatic method for assessing its risks. Your assessment should discourage using the trick, and if it does not, at least you will make an informed choice.

You should keep in mind that the GTT Framework does not depend on classifying each choice correctly. As with many classification systems, the boundaries of each category can be murky and debatable. Within negotiations, the boundaries can be further influenced by the context, such as whether the dispute is an employment or business one. The ultimate value of the framework is how it promotes your thoughtful and informed assessment of each negotiation choice.

Finally, the GTT Framework is not an alternative negotiation approach. It applies as an overlay to any negotiation approach, whether positional or adversarial, principled or problem-solving, or some other approach. Within your preferred negotiation approach, the framework illuminates the implications of your choices.

Nexus between Conflict and Negotiation Styles

You also should be attentive to how your conflict style can influence your negotiation style in order to avoid your natural conflict style impeding your negotiations. If you know that "compromising" is your conflict style, for example, you might try to offset your inclination to prematurely split the difference in your negotiations. You might slow down the negotiation pace and select the best objective standards, for example, instead of the first facially fair one. If you tend to "avoid" conflicts or "accommodate" to preserve relationships, you might compensate for this conflict style by conscientiously advocating your interests, a good negotiation practice, instead of settling for what might be comfortable to do.

When you are aware of possible *conflict* styles, you also are more likely to recognize the conflict styles of others, which can guide you in selecting your responses. For example, if the other person has a take-charge, competitive conflict style, you might use active listening skills like summarizing and asking suitable questions that can lead the person toward the issues you want to discuss, while reducing the risk of a contest over who is controlling the negotiation. If the other side insists that his issue gets addressed, you might agree on the condition that your issue is considered next.

If you think the other person has a compromising style, you ought to act reasonably and fairly, and with a degree of efficiency—values that compromisers subscribe to, when trying to persuade the other person. You may want to highlight how your proposal gives up something based on the principle of reciprocity while being fair to both parties.

Neither your conflict style nor their conflict style should monopolize the negotiations. Instead, you should consider which conflict styles are at play when selecting the moves that shape your negotiation style.

Modifiers, Caveats, and No-Go Areas— When This Advice Just Won't Apply

A key lesson is to avoid using tricks by mistake. What counts is not what you intend but what the other side believes.

Whether your move may be mistakenly seen as a trick can depend on the sensibilities or culture of the other side, as well as on the context of the negotiations. Some people may consider a good guy/bad guy ploy as a tactic, based on their sensibilities, while others may see the ploy as a trick. The same person may view insufficient settlement authority as a tactic in a dispute involving an insured claim, but as a trick when it happens in a business-to-business contract dispute. An inflated first offer of 90 percent above a reasonable settlement amount might be viewed as a tactic in some cultures and a trick in other cultures.

You can try to gauge whether your move will be perceived as a tactic or trick (or good practice) by asking yourself two questions: (1) How would you react if you were the target of the move? (2) How do you think the other side would react if they discovered your true intentions? The chapter in *The Negotiator's Desk Reference* illustrates how to use these two techniques to reduce the risk of the other side misunderstanding your move.

Conclusion

The benefits and risks of each negotiation choice can be assessed by applying the GTT Framework as illustrated throughout the chapter. However, the ultimate value of this tripartite schema is not correctly classifying each choice. The value is the analysis it promotes for forging an effective *negotiation style.*

This Ties in With:

Craver, Ch. 4, Classic Techniques; Liao & Zhang, Ch. 30, Chinese Wisdom & Your Style

4

Techniques of Distributive Negotiation

Charles B. Craver[1]

Introduction

Like it or not, many if not all negotiations include *at least* an element of hard bargaining, as the participants determine how to distribute the items on the table. This chapter is based on C. CRAVER, *Distributive Negotiation Techniques*, in 1 THE NEGOTIATOR'S DESK REFERENCE 75–89 (Honeyman & Schneider eds, 2017). The full references in that chapter can be found at www.ndrweb.com/chapter-6--public.html.

Why This Concept Might Change Your Thinking

Legal negotiators must understand the techniques that their counterparts may employ. This will also enable them to decide which tactics they should employ. Those who have reviewed concepts explored in

1. **Charles B. Craver** is the Freda H. Alverson Professor of Law at the George Washington University Law School, where he regularly teaches a course on legal negotiating. He has won teaching awards at three different law schools. Craver is the author of five books and coauthor of ten, and the author of numerous law-review articles on dispute resolution and employment law. Professor Craver received his J.D. from the University of Michigan in 1971, his Master of Industrial and Labor Relations (MILR) degree from the Cornell University School of Industrial and Labor Relations in 1968, and his B.S. from Cornell University in 1967.

this chapter can significantly improve their ability to achieve their basic negotiating objectives.

Action Plan—What You Can Do Differently Tomorrow

Even if you would never use some of these techniques, you still need to know them, so you can both recognize them and counteract their impact. They are organized in four major groups: building confidence, making offers, responding, and client authority.

Techniques to Build Confidence

Persuasive negotiators begin by articulating *principled positions* that logically explain what they are offering or seeking. This bolsters their confidence and undermines the confidence of less prepared counterparts. They also plan to make *principled concessions*. This lets their counterparts know why they are changing positions and why greater concessions are not presently warranted.

Some endeavor to gain a psychological advantage by controlling the day, time, and location for their interactions. When this works, it bolsters their confidence in subsequent handling of substantive issues. This approach helps them when counterparts begin negotiations by conceding these matters.

Others seek to control the bargaining agenda, trying to limit talks to topics that interest their own clients. They hope to resolve these favorably before even tackling the counterparts' items.

Most legal negotiations are one-on-one. But some parties attempt to gain a tactical and psychological advantage by adding people. They hope the extra participants will intimidate their lone counterpart, and help them in reading nonverbal messages emitted by the opposing individual.

Time constraints may affect your counterparts more than you. Whenever possible, negotiators should try to avoid revealing any time pressure. They should also try to induce clients to provide the time needed for best results.

Conversely, some negotiators act like wolves in sheepskin. They profess a lack of negotiating ability and legal expertise and try to evoke sympathy to lure unsuspecting counterparts into a false sense of security. They then ask their counterparts what they think would be fair, hoping for a significant move in their own direction.

Techniques Regarding Making Offers

Inexperienced negotiators frequently begin interactions with extreme positions, thinking that this anchors the deal their way. People facing truly unrealistic demands or offers should not be casual in showing displeasure, because this may lead counterparts to think their positions are not truly unrealistic.

When facing an unrealistic opening position, you may want to use probing questions. This separates the items into components. A series of questions—beginning with finite terms that do not lend themselves to puffing—is then designed to force counterparts to logically assess each aspect of their position. The sum total is likely to be more reasonable than the original figures.

Some do not like the time-consuming give-and-take of conventional bargaining. Instead of beginning with elevated demands or minimal offers, they determine where they believe rational parties would end up and begin there—but inflexibly. They see this as "best-offer-first" bargaining; their counterparts see it as "take-it-or-leave-it bargaining."

In multiple-issue negotiations, some attempt to disclose their own relative item values and to elicit similar information from their counterparts through multiple equal-value offers. They formulate different offers that vary what they seek and what they offer counterparts, but which are all of equal value to their side. This can help counterparts see the relative values of the items involved.

Negotiators occasionally phrase monetary offers in terms of a range instead of a single figure. But this approach may suggest uncertainty in the mind of the offeror. Recipients of such offers should focus on the most beneficial end of the spectrum.

Early in some interactions, negotiators occasionally make realistic offers or demands, with a time limit after which they will be withdrawn or reduced in value. But if you ignore the deadline and prior threats to end the interaction, you can frequently induce your counterpart to continue.

Negotiators occasionally find a counterpart who wants something their own side doesn't care about. They may disingenuously indicate that this item is important to their own side, and make a show of claiming it, hoping to trade it later for something of real value.

Techniques Regarding Responses

Negotiators frequently generate consecutive offers through the flinch: when they receive their counterpart's offer, they pull back and look shocked, physically indicating disappointment with the terms proposed. You should not allow such an actor to induce you to make consecutive concessions: stay with your articulated position, and evaluate what the other side is prepared to offer.

Anger, whether real or fake, at a critical moment may convince counterparts of the serious nature of one's position. It may intimidate opposing parties into making concessions. Aggressive behavior usually has the same intent as real or feigned anger. It is employed to convince counterparts of the seriousness of one's position. A few negotiators gain a bargaining advantage through seemingly irrational behavior. Some of them attribute the irrationality to their (absent) clients; others exhibit their own bizarre conduct. They hope to convince counterparts that their side cannot be dealt with logically. Opposing parties must either accept one-sided demands or assume there will be no settlement.

At a critical moment, participants occasionally walk out or hang up the phone to convince counterparts that further concessions won't happen. Never "run after" persons who have walked out or hung up, since they will see this as a sign of weakness.

Most legal negotiators make overt or implicit statements regarding negative consequences of no-settlement. Effective threats must be clearly communicated, and they must be proportionate to the action the user is seeking. Negotiators occasionally threaten dire consequences of no-settlement. They indicate that havoc can be avoided only if the other side agrees to set terms. Recipients of such threats must ask themselves whether the promised havoc is really likely, and how the event would really affect the *other* side. Negotiators occasionally use *affirmative promises* to encourage counterpart movement, by promising to reciprocate changes made by the other side.

Silence is an extremely effective bargaining technique, and it is often overlooked by negotiators. Less proficient negotiators fear silence. You can use silence to allow the process to unfold—and to reduce the elevated aspirations of counterparts.

Adept negotiators may use the "Br'er Rabbit" approach to obtain beneficial terms from win-lose counterparts. They subtly suggest to opposing parties that they or their clients would suffer greatly if certain action was either taken or withheld, when they hope to obtain those very results.

Passive-aggressive negotiators employ oblique but aggressive techniques. They are late for bargaining sessions or forget necessary documents. They exhibit personal ineptitude to generate concessions from impatient counterparts. Persons dealing with such bargainers should try to assume responsibility for the issues they think these individuals will fail to carry out.

Techniques Regarding Authority

Many negotiators like to indicate early on that they lack final authority to conclude the deal. Some who possess real authority still reserve the right to check with their absent clients and reassess the tentative terms before accords can become final. Other negotiators really do have constituencies that must approve before preliminary agreements can be operative.

You cannot bargain meaningfully with people who indicate they lack the authority to speak for their own clients; you end up bidding against yourself. Negotiators should not succumb to this approach. When counterparts indicate that they lack authority to negotiate, they should be told to obtain such authority before talks continue. When partners employ the good cop/bad cop approach, a seemingly reasonable negotiator softens resistance by appreciating "generous" position changes by the other side. But when a final accord seems on the horizon, the reasonable person's partner or client rejects the new offer as entirely unacceptable. Just as the counterpart is preparing to explode, the reasonable partner assuages their feelings and suggests that if some additional concessions were made, she could probably induce her seemingly irrational partner to accept the new terms. This works more often than it should.

Some crafty *nibblers* "agree" to final accords with apparent client authority. Days later, they contact counterparts and sheepishly indicate that their principals are dissatisfied and must have several position changes before they will accept the other terms. When their unsuspecting counterparts and their clients are psychologically committed to final deals and do not want these few items to negate previous efforts, they frequently agree to the requested modifications.

Conclusion

During "value claiming" or distributive elements of bargaining, most negotiators employ various techniques to enable them to claim more of the joint surplus than they give to their counterparts. It is important for negotiators to decide which tactics they should employ, and even more important for them to recognize and effectively counteract the techniques used by their counterparts.

This Ties in With:

Abramson, Ch. 3, Fashioning Style; Cristal, Ch. 23, No Trust; Wade, Ch. 50, Dobermans

5

Reflecting on Negotiating While Black

Michael Z. Green[1]

Introduction

The reality for black persons in America is that the world can sometimes look like a bleak and discriminatory place. The concept of performing certain activities "while black" has been used in a number of instances to capture the ongoing and unique experiences of black people in our society, including referring to "driving while black" when repeatedly being stopped by police officers. Expanding upon that concept by examining literature regarding what it means to be "negotiating while black" suggests how black persons can achieve positive negotiation results despite discrimination. This chapter is based on M. Green, *Negotiating While Black*, in 1 The Negotiator's Desk Reference 563–581 (Honeyman & Schneider

1. **Michael Z. Green** is a tenured faculty member at Texas A&M University School of Law in Fort Worth, Texas. His scholarship focuses on workplace disputes and the intersection of race and alternatives to the court process. He began full-time law teaching after completing the prestigious Hastie Teaching Fellowship and obtaining his fifth degree, Master of Laws (LL.M.), from the University of Wisconsin. A juris doctor *cum laude* graduate with a master's degree in human resources and industrial labor relations, both from Loyola University Chicago, he has authored numerous law articles and book chapters. Additional biographical information is available at http://law.tamu.edu/faculty-staff/find-people/faculty-profiles/michael-z-green.

eds, 2017). The full references in that chapter can be found at www.ndrweb.com/chapter-41--public.html.

Why This Concept Might Change Your Thinking

Looking at all the difficult experiences for a black person in our society (that is clearly not yet post-racial), one could easily view most transactions as not fitting the platitudes espoused in the dispute resolution community about resolving disputes in a creative way and expanding the pie beyond a zero-sum game. Rather the chances are that the black person may perceive the negotiation process as a game where the black person involved is merely a pawn destined to lose out, probably quite early in the game. These feelings can be especially strong in the workplace, where dispute resolution systems, either through the courts or as alternatives to the courts, fail to navigate the consequences of implicit bias and make it very difficult to establish the existence of explicit bias. In reviewing the studies that capture what it is to be negotiating while black, one can better understand the realities of this problem even if negotiation theorists have rarely addressed this subject in any comprehensive and prescriptive manner.

For decades, commentators have raised concerns about the prejudice involved with informal dispute resolution processes. For example, one study found that black car buyers were induced to pay much higher prices due to both the initial offer they received from the salesperson and the final purchase offer. During these negotiations, salespersons apparently believed that white males had better search details and were more informed about the dealer's actual costs than black purchasers. The Department of Justice has found similar situations involving discriminatory negotiations in car financing. Other studies demonstrate the existence of racial bias in closing costs or lending rates for homeowners, and in salary negotiations where black professionals are offered lower salaries or benefits. Troublingly, these biases even appear on online sites, where apparently black sellers of items, such as baseball cards or iPods, receive less money than whites, as described by various tester studies.

Action Plan—What You Can Do Differently Tomorrow

I will attempt to provide some prescriptions to advise those involved in a negotiation with a black person, especially with respect to matters of salary in the workplace. Imagine a negotiation about a starting salary between a black female, Samantha, and her soon-to-be supervisor, Jerry, a white male. As negotiation theory suggests, both parties should feel that the result leaves them better off than if they had not negotiated an agreement. Prescriptive approaches to negotiation have tended to counsel the negotiators to emphasize "their and their opponents' underlying interests rather than . . . positions." Overall, one of the biggest concerns is leveling the playing field in terms of providing information that Samantha would need to negotiate effectively with Jerry. This should include all facts related to the salary of Barry, a white male hired into a similar position by Jerry shortly before negotiations between Samantha and Jerry began.

One way for black persons to acquire additional information for a fairer negotiation can be through receiving common information available to all parties, possibly through posting it on the Internet and making sure that all parties have the same information. But as one study has explained, companies may be unwilling to establish any policies aimed at correcting any information discrepancies related to salary negotiations because this "would result in higher payroll expenses." Another way to improve the information disparity involves hiring more racially diverse employees in general, so they can provide a social network for sharing information with same-race applicants.

With technological advances, the use of the Internet may also help remove information disparities through developing networks that fairly disseminate information without consideration of race. For example, as mentioned earlier, various studies and litigation have shown that being black represented a negative result in auto purchase negotiations. However, another study has concluded that encouraging the use of web services that offer information on automobile pricing has helped level the playing field for minority purchasers during negotiations. Those authors also asserted that when obtaining information through an Internet referral service where party demographics are unknown, this process eliminates most of the offline minority premium.

As a result, and beyond attempting to examine the literature identifying harsh consequences when negotiating while black, this chapter has highlighted one overriding concern: unless the black person in the negotiation *has as much information* as a similar white counterpart, be it through social or Internet networks or some other means, and the white person negotiating with her *focuses* on excising any *conscious and subconscious* race-based stereotypes from the process, negotiating while black, even in 2019, and even with relatively well-meaning counterparts, means that unproductive obstacles still exist. Companies must find ways to address the stereotype threat black persons experience in being perceived as less qualified than their white counterparts because of race. This threat leads racial minorities to "cover" their identities and not rock the boat at work to protect themselves, but at their own expense in salary negotiations. If those companies do not act to address these concerns, they will lose out on finding and nurturing productive black talent in their workplace.

One way to prevent covering and stereotype threats from infecting workplace negotiations over key concerns such as salary is that the company should seek a very diverse leadership group, providing many examples of people who look like and reflect the background of the black person negotiating with that company. Then black persons can identify with successful people who look and sound like them, and thus have less apprehension about performing in a way that feeds into or allows a focus on negative stereotypes. Also, through mentoring networks and identity caucuses, black persons can meet similar role models who will provide a positive reflection and a social network of information and sources to level the negotiating playing field. These networks can help combat the application of negative stereotypes while also encouraging self-affirming opportunities to show that negative stereotypes do not match the black person involved.

A critical race scholar, Jerry Kang, has suggested that organizations should emphasize having a humble, mindful, and internally motivated mindset to do the right thing in addressing implicit bias in the workplace. Kang has also asserted that persons involved in making decisions should concentrate on looking for exemplars that counter stereotypical associations, and reflect on why certain biases occur while purposefully thinking about alternative choices and criteria. Finally, Kang has argued for the removal of unconstrained discretion and other approaches that contribute to the causal links that allow bias to manifest. As an example, an organization can develop standardized criteria and evaluation forms while also diversifying its decision-making process. Using structured interviews and metrics may help when checking short lists and applicant pools to counter bias and other tendencies that may not reflect the best choices for finding and cultivating talent in a nondiscriminatory way.

In returning to the negotiation between Samantha and Jerry, we can now look for the countermeasures that Jerry should take to root out bias and make sure that his negotiation with Samantha is not discriminatory. Instead of attempting to obtain the lowest salary when negotiating with Samantha, Jerry has to recognize that implicit and explicit biases may lead him to treat Samantha differently than Barry. One of Jerry's interests, not only as the person involved in the negotiations but as the future supervisor of both Samantha and Barry, should be to recognize that he cannot let Samantha join his organization with a salary drastically less than Barry's. As a result of this interest, Jerry should prepare to not let Samantha accept any offer that would look bad when it becomes evident that Barry and Samantha are performing similar work and have comparable job duties. Even if Samantha acts against her own financial interests in negotiations, possibly due to a lack of information or a desire to cover and respond to stereotype threat concerns, Jerry must ignore Samantha's behavior and make his final offer to Samantha more commensurate with Barry's salary. Then Samantha's experience of negotiating while black would not have been a negative one.

Modifiers, Caveats, and No-Go Areas—When This Advice Just Won't Apply

The prescriptions above focus on workplace salary negotiations, primarily in the private sector. The literature suggests that these concerns translate well in most situations where power imbalances exist and societal stereotypes can prevail, for example, in automobile purchases. But there may be other situations and dynamics where lawyers and neutrals involved might have to navigate additional hurdles. For example, this chapter does not discuss the ramifications when both negotiators are black but face stereotypical and biased expectations from their counterparts or superiors. Additionally, matters involving public concerns and political factors or broad group dynamics could add additional complexities beyond the scope of this chapter.

Conclusion

In 2003, Supreme Court Justice Sandra Day O'Connor explained how individual views may be affected by the "unique experience of being a racial minority in a society, like our own, in which race unfortunately still matters." When negotiating while black, we must take heed of this reality and plan accordingly.

This Ties in With:

Bear & Babcock, Ch. 6, Gender; Goh, Ch. 31, Mistakes; Kaufman & Blanchot, Ch. 32, International

6

Gender Gaps in Negotiation: Implications for Individuals and Organizations

Julia B. Bear[1] *and Linda Babcock*[2]

Introduction

Research shows that, on average, women tend to underperform in competitive negotiations on behalf of themselves compared to men. The long-standing wage gap and occupational segregation between men and women are in part explained by gender differences in negotiation that underscore these inequalities. Gender differences emerge in a variety of important negotiation outcomes, including negotiation performance, the propensity to initiate negotiations, and how negotiators are judged by others. In this chapter, we review recommendations regarding this issue on a personal level—how women can improve their negotiation performance—and on an organizational level—how organizations can address (and stop perpetuating)

1. **Julia B. Bear** is Associate Professor in the College of Business at Stony Brook University. She received her Ph.D. in organizational behavior from Carnegie Mellon University. Her research focuses on gender and negotiation.
2. **Linda Babcock** is the James Walton Professor of Economics at Carnegie Mellon University (CMU). She is the founder of the Program for Research and Outreach on Gender Equity in Society (PROGRESS) and the CMU Leadership and Negotiation Academy for Women. Babcock earned a Ph.D. in economics from the University of Wisconsin-Madison.

inequities. This chapter is based on J.B. BEAR & L. BABCOCK, *Gender Differences in Negotiation*, in 1 THE NEGOTIATOR'S DESK REFERENCE 595–605 (Honeyman & Schneider eds, 2017). The full references in that chapter can be found at www.ndrweb.com/chapter-43--public.html.

Why This Concept Might Change Your Thinking

Gender gaps in salaries and career advancement are problematic across industries and particularly in the legal profession. Among lawyers, men tend to earn significantly higher salaries and are more likely to be promoted to partner compared to women. Although attorneys may negotiate effectively on their clients' behalf, they also need to negotiate effectively for themselves and their own career advancement. Moreover, individuals who oversee the advancement of others should be cognizant of differences in negotiation between men and women to help address and mitigate these gender gaps. In the next section, we provide recommendations both for those who seek to improve their own negotiation performance, as well as for those in positions to address gender inequity from an organizational perspective.

Action Plan—What You Can Do Differently Tomorrow

Individual Recommendations

Preparation Phase

There are several evidence-based methods to help women improve their performance. Preparing for a negotiation while imagining that a negotiation is for a close friend (even when the negotiation is actually for oneself) improves women's performance. In addition, when women (prior to a negotiation) think about past events in their lives when they behaved assertively, their negotiation performance improves. Moreover, gender differences typically do not emerge in negotiations concerning relatively feminine topics—only those concerning more masculine topics—so focusing on gender-neutral aspects of a negotiation may be helpful. Finally, women's negative feelings prior to negotiating can be reduced by "priming power," that is, by recalling the experience of being powerful (having control over an outcome that is important to someone else).

In terms of formal training, research has revealed that training that includes both a skills component and a self-efficacy (the belief that one can negotiate) component is the most effective in improving women's negotiation performance. The way a negotiation is framed matters, as well. Gender differences in propensity to initiate a negotiation disappear when a request for greater compensation is framed as "asking" as opposed to "negotiating." Thus, psychologically reframing a negotiation as a problem-solving activity could help women increase their likelihood of initiating a negotiation.

Negotiation Phase

Women often face a catch-22 in negotiations: If they negotiate, they are seen as less likeable, but if they don't negotiate, they lose out on higher compensation and other rewards. Recent research has examined whether using certain types of strategies while negotiating or providing certain types of information can improve women's outcomes and reduce the potential for backlash, i.e., suffering social penalties due to negotiating for oneself. Women suffer less backlash when they frame their request for greater compensation in terms of how it will benefit the organization (for example, that their negotiation ability is a valuable skill that they bring to the job). Also, when women explicitly provide information that they are the family breadwinner, women are offered salaries comparable to those of men, while avoiding certain social penalties. Negotiating in a stereotypically feminine style, such as using tentative and deferential language, does not result in backlash, although it is ineffective in persuading the other side to grant the negotiation request.

Organizational Recommendations

We next consider the potential benefits and pitfalls of several evidence-based suggestions for organizations to level the playing field for women by mitigating the impact of gender differences in negotiation. Simply encouraging women to negotiate more assertively may backfire if women are then perceived as too aggressive. Furthermore, putting the onus on individual women ignores the broader societal systems that perpetuate stereotypes and gender gaps. Therefore, organizational interventions may have the best chance of creating equal opportunities.

Ban Negotiations in Organizations over Terms of Employment Contracts and Work Assignments

Gender differences in negotiating can create inequities if important rewards in organizations, such as salary, promotions, task assignments, and opportunities, are all allocated depending upon whether employees negotiate. One solution is to ban negotiation over these rewards altogether. Many organizations today are experimenting with this intervention as a way to make the environment fairer to women.

Though this intervention could indeed reduce inequities that occur due to negotiation, it may introduce other types of inequities, for example, if supervisors were to allocate these rewards in a discriminatory way. Another potential downside is that banning negotiation can result in inefficient outcomes. For example, if an employee were interested in trading a lower salary for more days off or some other benefit, this type of mutually beneficial trade would be prohibited. Perhaps the biggest downside to banning negotiation altogether is that it requires perfect enforcement, which is unrealistic in most organizations. In fact, men may decide that they can negotiate regardless of what the organizational rules specify, whereas women may follow the rules, thereby exacerbating gender differences in negotiation.

Greater Transparency

Another suggestion is to make decisions about salary and promotion more transparent. Some companies have adopted formulas for how salaries are determined and have communicated them clearly. Promotion decisions could also be made according to specified timelines and standards. Given that the greater the uncertainty about standards, the more likely gender differences are to emerge, it behooves organizations to make the process for obtaining raises, bonuses, promotions, and work assignments as transparent as possible.

Stop Asking about Salary History

When an employee is hired, employers typically ask candidates about salary history. This practice perpetuates the gender wage gap that is partially caused by gender differences in negotiation. Specifically, if men are earning more than women from the start of their careers, the difference is further compounded when moving to a new job or position because the original salary differential is re-created and even magnified by basing new salaries on salary history. Evaluating the appropriate salary for a job before a candidate is hired can help reduce the impact of gender differences in negotiation. In fact, the state of Massachusetts has already implemented legislation (the Massachusetts Equal Pay Law) such that employers are prohibited from asking about salary history until after an employment offer (with compensation specified) has been made.

Focus on Men's Negotiation Behavior, Not Just Women's

Another approach to influence practice would be to focus on men rather than just women, and to consider the ways in which men's greater likelihood to negotiate compared to women could be detrimental. Thus, it may be worthwhile to consider how men may be asking *too much* as opposed to just whether women are asking for *too little*. To be sure, there is no formula for the "right" amount of negotiation. Nevertheless, it is important to consider that past research has shown that men are more likely to be overconfident about their performance compared to women. In this way, organizations might consider how they respond to men's negotiation behavior and scrutinize whether men's demands are truly justified by their past performance. By calibrating men's rewards and not just women's, organizations can address the gender gap, as well.

Change Our Cultural Views about Women Who Negotiate

This is by far the hardest recommendation to implement but it is necessary to stop penalizing women who negotiate. Developing an inclusive organizational culture where a diversity of styles, personalities, and perspectives can thrive will go a long way toward leveling the playing field not only for women, but for others, as well. Moreover, this cultural change has reverberations for men. Just as women should not be penalized about negotiating for greater financial resources at work, men should not be penalized for negotiating for greater nonmonetary benefits such as flexible scheduling to accommodate family responsibilities.

Conclusion

There is a rich body of empirical research showing gender differences in negotiation, but it also shows that these gender differences are mitigated under various circumstances and thus are not "written in stone" by any means. Given the preponderance of evidence concerning this topic, it behooves organizational leaders to consider their role in the perpetuation of this gender gap. Organizations may be missing out on compensating and promoting talented women, and likewise, organizations may be overcompensating and promoting men whose tendency to negotiate may belie their talent. Overall, individual employees, managers, and leaders of organizations should consider how, when, and who negotiates in their organizations—and whether the patterns that emerge are to the benefit or detriment of the organization and its employees.

This Ties in With:

Green, Ch. 5, Negotiating While Black; Porter & Kolb, Ch. 14, Moves; Liao & Zhang, Ch. 30, Chinese Wisdom & Your Style

7

Negotiating with Social Intuition

Andrea Kupfer Schneider[1] *and Noam Ebner*[2]

Introduction

In negotiation, our success in achieving our goals has much to do with the way our counterparts feel about us. Do they trust us, like us, and empathize with us? Or, conversely, do they dislike us, suspect our motives, or doubt our veracity? Core negotiation issues such as trust, relationship, rapport, and power are all conveyed through intuitive communication. Our capacity to navigate this little-charted terrain

1. **Andrea Kupfer Schneider** is a Professor of Law at Marquette University Law School, where she teaches dispute resolution, negotiation, ethics, and international conflict resolution and is the director of Marquette's nationally ranked dispute resolution program. Andrea has written numerous books, book chapters, and articles on negotiation skills and styles, dispute system design, international conflict, and gender and negotiation. She was given the American Bar Association (ABA) Section of Dispute Resolution Award for Outstanding Scholarly Work for 2017. Andrea received her A.B. *cum laude* from the Woodrow Wilson School of Public & International Affairs at Princeton University and her J.D. *cum laude* from Harvard Law School.

2. **Noam Ebner** is a professor in the Negotiation and Conflict Resolution program at Creighton University's Department of Interdisciplinary Studies. Previously an attorney and mediator, he has taught mediation and negotiation in a dozen countries around the world. He was among the first teachers to engage in online teaching of negotiation and conflict studies and to explore the potential for Massive Open Online Courses (MOOC) in these fields. Noam's research interests include online negotiation and dispute resolution, trust and its role in dispute resolution, negotiation pedagogy, and online learning. Noam can be contacted at NoamEbner@creighton.edu; his work can be found at ssrn.com/author=425153.

is captured by the term *social intuition*. The chapter is based on A.K. Schneider & N. Ebner, *Social Intuition*, in 1 The Negotiator's Desk Reference 127–142 (Honeyman & Schneider eds, 2017). The full references in that chapter can be found at www.ndrweb.com/chapter-10--public.html.

Why This Concept Might Change Your Thinking

Social intuition includes a range of skills from different domains. One of these is empathy, including both the capacity to understand the other side's point of view and the ability to understand their emotions and feelings. A second area of skills relates to social awareness and social facility, often described as emotional intelligence. A third range of relevant skills has its source in nonverbal communication.

To fully understand the notion of social intuition, and to consider its practical implementations in negotiation, one must assess it from three different angles:

Self: Awareness of our *own* emotions, cognitive patterns, biases and attributions, and typical responses and reactions. Negotiators who have this awareness are likely to be more effective in projecting clear and congruent messages and to "come across" better. They recognize the effects that the other, the situation, or other factors are having on their own internal resources of energy, motivation, and focus.

Other: The ability to read your *counterpart*. In this aspect, you seek attunement to their emotional state through observing and understanding their signals. Negotiators who "read" their counterpart in this manner can gain an abundance of helpful information. They might be able to separate their counterpart's core concerns from tangential issues or recognize when their counterpart is aiming high rather than approaching their reservation point.

Each of these two aspects of social intuition benefits negotiators. Combined, they also set the stage for implementing a third element of social intuition, *bridging*.

Bridging: *Action* you take to form *connections* with the other through the interactional exchange—connections that support you in *affecting* the other. When bridging works well, both negotiators look and feel as if they are moving together, despite their substantive differences. The elements of situational awareness—the ability to read ourselves, read our counterpart, and read the situation—all come together as we take bridging actions.

Social intuition in negotiation is, therefore, the convergence of three essential areas of negotiator capacity: self-awareness, other-focused attention, and synching for effect.

Action Plan—What You Can Do Differently Tomorrow

In this section, we gather six interactional elements under the framework of social intuition and suggest some specific considerations for each.

Proximity: Space and proximity between negotiators involve obvious elements of self, other, and bridging.

Negotiators who lack a sensitivity for spatial boundaries have poor proximity intuition. Generally, the closer one person stands to another, the more intimate *or* aggressive the interaction becomes. Lacking a well-established, positive relationship with another, standing too close to them might seem either adversarial or overly familiar. On the other hand, distancing oneself from another might convey dislike or disinterest.

With developed proximity intuition, a negotiator understands their own proximity preferences. They can use their stance or movements appropriately to emphasize points. They recognize how the other responds to their own proximity-related actions and recognize their preferences of motion and personal space. They are then able to bridge through this element effectively. Such bridging can be performed passively, by retaining suitable distance from the other, or actively, through physical touch, moving closer, or making eye contact.

Body Language and Mirroring: During negotiation, awareness of your own body language (facial expressions, posture, and head movements, for example), and of its relationship to the words you are saying and the emotions you are experiencing, is crucial. It provides a window into how you are experiencing the negotiation—and into understanding how you are being read by others.

Awareness of your counterpart's body language uncovers their emotional stance toward you, their degree of confidence, and the spectrum of pressures they face. The degree to which their body language mirrors your own can reflect their state of rapport and trust in your joint interaction. Finally, the use of body stance, physical motion, and mirroring actions as bridging mechanisms are key elements of active listening.

Eye Contact: Eye contact is perhaps the most oft-discussed element connecting nonverbal communication and social intuition in negotiation. Be aware of the messages that your own instinctive eye movements send about yourself. Skilled negotiators are also able to view the other party's eyes and read their emotional cues. Finally, negotiators who demonstrate excellent social intuition during a negotiation understand both the cultural meaning of eye contact and the messages that can be signaled to another party through their eyes. As a result, they can use eye movement as a bridging mechanism, intentionally showing interest or disinterest in a deal, or avoiding showing an attitude they wish to hide.

Physical Contact: Most negotiations provide opportunities for physical touch. This might be limited to introductory or parting handshakes, or include a hand guiding a counterpart to a meeting room; it may be a welcome hug for a counterpart who is a long-standing acquaintance. Social intuition helps gauge the appropriateness of physical contact, if any, during a negotiation.

Keen social intuition will allow negotiators to react well to touch initiated by their counterpart, and to decide the value, suitability, and style of touch at any point during the negotiation: its formality, degree of intimacy, duration, degree of vigor, force, and more. Negotiators with social intuition recognize those moments and implement a suitable and effective physical bridging mechanism.

Pace: Social intuition can determine two elements of pace: the speed at which a negotiator speaks and the amount of time a negotiator allows for each communicative "turn"—the completion of a conversational expression by themselves or by the other—before moving on to the next turn (by giving your counterpart the floor or by interrupting them).

Negotiators can adjust their pace to mirror their counterpart's, generating rapport. They can interrupt in bonding ways, to connect, or disruptively, to throw the other off-balance. They can also affect the other's pace by various means—signaling them to speed up through hand motions or verbal prompts, expressly asking them to slow down, or making "time-out" gestures.

Tone: A negotiator's tone is another aspect of *how* to say something. Our tone of voice subconsciously changes as our emotions toward the conversation, its content, or our counterpart leak into our voice. We also intentionally use tone to emphasize a point, convey the importance of an issue, or nonverbally express an emotion.

Limited social intuition regarding tone leads to incorrect or imprecise inferences. Sometimes, out of frustration or anger, negotiators unknowingly change their tone. Oblivious to their counterpart's tonal expressions, they might ignore emotional warning signs—or miss windows of opportunity. They might speak in whatever tone comes naturally to them, without knowing (or even caring) how that is received by the other person.

On the other hand, negotiators who are socially adept in tone are aware of their own tone—their defaults, and the variances that appear under different emotional circumstances. They monitor these to avoid undesired emotional leakage. Negotiators aware of elements of tone regarding the other will note the other's baseline practices rather than assuming they will be similar to their own. They will notice variances in tone and strive to identify their meaning. They can modify their own tone to bring a precise level of understanding to, or draw a particular emotional response out of, another person.

Modifiers, Caveats, and No-Go Areas—When This Advice Just Won't Apply

Social intuition, including elements that space does not allow here (such as ritual, humor, and metaphor), is generally developed in a particular cultural environment. The degree to which our own, and our counterpart's, cultural settings overlap affects whether our social intuition will assist us—or harm us. As negotiators, we must constantly be aware of our own cultural background and its effects on how we think, process, speak, conclude, and act. We must seek to understand our counterpart, and in particular, some of the cultural aspects of the surroundings in which *their* social intuition developed. Finally, negotiators can use elements of similarity or difference in cultural backgrounds to bridge—for example, mirroring your counterpart's way of saying or doing things in a manner that demonstrates respect for their patterns. Conversely, a negotiator might wish to point out an element of cultural difference between you, so that while the difference still exists, it is now a target for mutual adaptation. Being curious up front, rather than making assumptions, helps prevent social gaffes and miscommunication, while still leaving space for the positive effects of social intuition.

Conclusion

While negotiators typically focus on the content of their verbal exchanges, our brains process information and reach conclusions based on subtler interactional elements. By being mindful of these elements, we can not only gain information, but also affect the other and shift negotiation interactions in our favor.

This Ties in With:

Newell, Ch. 18, Attention; Itzchakov & Kluger, Ch. 20, Changing Attitudes; Thompson et al., Ch. 21, Nonverbal

8

Whole-Brain Negotiation

Alexandra Crampton[1]

Introduction

A neuroscience approach provides a way to integrate emotions and other differences between individuals by examining how our brains evolved as a social species. This chapter links brain evolution within our species to explain how each of us becomes a mini-evolution of a "social self" who uses a brain that is both social and individual. We develop into adulthood as social individuals—or *socioindividuals.* Inattention to this process risks limiting negotiation tools to individual and rational analysis, which effectively leaves most of ourselves—and others—out of the negotiation. This chapter is based on A. Crampton, *The Social Brain*, in 1 The Negotiator's Desk Reference 115–125 (Honeyman & Schneider eds, 2017). The full references in that chapter can be found at www.ndrweb.com/chapter-9--public.html.

1. **Alexandra Crampton** is Associate Professor of Social and Cultural Sciences at Marquette University. She received her B.A. from Stanford and a master of social work and joint Ph.D (anthropology and social work) from the University of Michigan. She received negotiation training through the Program on Negotiation (PON) at Harvard Law School as a PON research fellow, which was followed by writing on negotiation pedagogy for NP@PON. She delivered the keynote for the 2015 Wisconsin Bar Association training on culture in dispute resolution, providing integration of neuroscience and culture concepts. Her mediation research and practice focus is on elder and family court mediation.

Why This Concept Might Change Your Thinking

The expression "mind over matter" describes a presumed separation and superiority of rational approaches. For example, lawyers may limit emotions to allowing parties to "vent" before more serious work begins. Deviations from rational analysis are then addressed as cognitive distortions to be corrected, rather than to be understood. However, limiting negotiation to "just the facts" can easily cause unnecessary alienation of your client, as well as other parties. In addition, considerations of social difference, such as gender and culture, are considered by novice negotiators as advanced skills—as if there is a basic, normal way to negotiate that only requires adaptation when parties deviate from basic expectations. This can easily lead to stereotyping and misunderstanding rather than better negotiation.

A whole-brain approach to negotiation debunks the presumption that people exist independently of their environment. This presumption is a contemporary cultural construct more than a social reality. This is because humans evolved as a social species that requires an extended time to develop an inner understanding of the world. It is through this mini-evolution of understanding that we also learn to navigate—and negotiate—our *outer* world. Through this process, each of us develops unique and yet common ways of social interaction, communication, and interpretation. Emotions are key to this, because we relate to others emotionally before we develop capacity for rational and more individualistic analysis. Differences are inevitable because no two people will perceive or interpret situations in the exact same way. Shared traits and learned differences among negotiating parties can be traced to comparison of past environments in which we were raised, educated, and later trained as professionals. To negotiate optimally, lawyers ought to leverage both our human capacity to share experience and to uniquely evaluate.

The overall lesson is "don't presume" that there is one superior case assessment, nor that the merits of any argument are based solely on the law and rational analysis. Instead, allow optimal answers to emerge through negotiation and to be context-dependent. They will be derived through the interdependent work of brains as social. Leveraging the *social brain* expands the range of potential outcomes within legal and ethical parameters that professionally constrain options and outcomes. This expansion comes through including parameters otherwise neglected (and suppressed) as nonlegal, nonrational, and therefore irrelevant. In fact, there is always a degree of false choice of rational vs. emotional, culture (or gender) neutrality vs. sensitivity, and personal vs. professional when negotiating. A whole-brain approach integrates emotional and relational elements of negotiation, with attention to personal differences. Rational judgment remains important, but it should not be the only tool for success.

Action Plan—What You Can Do Differently Tomorrow

Learn how the personal and emotional are *integral* to the rational and analytic. The reality is that we first develop a sense of self and how to negotiate within our environment as children, before we have developed capacity for rational understanding. Through ongoing interaction within social environments, neural connections are formed, and patterned responses coalesce into an internal "schema" used to interpret new stimuli and guide responses. From this socioemotional self, we eventually develop ever more sophisticated, rational capacities.

In adulthood, as we try to make decisions, the process is not one of first discarding emotional and irrelevant information to then progress to a conclusion. Instead, the process is of an internal "brain chatter," largely from past experience, that eventually converges into an answer. While we may search for this consciously as a rationalized response, neurobiological research shows how personal and emotional experience not only informs our rationalized arguments, but those of others, as well. Conscious judgment will be more accurate if the deeper contributions of a largely unconscious and evolving self can be considered prior to using rational judgment to evaluate.

Recognize the benefits of social rather than individual attempts at expertise. Two neural concepts useful for this are *blooming* and *pruning*. The brain evolved not only to perceive but also to filter. In brain development, there are periods of blooming, in which neural connections expand, and then pruning, in which connections are lost. This happens within the environments in which we are raised, socialized, and educated as professionals. A stimulating environment will encourage novel neural connections, which is followed by narrowing to expert response through neural pruning. Thus, each of us become experts through experience that we internally (neurally) tailor to our ways of understanding. This understanding, therefore, may be accurate and yet will always be incomplete. If another disagrees, you may not be able to simply argue for the superiority of your analysis. You may need to first back up and be curious—try to understand how another party, confronted with the same case, may have a very different analysis. This will be true for your client as well as for opposing parties. Exploring variable interpretations will open negotiation options without necessarily giving away your (client's) position or valuable information.

Address difference through learning about each party rather than by memorizing traits. Typical ways of learning difference and negotiation involve studying how other people vary (such as by gender, culture, ethnicity, or professional socialization) and then incorporating that into a negotiation strategy. This, however, can lead to stereotyping and overgeneralization. What is more important is to gain a general understanding of how people are variably socialized and how people's life experience variably develops within them different internal filters for understanding the world, as well as variable underlying needs and interests. A general understanding can allow you to ask more educated questions in learning about the other parties—but is no substitute for engaging *them* in learning what is important to them in *this* context of *this* negotiation. The need to back up and have more general conversation may seem superfluous only until appreciation of difference helps—when you get stuck.

Modifiers, Caveats, and No-Go Areas—When This Advice Just Won't Apply

Although the emphasis in this advice is on identification and leveraging of nonrational, socially derived parts of each person in negotiation, the takeaway is not to abandon the rational, nor your individuality. Entirely prosocial behavior can lead to worse negotiation outcomes if people agree with each other too quickly and do not first push to identify and evaluate all options. Intragroup harmony can lead to acceptance of distorted views or neglecting self-interest. Your ability to separate yourself from other parties and the negotiation process remains an important dimension to successful negotiation. The task in whole-brain negotiation is not a forced choice but rather, a creative tension between socioemotional and rational responses in which social interaction promotes shared understanding yet also allows individual judgment in final evaluation.

Conclusion

In Western legal training and ethics, there is often a choice between the individual and the collective. Consideration of how our brains evolved as a species and how each of us evolve through brain maturation usefully blurs this false distinction by showing how much the individual is formed through a collective and vice versa. We are born into a social environment already in play, and we first adapt to this environment before we develop capacity to then replicate and potentially modify this environment. Reliance on rational capacity for individual judgment is like starting the negotiation journey by planning the commemorative photo album, which will inevitably limit us to seeing what we already expect. This can easily alienate other parties and prevent optimal negotiation.

This Ties in With:

Schneider & Ebner, Ch. 7, Social Intuition; Shestowsky, Ch. 11, Persuasion

Section III

Making Your Case

Section III is about ensuring that however farsighted and generous you choose to be in a negotiation, your own needs are still met. The section begins with Chapter 9, which is about setting goals—or how to ensure that your aspirations are both high *and* attainable. Chapter 10 discusses six factors that influence whether you will get your way or not (all other things being equal), and then Chapter 11 is on how to distinguish between and work with two kinds of audiences that are responsive to completely different psychological approaches.

We turn next to Chapter 12, which boils down a bestseller into a brief treatment of how each party is likely to formulate (and believe) a completely different story of what is going on. Chapter 13 explains why and how the best salespeople listen far more than they talk—and what questions they ask when they do talk.

But when the story your negotiation counterparts are telling themselves is one that you must challenge, the moves and turns the discussion takes are likely to determine whether you get anywhere in your negotiations—and that is the final subject of this section, in Chapter 14.

9

Measuring Success

Andrea Kupfer Schneider[1]

Introduction

When you set out to negotiate with someone, how do you evaluate what you are really trying to achieve? Could it be an unfocused want or "anything above your reservation price"? Four keys to negotiation success are being optimistic; setting goals you can justify in public without laughing or lying; making them specific; and paying real attention to goals that cannot be expressed in a number. Finally, to achieve true success we need to get used to disappointment. This chapter is based on A.K. SCHNEIDER, *Productive Ambition*, in 1 THE NEGOTIATOR'S DESK REFERENCE 321–329 (Honeyman & Schneider eds, 2017). The full references in that chapter can be found at www.ndrweb.com/chapter-23--public.html.

1. **Andrea Kupfer Schneider** is a Professor of Law at Marquette University Law School, where she teaches dispute resolution, negotiation, ethics, and international conflict resolution and is the director of Marquette's nationally ranked dispute resolution program. Andrea has written numerous books, book chapters, and articles on negotiation skills and styles, dispute system design, international conflict, and gender and negotiation. She was given the American Bar Association (ABA) Section of Dispute Resolution Award for Outstanding Scholarly Work for 2017. Andrea received her A.B. *cum laude* from the Woodrow Wilson School of Public & International Affairs at Princeton University and her J.D. *cum laude* from Harvard Law School.

Why This Concept Might Change Your Thinking

Good negotiators spend a lot of time thinking about how to determine their best alternative to a negotiated agreement (BATNA) and to assess their interests. They may not spend equal time focusing on aspirations. And unless negotiators actually set a specific goal and try to reach it, they will undoubtedly fall short. Social science research confirms that negotiators with higher aspirations tend to achieve better bargaining results. Yet once negotiators start to focus more on aspirations, they also need to think about how aspirations should be set, and how to distinguish an aspiration from a reservation point. Moreover, negotiators should consider the psychology behind setting high aspirations, so that their overall satisfaction with their outcome accurately reflects their results. Finally, negotiators should consider aspirations broadly, focusing on more than money or other measurable criteria.

Action Plan—What You Can Do Differently Tomorrow

Justifiable Aspirations

The first step in setting goals is to make those aspirations reasonable and justifiable, for several important reasons. A negotiator will be more likely to succeed in convincing her counterpart to reach an agreement based on her aspiration level if she can argue that such an outcome is derived from objective criteria. Objective criteria help persuade both us and our counterparts about the fairness of our offer. We are able to argue more persuasively when we believe in the justice of our cause. Similarly, our counterpart is more likely to agree to our offer when it is fair in his or her eyes.

The availability of objective criteria also makes it easier for the negotiator to justify a refusal to make concessions. Demands that are not realistically grounded are harder to hold on to during the bargaining process. Similarly, demands that lack an objective justification encourage the opposing negotiator to make unprincipled counterdemands.

An additional reason that aspirations should be justifiable (versus laughable) is that overly aggressive aspirations can lead to a negotiation impasse, even when mutually beneficial agreements are possible. In circumstances in which determining where to set one's bottom line is especially complex, or the context is assumed to be competitive, aggressive aspirations are likely to also impact the perceived reservation point unrealistically. Thus, aspirations that are *too* high can indirectly lead the negotiator to reject proposed agreements that are actually within an objectively acceptable range.

Optimistic Aspirations

Negotiators should also establish *optimistic* aspirations, because as empirical evidence has shown, negotiators with higher aspirations tend to achieve better bargaining results.

There are different explanations for this. First, a negotiator's aspirations help determine the outer limit of what she will request. Because a negotiator will almost never achieve more than what she asks for, setting relatively high goals is important so that the negotiator makes suitably assertive demands from which she can bargain down (or up).

Second, optimistic aspirations can cause negotiators to work harder at bargaining to achieve their desirable outcome. Rather than getting frustrated and either walking away or giving in, the negotiator who *knows* she has high aspirations (and justifiable ones) will be willing to tolerate a longer give-and-take in order to approach her aspirations. In other words, higher aspirations can lead negotiators to be more patient in the negotiation rather than hurrying to a less optimal outcome.

Specific Aspirations

Finally, aspirations should be specific. A general goal of "doing well" or "let's see what they say" is insufficient to trigger the positive behavioral benefits of setting aspirations. Much in the same way that negotiators learn to define their BATNA and then use it to determine their bottom line, negotiators should take vague aspirations and turn them into specific goals for the negotiation.

Subjective and Objective Values

A last note on aspirations concerns subjective goals. Feeling good about the outcome of the negotiation is a separate goal that we have seen reflected in literature on fairness, trust, and procedural justice. Subjective valuation of an outcome may shed light on objective values, as well. We rarely know how we have done objectively in a real negotiation, as negotiators do not usually sit down and exchange information, comparing BATNAs, bargaining ranges, and goals. Psychologists argue that negotiator intuition and one's subjective assessment of the outcome is, therefore, as good as it gets for assessing motivations and tendencies of negotiators.

The subjective value of the negotiation also creates reputations that feed back into future interactions. In other words, if we create subjective value for the other side (our counterpart feels good), he or she is more likely to want to interact with us in the future in a positive way. This reputational value can add to one's objective outcomes in the future. Finally, this subjective value also makes it more likely that the agreement will actually be implemented.

The concept of subjective value can help us think more broadly about our aspirations in negotiation as we go forward, to set them optimistically, specifically, and justifiably. What kind of process do we aspire to establish? Toward what reputation should I aspire? How should I treat my counterparts (and be treated by them)? Setting goals for these subjective items should also increase our satisfaction with the negotiation outcome.

Modifiers, Caveats, and No-Go Areas—When This Advice Just Won't Apply

Sometimes, a negotiator may set low aspirations if the negotiator feels that she lacks enough information about the other side's interests and bottom line to confidently predict what results are possible. A negotiator may assume that she needs the deal more than her counterpart or may not understand why reaching a settlement is important to the other side. Without this information, she may set her goals lower than they should be from an objective perspective. Furthermore, negotiators often do not update their goals as new information is learned over the course of the negotiation.

A negotiator may also set low goals when she is relatively uninterested in the result or wants to avoid conflict with another person. Of course, these low goals may be appropriate—as long as the negotiator makes a *rational* decision about the relative unimportance of those goals.

Finally, negotiators often fail to follow the "optimistic but justifiable" approach to setting aspirations because this can result in disappointment when these goals are not achieved. Setting low or nonspecific goals maximizes the likelihood of success and thus protects self-esteem. The "high aspirations" negotiator may well have received much more money than the "low aspirations" negotiator, but he may be more focused on his perceived *loss* compared to his original aspiration. In order to avoid this disappointment, negotiators often set low goals. To make things worse, this disappointment from one negotiation can lead negotiators to set lower goals in future negotiations, again in a self-protective response.

Negotiators should instead focus on their *total* accomplishment rather than comparing their results to their goals. In other words, a negotiator should set goals for her outcome—but evaluate success based on her BATNA.

Conclusion

This chapter has argued that the importance of setting aspirations in negotiation is as important as thinking about our bottom lines. Aspirations should be justifiable, optimistic, and specific. Aspirations should also be broadened to include more subjective measures of success, to ensure good reputations and higher compliance with our agreements.

This Ties in With:

Guthrie, Ch. 10, Compliance; Shestowsky, Ch. 11, Persuasion; Abramowitz, Ch. 13, Sales; Groton et al., Ch. 53, Thinking Ahead

10

Courting Compliance

Chris Guthrie[1]

Introduction

Every lawyer negotiates, and every negotiation requires persuasion, so lawyers must know how to persuade. Lawyers are skilled at legal argumentation, which is a powerful form of persuasion well-suited to the courtroom. But even if the law, facts, and logic cut in her favor, a lawyer negotiating a deal or dispute can get only so far with legal argumentation at the bargaining table. To succeed in negotiation, lawyers need to supplement legal argumentation with the subtle skill of psychological persuasion. The purpose of this chapter is to explain how lawyers can use psychological principles of influence to help get their clients what they want in negotiation. This chapter is based on C. GUTHRIE, *Getting Your Way*, in 1 THE NEGOTIATOR'S DESK REFERENCE 331–338 (Honeyman & Schneider eds, 2017). The full references in that chapter can be found at www.ndrweb.com/chapter-24--public.html.

Why This Concept Might Change Your Thinking

Negotiation is a voluntary process in which either party is free to walk away at any time and in which each party needs the other in order

1. **Chris Guthrie** is the dean and John Wade-Kent Syverud Professor of Law at Vanderbilt University Law School.

to reach a deal. Because the parties are dependent on one another, a lawyer must view negotiation not as an out-of-court forum for legal argumentation, but rather as a process of psychological influence.

Relying on decades of empirical research, Professor Robert Cialdini has identified six principles of psychological influence shown to facilitate agreement: authority, liking, social proof, commitment and consistency, reciprocity, and scarcity. A lawyer who uses these principles of influence successfully is more likely to help her client get her way; a lawyer who is unaware of them is vulnerable to a counterpart who knows what they are and how they work. Thus, for both negotiation offense *and* negotiation defense, a lawyer should familiarize herself with these tactics.

Action Plan—What You Can Do Differently Tomorrow

How might a lawyer use the psychology of persuasion to facilitate her client's aims?

To begin, she should recognize that she is more likely to get what she wants if her counterpart views her as an authority figure (*authority*). People are more likely to defer to those they perceive as authorities, so a lawyer who can reasonably lay claim to stature in a field, or who can reasonably invoke a relevant authority figure, like a judge who has ruled in her favor in similar cases before, is more likely to induce the other party to comply.

People tend not only to follow authority figures but also to emulate and comply with those they like (*liking*). People tend to like those with whom they have something in common. A lawyer should therefore spend some time at the outset of a negotiation eliciting and identifying commonalities with her counterpart (e.g., shared profession, shared hobbies, friends and colleagues in common, family composition) and, throughout the negotiation, she should find opportunities to identify and reflect back her counterpart's cues (e.g., leaning back when she leans back). By creating this connection with her counterpart, she can accomplish two things. First, she can build rapport, which facilitates agreement. Second, she can model behaviors she would like to induce her counterpart to mimic, because people have a tendency to take cues from another person's behavior to guide their own (*social proof*). This is particularly true when the person they are observing is someone with whom they identify. So, for instance, a lawyer who has garnered her counterpart's affection at the outset of the negotiation might describe the negotiation as a shared search for win-win outcomes, with the intention of inducing her counterpart to view the negotiation the same way and to conduct herself accordingly.

Once a lawyer has established her bona fides as an authority figure, connected with her counterpart to facilitate affection, and modeled desirable behavior, she should then seek to induce small commitments from her counterpart with an eye toward eventually securing larger ones (*commitment and consistency*). Research on commitment and consistency shows that once a person takes a stand or makes a commitment, she will feel both internal and interpersonal pressure to behave in accord with the position she has taken. So a lawyer may benefit in negotiation by encouraging her counterpart to make small commitments early. Perhaps, for example, she can persuade her counterpart to agree to a minor substantive term such as a confidentiality clause or a non-disparagement clause or a no-publicity clause. By inducing one's counterpart to make a small commitment like this, the lawyer may be able to obtain more substantial commitments later in the process. Her counterpart may simply feel duty bound to comply *due to her own compliance earlier in the process*. This is likely to work particularly well if her counterpart previously agreed to embrace an abstract principle (such as equitable division or what a court would do) and is subsequently asked to agree with the execution of that principle (*therefore, my client should receive X*).

People feel obligated not only to behave consistently with prior behavior but also to reciprocate the behavior of others. In other words, people feel obligated to repay what they have received from another (*reciprocity*). If one person sends a holiday card to another, that person, even if a stranger, will likely feel obligated to do the same!

A lawyer can use reciprocity in at least three ways to persuade her counterpart to make a meaningful concession at the bargaining table. Most obviously, she can make a concession herself, and this can create in her counterpart a sense of obligation to respond similarly. If she started from a more favorable position than her counterpart, the reciprocal concession she induces her counterpart to make is likely to work to her client's advantage in a distributive negotiation.

Relatedly, a lawyer can use reciprocity to "logroll" in negotiation. That is, she can agree to make a concession on an issue that might matter less to her client, to induce her counterpart to make a concession on another issue that matters more to her client. Reciprocity can facilitate this mutually beneficial *quid pro quo* or exchange of favors.

Third, and somewhat less obviously, a lawyer can request a substantial concession, expecting to get turned down, and then make a more modest request. In many instances, the lawyer's counterpart will feel obligated to respond to this ostensible "concession" and comply with the more modest request. Cialdini calls this powerful tactic the "rejection-then-retreat" strategy.

Finally, a lawyer might use *scarcity*—the idea that opportunities seem more valuable to us when they are at risk of becoming unavailable—to her client's advantage in negotiation. Scarcity can induce compliance in part because it works hand-in-hand with "loss aversion," a well-known psychological phenomenon demonstrating that we generally find losses much more painful than we find equivalent gains appealing and are therefore motivated to avoid losing something.

The lawyer who appreciates the impact that scarcity is likely to have on her counterpart may try to create the impression in negotiation that opportunities to settle are limited and time is running out. For example, she might extend an offer but give her counterpart a limited window within which to accept it. Likewise, she might make an offer immediately prior to an expected judicial ruling that might be harmful to her counterpart's case, or she might make an offer of judgment under Rule 68 of the Federal Rules of Civil Procedure. In each instance, her counterpart might feel more motivated to settle due to the limited availability of the offer (and indeed, the scarcity principle undoubtedly helps explain the apparent abundance of settlements on the courthouse steps).

Modifiers, Caveats, and No-Go Areas—When This Advice Just Won't Apply

A lawyer *can* use authority, liking, social proof, commitment and consistency, reciprocity, and scarcity to induce her counterpart to settle on terms that are favorable to her client. But *should* she?

A lawyer should try to obtain the best possible outcome for her client, but she should do so in ways that comport not only with the formal ethical rules, but also with her own sense of professional responsibility and personal ethics. (Would I want my mother to know I used that tactic? Would I want my counterpart to use that tactic? How would I feel if the local newspaper ran a story about the negotiation?)

Most lawyers will feel comfortable employing these tactics; indeed, many lawyers already use them, even if they do not apply Cialdini's labels to them. Like other negotiation tactics, these compliance tactics often prove effective and do not automatically run afoul of any formal ethical rules. Other lawyers, however, might feel uncomfortable using at least some of these tactics. For example, a lawyer who attempts to garner his counterpart's affection solely to facilitate agreement, or who attempts to secure a small commitment from his counterpart solely as a way of obtaining a larger one later, might feel as though he is treating his counterpart as a mere instrumentality.

Conclusion

The lawyer, as a professional, must decide for himself or herself whether and how to employ these powerful persuasive devices at the bargaining table.

This Ties in With:

Shestowsky, Ch. 11, Persuasion; Heen & Stone, Ch. 12, Your Story & Mine

11

Psychology and Persuasion in Your Negotiation

Donna Shestowsky[1]

Introduction

Persuasion is both an art and a science. It is an *art* because persuasion strategies can be used in both subtle and obvious ways. It is a *science* because researchers have uncovered systematic patterns in the effectiveness of certain strategies and how they work in different contexts. Good negotiators have an intuition for the art of persuasion; *expert* negotiators also understand and apply the scientific knowledge about what works. This chapter summarizes the relevant empirical research that can help you improve your negotiation strategy in both deal-making and settlement contexts. This chapter is based on D. Shestowsky, *The Psychology of Negotiation: Using Persuasion to Negotiate More Effectively*, in 1 The Negotiator's Desk Reference 339–350 (Honeyman & Schneider eds, 2017).

1. **Dr. Donna Shestowsky** is Director of Lawyering Skills Education and Professor of Law at the University of California, Davis. She earned a J.D. and Ph.D. (psychology) from Stanford University, and a B.A. and M.S. (psychology) from Yale University. She is the principal investigator of a multi-court research project, funded by the National Science Foundation and the American Bar Association (ABA), which examines how litigants evaluate procedures. Her commentary has appeared in national sources such as CNN, NPR, and the *New York Times*.

The full references in that chapter can be found at www.ndrweb.com/chapter-25--public.html.

Why This Concept Might Change Your Thinking

To be an expert negotiator, it is critical to use the psychology of persuasion both proactively and reactively. Proactively, incorporating psychological principles into your negotiation toolkit will help you be more persuasive as you advocate for your own proposals. Reactively, knowledge of these principles will help you identify and guard against situations in which others subtly attempt to persuade you to act against your client's best interests. Overall, being able to identify and respond appropriately to opposing counsel's attempts at persuasion can mean the difference between being at their mercy and resisting their appeal.

Action Plan—What You Can Do Differently Tomorrow

There Are Two Routes to Persuasion

Although legal education focuses on helping lawyers develop strong arguments (i.e., arguments that offer clear, logical, and relevant reasons in favor of their position), psychological research reveals that strong arguments often fail to persuade because people do not always have the ability or motivation to think deeply enough to recognize and respond to strong arguments. In fact, there are two distinct routes to persuasion, one that depends on the content of arguments (*central route persuasion*) and one that does not (*peripheral route persuasion*). Central route persuasion occurs when negotiators are both able and willing to think deeply about your arguments and therefore are more likely to recognize and support a strong proposal. In contrast, when negotiators are not willing or able to think deeply, they use peripheral processing, which involves considering your arguments more superficially. In these cases, individuals are apt to use *peripheral cues* (peripheral to the merits or content of your message) as heuristics or mental shortcuts to make decisions. At these times, strong arguments will not have their intended effect, while strategies that focus on how a proposal is "packaged" are likely to be more successful.

People who are both able and motivated to think deeply are best persuaded via the central route. The ability to think deeply is influenced not only by individual characteristics such as intellectual ability, but also by situational factors such as being tired, hungry, distracted, or preoccupied with other projects or personal matters. Generally, behaviors that reflect attentiveness and engaged thinking suggest that the other party will be responsive to central route persuasion.

Similarly, opposing counsel's motivation to think deeply can be the result of either situational factors, such as his viewing the focal issues as highly personally relevant, or personality traits, such as his general motivation to think deeply. Behaviors demonstrating boredom, laziness, or distraction (e.g., opposing counsel often asks you to repeat yourself or raises issues that are clearly irrelevant to the focal topic) suggest that he is engaging in peripheral processing, and thus peripheral route persuasion will be more effective.

Although both routes to persuasion can produce the same level of influence in the short term (even during the negotiation session itself), decisions made via the central route are more likely to persist over time, resist subsequent persuasive attempts, and promote behavioral adherence to the terms of the agreement. Thus, when you want long-term voluntary compliance with the negotiated outcome, and you can offer strong, win-win arguments in support of your proposals, it is critically important to persuade opposing counsel via the central route. While you cannot change the personality traits of opposing counsel that limit his ability and motivation, you can often shape situational factors to increase the chances he will think deeply enough to recognize the wisdom of your proposals.

Strategies for Persuasion by the Central Route

If you can make a strong case for your proposal, you want opposing counsel to engage in central processing when he encounters your pitch. But you want him to process your pitch deeply *only* when it has intrinsic value to him (as well as to your client). If the merits are not strong, deep processing will make your opponent more likely to realize this and consequently reject the proposal. However, when you have great win-win ideas, encouraging deep processing can help you succeed in selling those ideas. Several strategies can help you accomplish this goal. First, ask questions rather than making assertions, requests, or demands. Second, frame the reconciliation of competing interests as a puzzle or problem that requires coming up with an objectively reasonable or accurate solution. Third, reduce distractions that may interrupt deep thinking (e.g., consider using email—when we communicate via technology, we generally pay less attention to the other party and more attention to their message). Fourth, make clear and concise arguments—for example, avoid jargon that opposing counsel might not understand. When arguments are complex and protracted, the other party is more likely to tune out and not expend the effort required to understand them. Finally, induce a sense of individual responsibility for the terms of the agreement. This strategy is most relevant when you are negotiating against a team because it helps combat *social loafing*, the tendency for individuals to put less effort into a task when they share responsibility for the outcome as part of a group because they assume their teammates will do the hard thinking and they, therefore, need not do it themselves. Encourage each member of the opposing team to think for himself by asking questions of those who are quieter or by proposing a general brainstorming session in which everyone is expected to participate.

Strategies for Persuasion by the Peripheral Route

If you perceive that opposing counsel lacks the motivation or ability to scrutinize your arguments, it will likely be advantageous to set the stage for peripheral cues by promoting decision-making via heuristics. One particularly well-researched peripheral cue is the expertise heuristic—people will be more persuaded by "experts," believing that they have done the thinking for them and that they themselves can therefore simply follow the experts' suggestions. You can capitalize on this heuristic by speaking quickly (rapid message delivery is generally associated with greater perceived credibility), having a high-status member of your team conduct the negotiation, emphasizing your significant knowledge base or accomplishments in a domain relevant to the negotiation, or by beginning negotiations by summarizing your background in a way that emphasizes your status. To take full advantage of peripheral route persuasion, you should develop a plan for how to make such cues salient during your negotiations.

Select (or At Least Consider) Your Audience

Ideally, you should prepare to use both central and peripheral strategies and then employ each as the situation dictates. If your best strategy involves central route persuasion and you have the opportunity to choose which representative of the opposing party you will meet with, then you should select someone who can process arguments thoughtfully and who is highly motivated to think. When observing people working as part of a team, you can identify these individuals by noting who tends to talk most frequently and is highly engaged in group meetings. When peripheral processing is more desirable, you might invite someone who has been less participatory in prior group meetings (i.e., someone who seems to engage in social loafing) and plan to make use of peripheral cues. If the opposing counsel's ability or motivation to think is uncertain (which is often the case), you should employ strategies that promote careful thinking when you offer objectively strong arguments to support your proposals and supplement this approach by using peripheral strategies.

Conclusion

As stated at the outset, *expert* negotiators understand and apply scientific knowledge about the psychology of persuasion to their negotiations, and also have a knack for the art of persuasion. By adding the persuasion skills described above to your toolkit, you can negotiate with the confidence that you are doing your best to advocate for your clients.

This Ties in With:

Guthrie, Ch. 10, Compliance; Heen & Stone, Ch. 12, Your Story & Mine

12

Your Story and Mine

Sheila Heen[1] *and Douglas Stone*[2]

Introduction

Each party to a conflict will see that conflict differently. Here we consider why that matters, and we offer two important communication tools to help you manage these differences effectively in a negotiation. This chapter is based on S. Heen & D. Stone, *Perceptions and Stories*, in 1 The Negotiator's Desk Reference 351–363 (Honeyman & Schneider eds, 2017). The full references in that chapter can be found at www.ndrweb.com/chapter-26--public.html.

1. **Sheila Heen** is a founder of Triad Consulting, a Lecturer on Law at Harvard Law School, and coauthor of two *New York Times* best sellers, *Difficult Conversations: How to Discuss What Matters Most* (Penguin 1999) and *Thanks for the Feedback* (Penguin 2014). In private practice, she helps executives navigate strong disagreement to make tough decisions while preserving relationships with each other, with employees, and with clients. Her public-sector work has included work in Barrow, Alaska, with the Inupiat Eskimos who own the North Slope, in Cyprus, with Greek and Turkish Cypriots, and at the White House. She can be reached at heen@post.harvard.edu.

2. **Douglas Stone** is a founder of Triad Consulting and a Lecturer on Law at Harvard. He consults for a broad range of organizations, including Merck, Honda, Fidelity, the World Health Organization (WHO), and at the White House, and lectures widely on leadership, negotiation, and communication. Doug is coauthor of *Difficult Conversations* (Penguin 1999), which is available in twenty-five languages and a *New York Times* business best seller. This book is used as the standard communication text in many business and law schools, and in organizations around the world. Doug is also coauthor of the bestselling *Thanks for the Feedback* (Penguin 2014). He can be reached at dstone@post.harvard.edu.

Why This Concept Might Change Your Thinking

We're all aware that human beings take in information from the world around us in ways that are incomplete and distorted, and that any two people will take in different information. It could hardly be otherwise; we have different interests (e.g., a person in a wheelchair will notice different things about a city sidewalk and curb-cuts than a person who is not in a wheelchair.) We have different access to information based on who and where we are in the world (e.g., I am a managing partner at my firm, you are a non-equity partner. I have access to the financial information upon which income distributions are determined; you have access to the countless sacrifices you made to bill the hours you billed). And as a rule, I have better access than you to my intentions and you have better access than I to the impacts of my actions on you.

With differing values, goals, experiences, predictions, roles, and self-interest, we also make different *meaning* from whatever data we take in. I see the appointment of a woman of color to the board of directors as broadening the board's range of voices; you see an inadequate and cynical response to the lack of diversity.

Beneath awareness, our brains format information and meaning into stories. We tend to cast ourselves as the hero or the victim—as injured or underappreciated. We tend to cast the other as villain or oppressor, who harms or dismisses us. We are quick to believe that the other is to blame and that we ourselves are blameless.

Yes, our stories reflect more than self-interest. But when taking in information and making meaning from that information, we all share certain default tendencies. (Ironically, one of them is perceiving these distorting tendencies in others, but not in ourselves.)

The ways people process the world into stories has profound implications for how we understand and manage conflict. Our ability to persuade someone depends on our ability to understand them. The reason is simple: *people don't change their minds until they feel understood*.

Action Plan—What You Can Do Differently Tomorrow

Below we discuss two powerful tools that will help you manage conflict and negotiate across differences more effectively.

1. Frame the Conflict from the Third Story

As noted above, any conflict between two sides has, well, two sides. I have my story and you have your story; I think I'm right and you think you're right. We both assume there are just two ways to tell the story of the conflict.

But we can always tell a third story—the way a mediator or disinterested observer might describe the conflict. It will be different from either my story or yours in one key way: instead of framing the two stories as a competition between right and wrong or better and worse, it frames them as merely *different*.

The third story offers both sides an inviting and constructive container for the conversation; it shifts the purpose away from the implicit question "which one of us is right?" and toward the questions "why do we see this differently?" and "how can we best manage these differences?"

Significantly, you don't need a mediator in order to use the third story. As a party to the conflict, or as an attorney to a party, you can start the conversation: "You and I see this differently. Let's try to figure out why. Once we understand why we see this differently, we'll be in a better position to problem-solve, and perhaps, reach agreement."

2. Listen Well: Inquire, Paraphrase, and Acknowledge

We often assume that the advice to listen is about being well-mannered or friendly. Those qualities are fine, but not enough. Listening is about bringing your *assumptions* about what you do and don't know (about what others think and feel) in line with what you *actually* do and don't know. We tend to assume that others see what we see and make meaning of the world as we do. As we discussed above, often they don't.

When you clarify the other person's interests, you are in a much better position to craft an outcome to a negotiation that meets those interests (and optimizes value for both sides). Inquiry is also the only way to meet one specific interest: the desire to feel heard. That doesn't guarantee a deal, but failure to meet that interest can destroy a deal.

Finally, and counterintuitively, using inquiry well makes you more persuasive. We often conceptualize persuasion as moving information from my brain to your brain: "I'll advocate—I'll pour my information and meaning-making into your head. And because they make sense, you'll agree with me."

The pouring metaphor assumes that the other person's brain is empty. But other people's brains are not empty any more than yours is. Especially in the context of conflict, the person you are trying to persuade is filled with their own thoughts.

Thoughts don't just take up space. Thinking is an activity—a conversation with oneself—that absorbs our attention. If I am listening to my own thoughts, I am not listening to you. Common thoughts in the context of conflict or negotiation are:

You're wrong.
What you don't realize is. . . .
This isn't fair.
This is your fault, not mine.
I'm fearful that. . . .

When you are talking to me, you are competing with the conversation I am having with myself. When I feel unheard, afraid, or unjustly treated, my self-conversation becomes louder. My thoughts block me from hearing your thoughts. If I am focused on my own thoughts, then no matter how brilliantly you present your ideas, they won't persuade me—not because they are unpersuasive, but because they are unheard.

Inquiry is important to persuasion because it's the only tool that gives you access to another person's thoughts, to their internal conversation. If the other person is thinking, "I feel unheard," the only way to lower the volume on that internal conversation is to listen to them. If they are thinking, "what you don't understand is . . .," the only way to lower the volume is to try to understand. If they are thinking, "I'm angry because this is not fair," the only way to lower the volume is to help them get that concern on the table.

Yet we often do the opposite. When they are thinking, "I feel unheard," we notice that they aren't taking in what we are saying, so we advocate more loudly. If they are thinking, "I feel unheard," and we say something like, "Here are more reasons you are wrong!"

the impact isn't that they feel more wrong, it's that they feel more unheard. Their internal conversation gets louder. Our ability to persuade is diminished even further.

Listening well, then, helps the other person turn down the volume on their self- conversation. They no longer think, "I don't feel heard," or "what you don't understand is . . .," because they do feel heard and understood.

Listening well is *not* about asserting that you understand the other person. It requires that you ask questions from a place of genuine curiosity: "Say more about why that felt dismissive." "Help me understand how you're tying these two ideas together." "What's at the heart of this situation from your point of view?" "What are you concerned might happen if we do it my way?" (Note that good "questions" don't have to end with a question mark to qualify as useful inquiry.) As you get answers, it's important occasionally to paraphrase and to acknowledge key emotions you hear. This helps convey that you understand the other person, or conversely, that you don't, which then gives them the chance to clarify.

Modifiers, Caveats, and No-Go Areas— When This Advice Just Won't Apply

Being good at advocacy is still needed, and it is just as important as being good at inquiry. Some people who are good at inquiry struggle with advocacy, and some who are good at advocacy struggle with inquiry. But a good negotiator or conflict manager can and should be skilled at both.

Is it best to listen *before* one advocates? Often . . . but not always. If your primary purpose is to communicate a message, then you have to start there. It's unhelpful, for example, to inform someone they are being fired or that you are breaking up with them by asking, "How do you think things are going?" But other things being equal, you are better off listening well and then advocating.

Conclusion

There are no magic words that make conflict disappear, nor any spell you can cast to ensure that you always win the day. We each see the world from our own vantage point. Conflict is the inevitable result.

But framing conflict from the third story, and then listening well before you advocate, can meaningfully reduce conflict and improve your outcomes.

This Ties in With:

Guthrie, Ch. 10, Compliance; Shestowsky, Ch. 11, Persuasion

13

Modern Consultative Sales Theory

Ava J. Abramowitz[1]

Introduction

I remember clearly how much I loved *Getting to Yes* the first time I read it. And I distinctly remember thinking, "But how exactly does one do that?" Yet over the years, nothing I read told me *precisely* how one gets another to come to yes, until I read the formative book behind modern consultative sales theory—*SPINSelling*—and learned that:

- Problem-solving is the purpose of consultative selling.
- Developing shared understandings through effective information-seeking is the medium.
- Coming to a solution that all parties want to implement is the result.

As that is what negotiation is all about, consultative selling changed my client services, my negotiation style, the outcomes reached at the

1. A former assistant U.S. Attorney for the District of Columbia, **Ava J. Abramowitz** mediates for the U.S. Court of Appeals for the District of Columbia and for the U.S. District Court for the District of Columbia. A Professorial Lecturer in Law at the George Washington University Law School, she is the Long Range Planning Officer of the American Bar Association (ABA) Dispute Resolution Section and former co-chair of its Mediation Committee.

table, and ultimately the success of my clients. This chapter is based on A. ABRAMOWITZ, *What Negotiators Can Learn from Modern Sales Theory*, in 1 THE NEGOTIATOR'S DESK REFERENCE 421–433 (Honeyman & Schneider eds, 2017). The full references in that chapter can be found at www.ndrweb.com/chapter-31--public.html.

Why This Concept Might Change Your Thinking

While all of us who graduated law school are steeped in advocacy, there is quantitative, empirical evidence in other fields that direct persuasion—the "advocacy" we were taught in law school—doesn't translate well at the negotiation table. *Effective persuaders "sell" not by telling, but by asking*—by exploring with the Other the problems facing them both. Moreover, expert persuaders reach agreement not by pressure but by developing with the Other a solution all parties are willing to implement. They do it by asking four types of questions, in any order that makes sense: Situation Questions, Problem Questions, Implication Questions, and Need/Payoff Questions. To get to "yes," you have to do your homework, ask these questions, and listen afresh, ever curious about how the Other sees the world and why. Only after you both have a shared understanding of each other's explicit needs, uncovered during the question-answering process, should the contours of a deal meeting those needs be etched. Hence, the term "consultative selling."

"Hey, I ask lots of questions." I'm sure you do, but if you are a well-trained lawyer, you probably ask just two of the four types of questions—Situation Questions, about the facts, and Problem Questions, about the issue at hand. That's what we are taught; that's what we lawyers do. As a result, we may be able to provide a *legal* analysis of our client's problem, and even offer a legal solution, but in doing so we face real dangers. Research into consultative selling found that asking just Situation and Problem Questions increased the chance that a solution proposed thereafter would be rejected. It also increased the chances of impasse. It was Implication Questions—about the seriousness, the consequences, and the effects of the problem—that produced a desire to find solutions, and Need/Payoff Questions, about value and usefulness, that produced viable solutions. Moreover, in limiting ourselves to just Situation and Problem Questions, we risk solving *our* (often legal) view of our client's problem but not *their* (usually more complicated) view of the problem—and it is *their* view that counts. The same dangers apply later with the Other at the negotiation table.

Simply put, problems that need to be negotiated generally are not simple. Often, due to the nature of the problem, the cost of the solution, and the attendant risks and rewards of proceeding or not, the stakes are high in deciding what to do. The approaches taught by consultative selling make building common ground and devising shared *and implementable* solutions to even the highest-stakes problems substantially easier.

Action Plan—What You Can Do Differently Tomorrow

Let me be quick to say that consultative selling skills are counterintuitive and hard to come by, especially for lawyers geared by their training to issue-spot and solve problems. "You have a problem," we say to our clients. "I and my colleagues will make it go away or at least dull over time." Consultative sellers don't do that. They explore the problem right in front of the buyer, picking at its contours, prodding its implications, until both the seller and the buyer wince at the severity of its consequences and the looming risks of standing pat. Now they merge heads to develop a solution that will pass the test of time. Even then, they continue to pick and prod, uncovering, exploring, and addressing every weakness of the proposed solution. Better, they reason, that it fall apart in front of us, where we can pick it up, dust it off, and build success into the effort.

Only when implementability poses no foreseeable risk, or at least a reasonably manageable risk, and also holds a real, measurable promise of success, do they close the deal. To them, no contract with the potential of a lawsuit is worth signing.

Still interested? Try these first steps:

Step One: Before you sit down to negotiate, plan the key questions you need to ask—the key problems and attendant implications you need to explore. Experience shows that if questions are not planned, questions are not asked.

Step Two: Once you sit down with the Other, start your explorations looking for areas of agreement. Negotiation, like high-end sales, is too fragile a process to start with disagreement. Ask questions and listen to the answers with the goal of understanding the Other and ultimately finding common ground. Even then, don't assume you are so well-trained that you get it. Test your understanding. Share with the Other what you heard and don't move on until the Other gives you the signoff that what you heard is what they meant. Respond only after you get that confirmation.

Step Three: With signoff in hand, you have two choices. If you can find a way to agree with anything you just heard, build on that agreement. Supporting the Other's ideas is a powerful way of building common ground. If you disagree, though, keep your disagreement to yourself. Instead, use the reasons you would say no as impetus for your questions. Noodle it through with the Other. If their analysis is wrong, they can gently learn for themselves its weakness. If your analysis is wrong, you can set it aside without the Other ever knowing how wrong you can be.

Step Four: Don't jump to solutions. Doing so invites disagreement, even impasse. Take the time necessary to ask Implication and Need/Payoff Questions, as they are the ones that correlate most highly with successful outcomes. Use those questions to get behind positions and come to understand what is triggering them. That's the way to best explore for interests and mutual needs. Only with everyone's explicit needs front and center can you both set about designing a mutually beneficial solution.

Step Five: Think implementation from the outset and revisit it continuously. How is it going to work? What happens if . . . ? How can we build success into this effort? Just remember, your value to your client doesn't get measured when *your* work is successfully done. It gets measured when *their* work is successfully done.

Step Six: Know that the parties have to go through stages before they are willing to move. They have to recognize that they have a problem that needs to be solved. They need to try on various solutions for size, assessing each one for risk and reward. Give the Other the freedom needed to go through those stages, or else they will stay right where they are.

Step Seven: Don't minimize the consequences the Other is facing. That's another quick way to impasse. "If I were you . . ." never works. You are not they. Do what the best consultative sellers do: Avoid buyer objections. Help the Other struggle through it for themselves. Ask Problem and Implication questions. Give yourself the freedom to work *with* the Other. Through Implication and Need/Payoff Questions, let *them* discover the solution with you. It is the shortest route to finding the common ground you both want to build on.

Conclusion

Can we be disciplined enough to use such a process? Do we know how to help build success into an endeavor? Or are we too busy building in language to pawn off risk and liability? Consultative sales skills require a sea change from the legal thinking most of us were taught in school. For some of us, using those techniques may at first prove too heavy a lift. But for all of us, learning to walk was a heavy lift. We didn't judge ourselves as inadequate when we fell. We just picked ourselves up and tried again until one foot came after the other. Same with consultative selling. One by one we can reframe it into a key negotiator skill. It will just take time—and, yes, we can do it.

This Ties in With:

Abramson, Ch. 3, Styles; Guthrie, Ch. 10, Getting Your Way; Shestowsky, Ch. 11, Persuasion; Liao & Zhang, Ch. 30, Chinese Wisdom & Your Style

14

It's More Than What You Think: Moves and Turns in Negotiation

Jessica Porter[1] *and Deborah Kolb*[2]

Introduction

All negotiations occur on multiple planes: at the same time we bargain about the substantive issues, we're also negotiating about our roles, power, and position. On that plane, what we call the *Shadow Negotiation*, parties use *strategic moves* to enhance their position. Those moves, if not understood, can throw you off balance and make you defensive. When we feel defensive, we *defend,* by using *countermoves,* which tend to keep the power dynamic in place. We offer a different strategy—helping negotiators anticipate moves and

1. **Jessica Porter** is a writer and researcher who consults with organizations around issues of leadership development, gender and diversity, and creating change. She is the coauthor *of Negotiating at Work: Turn Small Wins into Big Gains* and was the lead researcher of *Sleeping with Your Smartphone: How to Break the 24/7 Habit and Change the Way You Work*, by Leslie Perlow. Jessica is a doctoral student at Antioch University, studying leadership and change.
2. **Deborah Kolb** is Deloitte Ellen Gabriel Professor for Women and Leadership (Emerita) and the cofounder of the Center for Gender in Organizations at the Simmons College School of Management. She is an authority on gender issues in negotiation and leadership and the author of several books on the subject. Her most recent, *Negotiating at Work: Turn Small Wins into Big Gains*, was named by Time.com as one of the best negotiation books of 2015. Deborah received her Ph.D. from MIT's Sloan School of Management.

turn them to refocus the negotiation to get it back to a level playing field. Whether you're negotiating on behalf of your client or your career, knowing how to *turn* moves can help restore your authority, engage the other party, and maintain a strong position in the negotiation and in your organization. This chapter is based on D. KOLB & J. PORTER, *Power at Play in Negotiation: Moves and Turns*, in 1 THE NEGOTIATOR'S DESK REFERENCE 365–378 (Honeyman & Schneider eds, 2017). The full references in that chapter can be found at www.ndrweb.com/chapter-27--public.html.

Why This Concept Might Change Your Thinking

Understanding Strategic Moves

A negotiator's *power* is not just based on the strength of their position, but is related to how competent and credible they are perceived to be. To an extent, we form conscious and unconscious judgments of each other's competence based on fixed aspects of identity such as age, race, gender, or status. At the same time, competence and credibility are socially constructed within interactions of the negotiation itself. Each party presents a *face* in the negotiation—they manage impressions of themselves to strengthen their legitimacy and position.

Negotiators are always managing the impressions of themselves and their counterparts, using strategic moves to challenge authority and credibility. When your self-presentation is challenged, it can, if you are not prepared, undermine your confidence. It's hard to advocate for your client when you're coming from a "one down" position. Based on our research, we've identified some typical strategic moves that negotiators use to gain the upper hand.

Challenging Competence or Expertise

This is a common move to undermine you by making a comment or gesture that explicitly or implicitly questions your competence or expertise. They might mention your age or level of experience or joke about where you went to law school. Even subtle jibes at your competence can make it hard to speak with authority.

Demeaning Ideas

The other person might attack your proposal in ways that give you little room to respond. They might express disbelief or even outrage at what you have proposed, making you and your idea sound ridiculous. They may demean you by suggesting that you have not adequately thought it through. These moves make it difficult to argue for what might otherwise be a reasonable idea.

Criticizing Style

With phrases like "Don't get so upset," they're casting you as the subject of the move. These moves present a negotiator as overreacting, inconsiderate, or irrational. This type of move often plays to cultural stereotypes, such as accusing a woman of becoming emotional.

Threatening Moves

These can take many forms, including ultimatums, threats to end negotiations, or implying there will be unpleasant consequences if the other person doesn't back down.

Appealing for Sympathy or Flattery

Not all moves are critical of the other person. Flattery and appeals for sympathy can be equally powerful in undermining your agency. If someone smothers you with praise, they may be counting on you to back down. Likewise, appeals for sympathy can be difficult to navigate, such as when the other party asks you to prioritize their needs and help them save face. By enlisting you to help them, they make it difficult to advocate for what you want.

Action Plan—What You Can Do Differently Tomorrow

Develop a Repertoire of Turns

When you are put into a defensive position, your client may start to question your value. If you are negotiating for yourself—for more responsibility, a prime case or client, or advancing your career—becoming defensive can not only set you back in the negotiation, it can create a lasting impression with your colleagues that might impact your career down the road.

Taken unaware by strategic moves, negotiators tend to react, almost instinctively, with a countermove. Countermoves keep the action in the frame of the move—suddenly, you're defending your competence or insisting that you're not being emotional, rather than concentrating on the issues of the negotiation itself. There is another way to respond to moves—you can *turn* them—shift the direction of the negotiation. Rather than staying in a defensive position, a turn changes the conversation's direction; turns are moments of potential resistance.

Here are six types of turns that can be used to reframe the negotiation after a strategic move:

1. ***Interruption:*** Interruptions can take many forms. They can be a pause, sitting silent for a minute or less. You can stand up, get a cup of coffee, take a restroom break, or suggest a longer break. Interruptions of *any* length break the action and change the dynamic. You get a chance to collect your thoughts and the interruption helps reset the conversation.
2. ***Naming:*** To name a move shows that you recognize the tactic. Statements such as, "I see what you're doing here," or "it seems like you might be trying to lower my expectations" can be an effective way to call out the move. In some—but not all—naming turns, you may want to frame the turn so the other party can save face (so smile when you do this).
3. ***Questioning:*** Like naming, this turn recognizes the move as a possible tactic, but does so with a more inquiring stance. Questioning a move is a subtle way to call a bluff. Questions like "What would you do if you were in my situation?" or "Can you help me understand how that is relevant?" can be very effective. They give the other person pause and often change the direction of the conversation.
4. ***Correcting:*** A correcting turn suggests different ways of seeing the situation, substituting a different perspective to what was implied. When moves imply criticism, you can correct an impression by providing a different, positive version of the situation. These turns can be particularly useful to counter stereotyped moves. For instance, you might respond to the move "Don't get so upset" by saying, "I am passionate when issues matter to me."
5. ***Diverting:*** A diverting turn shifts the focus to the problem itself; therefore, it is a way to depersonalize a move. One diverting

turn is simply to substitute a better idea. If you've prepared by thinking through multiple options, you can divert a turn by introducing one that has not yet been discussed. "Let's not get stuck on this. We have a problem to deal with."

6. ***Focusing on the future:*** Another turn you can use to turn a move is to shift the focus to the future. You may acknowledge the past, even admitting a prior mistake or problem, but move past it to the current problem. "I'm sure you'll agree that we need to work this out if we are going to move ahead on this."

Use Restorative and Participative Turns Strategically

Using turns to reframe the negotiation is effective, but we have to prepare to execute them effectively. It helps to consider what types of moves your counterpart might make—what do you know about the other person, and where might you be vulnerable? We've all had interactions that left us frustrated and churning, only to come up with the perfect response hours later. Thinking about the moves you might encounter in advance, and how you might turn them, increases your ability to respond effectively in the moment.

Which turns you use will depend on the type of move you're responding to, where you are in the negotiation, and what feels most comfortable to you. Early in the negotiation, a move that undermines you threatens your ability to reach a deal. When one person is positioned below the other, there's less incentive to achieve mutual gains. In those cases, *Restorative Turns* can be used to reclaim authority and foster interdependence in the negotiation. Naming and Correcting turns are usually in this category—they can help level the playing field and allow a negotiator to reclaim power in the relationship.

Once negotiators' authority and credibility have been established, in later stages of the negotiation, *Participative Turns* can be effective to help keep the dialogue moving along productively. These are turns that seek to engage the other party in problem-solving. Questioning and Diverting are useful strategies when you want to turn a move in a way that establishes a more interactive frame. They help position you as a collaborative negotiator and enlist the other party to join you in the process.

Conclusion

How you fare in a negotiation is not just a matter of how well prepared you are and the strength of your case. Understanding and managing the shadow negotiation helps you feel more confident and reinforces perceptions of you as a savvy negotiator.

This Ties in With:

Craver, Ch. 4, Classic Techniques; Bear & Babcock, Ch. 6, Gender; Amsler, Ch. 45, DSD

Section IV

Strategies of Communication

Section IV addresses the postmodern era of communication and the challenges of listening well. Chapter 15 surveys the confusing panoply of communication options now available and outlines a way to use them more tactically. In Chapter 16, we move to what has probably become the baseline method of ordinary, day-to-day communication, particularly for components of a negotiation that has yet to be framed in complete documents—e-mail.

Two very different groups have specific needs and uses for technology in their negotiations: lawyers and the young. Chapter 17 analyzes lawyers' needs and how technology is changing their practice. Chapter 18 focuses on the youngest adult generation—such avid users of technology that it is barely possible to pull their attention from it.

Chapters 19 to 21 focus on more than talking. In Chapter 19, the author argues that listening can be used in a disciplined way to avoid either cooperating or competing too much. Chapter 20 demonstrates some key findings from clinical psychology: it focuses on actually *understanding* what you hear, to make you more persuasive.

Yet, listening is not everything. Chapter 21 analyzes nonverbal communication as a whole, it demonstrates how many different forms it can take, and it shows how you can employ nonverbal communication consciously.

15

Hold the Phone: Choosing Modes of Communication

Andrea Kupfer Schneider[1] *and Sean McCarthy*[2]

Introduction

Technology shapes and affects both the negotiation process and negotiators themselves. We all use multiple modes of technology-based communication, such as email, videoconferencing, text messaging, and more. Choosing which mode and when to use it is particularly important—especially given the reality that many negotiations will consist of more than one mode. The question, then, is *which* mode of communication to choose, *in what context*, and *at what point* in the negotiation. This chapter is based on A.K. SCHNEIDER & S. MCCARTHY, *Choosing Among Modes of Communication*, in 2 THE NEGOTIATOR'S DESK REFERENCE 107–114

1. **Andrea Kupfer Schneider** is a Professor of Law at Marquette University Law School, where she teaches dispute resolution, negotiation, ethics, and international conflict resolution and is the director of Marquette's nationally ranked dispute resolution program. Andrea has written numerous books, book chapters, and articles on negotiation skills and styles, dispute system design, international conflict, and gender and negotiation. She was given the American Bar Association (ABA) Section of Dispute Resolution Award for Outstanding Scholarly Work for 2017. Andrea received her A.B. *cum laude* from the Woodrow Wilson School of Public & International Affairs at Princeton University and her J.D. *cum laude* from Harvard Law School.
2. **Sean McCarthy** is the director of compliance at Eastern Michigan University and a graduate of the University of Minnesota and Marquette University Law School. He is a lifelong fan of the Minnesota Vikings and football guy Mike Zimmer.

(Honeyman & Schneider eds, 2017.) The full references for that chapter can be found at www.ndrweb.com/chapter-59--public.html.

Why This Concept Might Change Your Thinking

Thinking about the modes of communication in negotiation forces us to examine two key concepts—media richness and interactivity. Face-to-face conversations are considered media "rich" because they allow tracking of multiple social cues. In face-to-face conversations (in person *and* online via video), you can interpret body language, tone, eye contact, and facial expressions, in addition to hearing the content of the conversation. Phone conversations provide some of this; through the tone, pauses, and inflections of conversation, these para-verbal cues tell us something of how the other party is feeling, in addition to the content. Email (or texting), on the other hand, does not incorporate those contextual elements.

Interactivity refers to whether the communication is synchronous (occurring at the same time). Face-to-face conversations are, by their very nature, synchronous conversations. In other words, both parties are engaged at the same time. Even when one side is talking, the other person is interacting through their body language and responses. Online communication may occur simultaneously, particularly with texting, but only if both parties happen to be on their devices at the same time and choose to engage that way. Often, our emails are sent without direct knowledge of whether the other party is available to read one at that time (or even within a short period of time.) In face-to-face conversations we often take turns—question, response, follow-up question, response, etc. Via email, particularly when one of the parties is in meetings or otherwise unavailable, the communication can stack up. Notably, many of us also tend to read emails from most recent to least recent—meaning that we read them in the opposite order in which they were generated.

The asynchronous nature of email also means that while our "work" hours might be over for the day, our work communication via email or text may continue (for better and worse.) We might be reading email about important subjects over dinner in the evening, while watching television, or in the midst of putting kids to sleep. We might be reading over a small phone versus a larger computer screen.

Not surprisingly, varying modes of reception (phones, tablets, computers, etc.) can also affect the quality of our reading.

Action Plan—What You Can Do Differently Tomorrow

Understanding the Differences in the Modes of Communication

There are four key elements that intersect with each mode of communication, depending on the level of media richness and interactivity that each mode provides: the typical type of contents in the communication; the level of nonverbal cues that can be sent and received; the timing and sequencing of the communication; and the level of trust and relationship that the communication mode tends to encourage. The table below charts this:

Table 1 Differences in Modes of Communication

	Content	Nonverbal Cues	Timing	Trust/ Relationship
Face-to-Face	All things personal and/or professional	High level of verbal and nonverbal cues	Simultaneous	Easy to build rapport
Phone	All things personal and/or professional	Para-verbal only	Simultaneous	More challenging
Email	Tends to be more task-oriented	Only if added deliberately	Dependent on access to device and promptness of reply	Most challenging
Video Conferencing	Depends on platform expectations (i.e., FaceTime v. Zoom)	High level of verbal and nonverbal cues (but technologically dependent)	Simultaneous	Can be easier, but technologically dependent

First, the difference between modes of communication is often in the content. In face-to-face conversations, the conversation often rapidly switches between the personal and the professional, the mundane (the weather) and the more on-point. In email communications, the content tends to be more task-oriented. What do we need to get done? What is the answer to *X*? This is less personal, unless we take the time in the email (often at the beginning or end or both) to add the personal touches. We are more likely to schmooze automatically at the beginning of a face-to-face negotiation; this same impulse does not necessarily occur online. Some modes provide much higher levels of nonverbal cues than others, and the timing of these modes can vary.

Finally, developing relationships and trust over email is more challenging. Parties can be more adversarial with each other via email (and even over the phone) compared to face-to-face negotiations. Parties tend to share less information and cooperate less in the process of negotiation via email, resulting in lower levels of trust and higher potential for deceptive practices. And without the facial and verbal cues of face-to-face communication, people often assume the worst and are more likely to attribute poor motives to our counterpart.

Understanding Your Defaults

It is important to examine yourself and your counterpart in terms of "default modes" of communicating. Ask yourself a simple question. When you pull out your phone, what is the first app that you examine? Do you check your voicemail? Your text messages? Your email? Or your social media? This is your default—at least with your personal communications—and the mode of communication with which you are most comfortable. Perhaps equally important to your comfort level is your skill level at each of these modes. Examine all the modes and think about your strengths and weaknesses. Do you prefer to make requests in person or via email? When you have a question for a colleague, do you email him or her or pick up the phone? Is the response something you will want documented/in writing? One approach in negotiation is to communicate through *your* most effective mode—as long as that mode seems acceptable to the other party.

Understanding Their Defaults

At the same time, of course, it is crucial to learn about the modes of communication in which your counterpart prefers to negotiate. This does not mean that you always choose that particular mode—rather, that you have thought about this choice consciously. So first, think about their habits when communicating with you. Do they show a preference for email, phone, videoconference, or face-to-face? And how technologically savvy is your counterpart?

As the relationship evolves, like many work relationships, a continuing awareness of modes of communication is useful to keep in mind. The formality of the relationship might relax so that the tone of your emails is more casual, or perhaps you are texting short notes. And the technology or social media itself may change, allowing different modes of communication, as well—think about the onset of Skype or FaceTime and how phone calls can now include that face-to-face component in order to build rapport.

Thinking Strategically about How to Communicate

Having now thought about both your defaults and your counterpart's, there are a few more elements to consider—the importance of the issue or your interests; the context, including formality, and your counterpart; the need for a prompt response; and the sequencing of communication.

For very important issues or interests, we want to consider the modes carefully. Will face-to-face be most persuasive (or most useful for reading their body language)? Or would email give us the ability to fully and completely explain our interests in detail, and give our counterpart time to contemplate our proposal? The formality and our relationship also need to be considered. A short text or phone call letting someone know you are running late is perfectly appropriate. Asking someone for a raise via text message, however, would likely be viewed as unprofessional (at least, for now).

You will want to consider the promptness of your communication and the reply. When time is of the essence, which mode will get the response quickest? And this could also be part of a sequence of communications. You might, for example, stop by someone's office and then follow up with an email if they are not there. Or you might send a long email explaining a complicated issue but leave a quick voicemail (or text) letting them know that. You might use different modes of communication for record-keeping versus getting a response. After meeting in person, it could be very helpful to write the details in an email, confirming both of your understandings of the conversation.

Or you might use certain modes, like face-to-face, Skype, or phone calls, for relationship-building in advance of a longer email request. Each of these choices can help increase your effectiveness in a negotiation when carefully considered as part of your overall strategy.

Conclusion

Thinking about the mode of communication is crucial to negotiation. Each mode can play to your strengths (or weaknesses); can help be more persuasive (or less); and can build (or harm) relationships. Thinking carefully about this element of negotiation will add to your effectiveness and your ability to get what you want.

This Ties in With:

Ebner, Ch. 16, Email; Rabinovich et al., Ch. 17, Online

16

Email Negotiations

Noam Ebner[1]

Introduction

Negotiation interactions increasingly take place online, via a variety of e-communication channels. While personal communication preferences are diverse, email continues to be the primary channel for professionals' electronic communication, including negotiation. This chapter highlights six particularly challenging elements for negotiators interacting via email. It is based on N. Ebner, *Negotiating via Email*, in 2 The Negotiator's Desk Reference 115–132 (Honeyman & Schneider eds, 2017). The full references in that chapter can be found at www.ndrweb.com/chapter-60--public.html.

Why This Concept Might Change Your Thinking

Given the broad definition granted to the term "negotiation" in this field's literature, the many types of interactions and relationships we now conduct online, and industry practices, legal professionals often

1. **Noam Ebner** is a professor in the Negotiation and Conflict Resolution program at Creighton University's Department of Interdisciplinary Studies. Previously an attorney and mediator, he has taught mediation and negotiation in a dozen countries around the world. He was among the first teachers to engage in online teaching of negotiation and conflict studies and to explore the potential for Massive Open Online Courses (MOOC) in these fields. Noam's research interests include online negotiation and dispute resolution, trust and its role in dispute resolution, negotiation pedagogy, and online learning. Noam can be contacted at NoamEbner@creighton.edu; his work can be found at ssrn.com/author=425153.

engage in email negotiation. Two lawyers emailing offers and counteroffers late into the night to settle before a hearing; a client retaining an attorney across the country, agreeing on her fee, and attaching a signed representation agreement; a corporate counsel writing the head of HR requesting a change in the firm's employee contracts—all are negotiating via email.

Intuitively, we know that some information is easier to communicate face-to-face, whereas other messages would be better off written in an email. But why is this so?

Choice of medium matters. Communication media affect and change the content and dynamics of communication conducted through them.

Two primary media characteristics generate differences between email and face-to-face negotiation. One is "media richness"—how well can the medium convey contextual cues that provide meaning and nuance to the words that are transmitted? Face-to-face communication, replete with facial expressions, tone, etc., is a "rich" medium. Conversely, email is "lean": it transmits neither visual nor audio cues.

Another is email's asynchronous nature compared to face-to-face interaction. Minutes, hours, or weeks can pass between the time a negotiator sends a message and the time their counterpart reads or responds. Reading messages out of order is common. And one cannot, on the spot, question or correct their counterpart.

These challenges are compounded by the very developments that have made email use so ubiquitous. For example, most emails are now read on mobile devices, not on computers. We walk about with our inbox in our pocket, reading and writing negotiation emails on buses; while watching the kids at the playground; and (some) even while *driving*.

Action Plan—What You Can Do Differently Tomorrow

Six Major Challenges, Six Sets of Solutions

1. *More contentious, and less cooperative, process:* Parties to email communication act more contentiously, with more frequent occurrences of insults, hostile behavior, and threats. These stem from physical distance, reduced social presence, reduced accountability, and a sense of anonymity. Combined,

they result in diminished process cooperation and increased competitive behavior.

1. Prefer email, when you feel that transmission of visual and verbal cues might set people off rather than facilitate constructive conversation; when you think your voice, or the voice of someone else in the conversation, might go unheard; or when you are concerned you might suffer from the impact of conflict-triggering unconscious biases, such as gender, race, etc.
2. It is easier to cause harm or act contentiously toward a distant, faceless other. Make yourself human, present, and real in the other's eyes. Share personal information and reduce the perception of distance through shared language or shared geographical or cultural references.
3. Remember, there is a real person behind the other screen, whether they have proactively unmasked themselves or not.
4. Vary the interaction pace. Answering at the pace that works best for you allows you to avoid banging out that knee-jerk response you will later regret. Read any received message twice before responding and delay sending anything written in a spate of annoyance—reread it a little later.
5. Use process-cooperative language overtly, setting a tone your counterpart can mimic. Rather than responding from your smartphone—on which you will peck out the fewest words possible—consider responding a little later from your computer, where you can craft a longer message, replete with intentionally cooperative wording.

2. ***Fewer, or less, integrative outcomes:*** As process cooperation diminishes, so too does information exchange, resulting in lower rates of integrative agreement, lower-value integrative agreement, and more potential for impasse in email negotiations.
   1. Facing a negotiation in which an integrative outcome is absolutely *crucial,* consider picking up the phone or getting on a plane.
   2. Use interest-related language intentionally, and often, when discussing your own position and inquiring about theirs.
   3. Portray integrative offers or ideas through use of charts, graphs, and presentations—all easily attached to an email.

   4. Every new message is an opportunity to set a new frame around the interaction. Intentional and repeated integrative framing might change the negotiation's overall dynamic. Use the subject line of the email to this end.
   5. If you are worried about whether you might not be communicating enough, you probably are not; more communication often translates into higher joint gain.
3. ***Diminished degree of inter-party trust:*** Communicating via email entails significantly lower levels of interparty trust, reducing cooperation and integrative outcomes.
   1. Bonding—building an *ad hoc* relationship with your opposite—helps build rapport and trust. Light, social conversation does not come very naturally over email; engage in it anyway!
   2. Mix media, when possible. In the face of preliminary *dis*trust, consider a preliminary face-to-face or videoconferencing meeting. At any point, consider using the very smartphone you are reading email on to *call* the other party in response to their message.
   3. Show e-empathy. Displaying empathy for a counterpart via email builds their trust in you. Don't neglect this just because the medium seems to be cold, formal, or impersonal.
4. ***Increased attribution, increased misinterpretation:*** Communicating through lean media increases the odds that our counterpart will misread our message, interpret it negatively, and attribute all this to our sinister intentions or bad character—and that we will do the same to their messages.
   1. Constantly remind the other of the real person opposite them. Use physical imagery for this purpose: Mention the city you are in, your surroundings (your office, hotel), the local weather, etc.
   2. Taking into account negative interpretations, clarify *much* more than you would face-to-face. Use "In summary" sentences to highlight your main points, and use the subject field to provide your counterpart with an initial interpretive frame.
   3. If writing on a smartphone causes you to respond in short, terse, messages, consider how they might read to your counterpart. Hold off and respond on a different device, or include

a tagline indicating that you are writing on a phone. Similarly, don't read too much into your counterpart's style or wording.

4. Waiting and perceived delay cause anxiety, which is conducive to negative attribution. Don't expect immediate answers to your own emails, and do your best to respond promptly to your counterpart.
5. Careful with the jokes. Humor has its benefits in negotiation; however, text-based humor is often misunderstood, misinterpreted, and misattributed.

5. ***Diminished privacy:*** In email negotiation, you never know who is "in the room" with you. Your opposite may show your email to their boss or to your competition. Information you transmit is forever archived beyond your control and might reach people with whom you had no wish to share it.
   1. Consider each address field carefully. To whom should a message be sent? Should anyone appear in the CC field or invisibly lurk from the BCC field?
   2. Archive the interactions, review them when things get unclear, and refer to them if your counterpart is inconsistent. Share messages with others to consult about the process.
   3. As online activities increasingly become public, sought out by future opponents and admissible in court, be very cautious of what you write in any email.
6. ***Diminished party focus:*** Communicating via email, negotiators suffer low cognitive retention of previous messages, and diminished concentration. We often write when distracted; we are not as good at multitasking as we like to think, and multitasking negotiators achieve lower outcomes.
   1. The greater the importance of the negotiation, the more focus pays off. Read and write messages in an environment that allows you to concentrate. Close other windows while reading and writing email, and always finish responding to one email before moving on to another.
   2. Don't trust your memory. Read your counterpart's entire message, carefully, before you reply. Did you take a break in the middle of your answer, to deal with other urgent multitasking? Read the email again, *and* the written part of your own response, before resuming your reply.

Modifiers, Caveats, and No-Go Areas—When This Advice Just Won't Apply

There are two caveats to the advice in this chapter. First, while we are likely to continue to adapt to text-based negotiation over time, leading to some diminishing of the effects described in this chapter, email is also likely to change, as it has in the past. Any advice given in this chapter should be revisited as time goes by.

Second, email brings us into contact with global counterparts at an unprecedented rate and adds to the likelihood of cross-cultural communication. Writing from the familiar surroundings of our office, we need to be particularly mindful of this.

Conclusion

Communicating by email, negotiators face a rougher playing field, a likely more contentious opposite, and numerous process challenges. The good news is that, armed with some knowledge and a healthy dose of awareness, negotiators can navigate these challenges, and even turn the medium to their advantage.

This Ties in With:

Schneider & McCarthy, Ch. 15, Hold the Phone

17

Online Negotiation

Orna Rabinovich,[1] *Ethan Katsh,*[2] *and Colin Rule*[3]

Introduction

The field of online dispute resolution (ODR) has experienced substantial growth in the last decade, extending beyond e-commerce and social networks to disputes arising in a range of settings. Beyond online platforms, we now see courts, public entities, and local enterprises developing online channels for addressing complaints and

1. **Orna Rabinovich-Einy** is an associate professor at the Haifa Law Faculty. Her areas of expertise are online dispute resolution, alternative dispute resolution, and civil procedure. She has published widely on the impact of technology on dispute resolution, the relationship between formal and informal justice systems, and dispute systems design. Most recently, she has coauthored a book with Ethan Katsh entitled *Digital Justice: Technology and the Internet of Disputes*. Rabinovich-Einy holds a J.S.D. from Columbia University. She was admitted to the Bar in Israel (1998) and in N.Y. (2001), and was certified as a mediator in N.Y. (2003).
2. **Ethan Katsh** is Professor Emeritus of Legal Studies at the University of Massachusetts and Director of the National Center of Technology and Dispute Resolution (www.odr.info). He is widely recognized as one of the founders of the field of online dispute resolution (ODR). With Janet Rifkin, he conducted the eBay Pilot Project in 1999, which led to eBay's current system that handles over 60 million disputes each year. He has published widely about law and technology and, most recently, is coauthor *of Digital Justice: Technology and the Internet of Disputes* (Oxford University Press 2017.)
3. **Colin Rule** is cofounder and COO of Modria.com, an ODR provider based in Silicon Valley. From 2003 to 2011, he was director of Online Dispute Resolution for eBay and PayPal. He is currently co-chair of the Advisory Board of the National Center for Technology and Dispute Resolution at UMass-Amherst and a non-resident Fellow at the Gould Center for Conflict Resolution at Stanford Law School. Colin is the author of *Online Dispute Resolution for Business* (2002) and (with Amy Schmitz) the book *The New Handshake: Online Dispute Resolution and the Future of Consumer Protection* (American Bar Association 2017).

disputes. As our society digitizes, the way we resolve our disputes is digitizing as well. Technology enables us to cross jurisdictions with a few swipes of our finger on a tablet, so our problem-solving processes must evolve in the same way. These developments are at the heart of what lawyers do as experts advising clients on procedural options, representing clients in various fora, and designing ODR tools and systems. The law, and dispute resolution more broadly, is being disrupted by technology, and lawyers should be aware of what this disruption means for their profession. This chapter is based on O. Rabinovich, E. Katsh, & C. Rule, *Lawyers and Online Negotiation*, in 2 The Negotiator's Desk Reference 187–200 (Honeyman & Schneider eds, 2017). The full references in that chapter can be found at www.ndrweb.com/chapter-64--public.html.

Why This Concept Might Change Your Thinking

ODR has introduced new tools into the toolbox of dispute resolution practitioners: online processes that are impossible (or at least highly impractical) to conduct face-to-face, online-offline hybrid processes, and new capabilities injected by technology into more familiar face-to-face processes. Lawyers need to be knowledgeable about the advantages and challenges introduced by these new online processes, including automated negotiation, crowd-sourced justice, and problem diagnosis.

These processes are different from traditional dispute resolution in several significant respects: they are delivered online, the parties can use them asynchronously, they leverage the processing power of machines, and they leave a digital record. These traits significantly enhance the efficiencies associated with ODR, allow for processes to be tailored to a party's particular circumstances, and ensure that information can be conveyed in simple, accessible language. Beyond reducing such barriers to dispute resolution as costs, time, and complexity associated with face-to-face procedures, technology can also lower strategic and cognitive barriers to dispute resolution, as evidenced in blind bidding and negotiation support systems that have been developed in the field. These tools encourage parties to reveal their true bottom lines, as well as maximize joint gains, by collecting each party's confidential preferences and sharing information via algorithms so as to optimize the likelihood of an efficient resolution.

The use of preconfigured text and pre-framed options curbs animosity and loaded language, and focuses parties on finding a solution rather than blaming their counterpart.

Action Plan—What You Can Do Differently Tomorrow

These developments are likely to transform legal practice on several levels. For one, as use of ODR expands, lawyers will have to advise their clients as to circumstances where they should use such processes, and in some instances may need to take part in these processes on behalf of their clients. Even though online negotiation and other ODR processes were originally offered mainly for small-scale disputes, as their use expands, they are being applied to the higher-value and more complex disputes in which lawyers are involved.

Second, technology will change the role of the lawyer. Among the most advanced ODR mechanisms are those that facilitate negotiation, many of which require lawyer involvement in the design phase, while others involve lawyers as online facilitators or reviewers of resolutions reached by the parties. In the Netherlands, for example, lawyers have reviewed divorce resolutions reached by the parties to ensure that they met legal and other requirements.

Third, lawyers will increasingly use ODR-inspired tools to communicate with their clients and with lawyers on the other side, in some cases engaging in direct negotiations, and in other cases exploring the parties' rights and interests.

Finally, lawyers can also play an important role in posing key questions to their clients regarding dispute systems design: How can a resolution effectively prepare for future disputes that may arise? What concerns should be anticipated in starting up a business or structuring a transaction? Or, what provisions should be inserted to manage future workplace conflicts? In many of these contexts, an understanding of the role of technology in dispute systems design can help lawyers provide valuable advice on how to structure better dispute resolution systems, which both resolve disputes in a fair and effective manner and prevent disputes from arising, thereby bringing value to their clients even before disputes arise.

The introduction of technology into dispute resolution also raises complex practice and ethical challenges for mediators, negotiators, and lawyers. For example, the ability to record all negotiation communications raises concerns about confidentiality and privacy. The ability to instantly access all sorts of information in the midst of a negotiation may lead to the introduction of information that can bias or derail an otherwise promising agreement. Negotiation partners may not be able to resist the temptation to secretly loop third parties into online communications or to Google the background of their counterparts to learn about unrelated but compromising events in their past.

Also, most ethical standards focus on the behavior of individual participants in a dispute resolution process, but technology also introduces the role of a systems designer/programmer, with its own unique ethical dilemmas and risks of systemic bias. These questions have not been adequately addressed in dispute resolution training materials and ethical standards, but as ODR expands, that will need to be rectified. New standards addressing transparency, accessibility, impartiality, and confidentiality in online systems will need to be drafted, promoted, and included in training materials. Lawyers, negotiators, and ODR system providers will need to be held responsible for adhering to these standards of practice and monitored over time by outside auditors.

Modifiers, Caveats, and No-Go Areas—When This Advice Just Won't Apply

Since ODR processes are delivered online, rely on automation, and leave a digital trail, their use may not be desired precisely where such traits are problematic. One context in which use of ODR is problematic is where digital access is limited. While smartphones and improved technological infrastructure have significantly enhanced access, even in third-world countries and for disempowered communities, the digital divide still exists. While we see this as a barrier that will be eliminated in time, these days, it still merits consideration in designing and implementing ODR systems and tools. Second, there may be contexts in which a physical encounter is necessary, either to ensure that a party feels they had a chance to "tell their story" in person or because the complex nature of the dispute requires highly intricate human involvement and skills, some of which must be delivered in person, at times through subtle body language. In addition, clients may be wary of using ODR where a high degree of confidentiality is necessary. While online communications can be protected, they can never be as safe as an undocumented face-to-face meeting. A final related point that merits consideration is that technology is not neutral, and its design could benefit some parties at the expense of others. These parties may belong to a particular gender, race, or age group, or may be "one-shotters" as opposed to repeat players. Whatever the nature of the parties, these dynamics require sophisticated oversight and a nuanced understanding of the connection between procedural choices and substantive outcomes on the one hand, and on the other, the unique ethical dilemmas that the online setting may give rise to.

Conclusion

As our lives become increasingly digital, so do our dispute resolution processes, formal and informal. This reality has rendered online dispute resolution as essential component of the lawyer' toolbox, requiring lawyers to be familiar with the range of procedural options that exist, as well as understand the implications for their clients of choosing particular procedural avenues for addressing conflict or in designing conflict management systems.

This Ties in With:

Schneider & McCarthy, Ch. 15, Hold the Phone; Ebner, Ch. 16, Email

18

Negotiating Attention with the Digital Generation

Lauren A. Newell[1]

Introduction

Today's youth—the Digital Generation—are tomorrow's negotiators; some may appear in your cases already. (And, if you are a young lawyer, you may find that this description applies to you personally.) They are known for their love of information and communication technologies (ICTs), such as cell phones and computers, and are criticized for their poor attentional capacity. This chapter offers negotiators of all generations practical suggestions for improving focused attention and explains why elder generations may need a different approach for negotiating with the Digital Generation. This chapter is based on L.A. NEWELL, *Reclaiming Attention in the Digital Generation Negotiator*, in 2 THE NEGOTIATOR'S DESK REFERENCE 201–214 (Honeyman & Schneider eds, 2017.) The full references from that chapter can be found at www.ndrweb.com/chapter-65--public.html.

1. **Lauren A. Newell** is a professor of law at the Ohio Northern University Pettit College of Law, where she teaches courses on negotiation, business organizations, and securities regulation. Her research focuses on the psychological aspects of negotiation and lawyering, including the emotional dimension of negotiation and the impact of new technology on negotiation and lawyering. Prior to joining the Ohio Northern faculty, Professor Newell practiced corporate law in New York City at the law firm of Boies Schiller Flexner LLP. She received her J.D. from Harvard Law School and her B.A. from Georgetown University.

Why This Concept Might Change Your Thinking

Negotiation requires strong powers of attention because it makes demands upon negotiators' cognitive abilities, emotional competencies, and impulse control capabilities. Digital Generation negotiators' ICT usage contributes to attentional problems in four respects. First, ICT exposure may be changing the Digital Generation's brains in ways that affect how—and how well—they pay attention.

Second, ICTs are *designed* to distract users with alerts. These distractions cause the Digital Generation constantly to shift attention between multiple tasks, which impairs their memory and makes them less cognitively efficient and accurate.

Third, ICTs contribute to cognitive overload. An overloaded brain suffers a reduced attention span, more restlessness, impaired cognitive abilities, decreased learning, and weaker understanding.

Fourth, ICTs trigger stress and anxiety through incessant interruptions. They compound this stress by putting the Digital Generation's brains continuously on alert for new information, without a chance to rest and relax. ICTs also create stressful societal expectations of always being reachable and responding without delay, by making constant connectivity and instant responses possible. Altogether, ICTs make the Digital Generation a different generation of negotiators.

Action Plan—What You Can Do Differently Tomorrow

No matter what generation you belong to, you can take immediate steps toward improving your and your counterpart's attention in a negotiation. The solution is not simply to turn your ICTs off. This is unrealistic for the Digital Generation, given their near obsession with ICTs. Moreover, research suggests that separating the Digital Generation from their devices can actually make them suffer from genuine anxiety, which is counterproductive. Here are two proven alternatives—meditation and scheduled technology breaks.

Starting at "square one," if *you* are a Digital Generation negotiator, you should first make an up-front investment in learning how to meditate. Regular meditation practice has numerous well-documented benefits, among them strengthening attention. Organizations, including schools (from elementary education to law schools), employers (such as Google and JPMorgan Chase & Co.), and professional associations (e.g., the American Bar Association), offer instruction in meditation practice. If you have access to this type of training, you should take advantage.

Otherwise, you should develop a meditation practice on your own. Meditation training is widely accessible through informal meditation groups, books and audio programs, smartphone and tablet apps, and podcasts, many of which are free. These informal channels can help you overcome any cost or access barriers to learning to meditate. Once you know how to meditate, you can do it anywhere and any time, as it suits your schedule. The key is to do it consistently: changing the brain through meditation requires at least twenty minutes of regular practice, preferably daily. Investing in meditation provides a flexible and cheap, yet highly impactful, solution to an attentional problem.

The second part of your action plan is to take "technology breaks"—designated times during the day that are reserved for checking messages and otherwise interacting with your ICTs. Between each technology break, you focus intensely on your tasks and put aside your ICTs. Technology breaks in a negotiation might look like this: During preparation for the negotiation, you set a countdown timer on your phone or computer to alert you every fifteen minutes that it is time for a technology break, and a second countdown timer to alert you when the break is over. Otherwise, during the fifteen-minute work period you silence your ICTs, turn off (or turn away from) your monitors, and disable visual alerts. The process would be similar during the negotiation itself, with all negotiators committing to set aside their ICTs during the designated work period. You could negotiate the frequency of technology breaks at the beginning of the negotiation session with the other agenda items, such as meal breaks or break-out sessions.

The time in between technology breaks could be as long as several hours or as short as fifteen minutes. The interval should be as long as you can realistically commit to focusing before turning to your ICTs. This may vary depending upon what you are doing and how engaging you find it. You may be able to focus longer *in* the negotiation, while having an intense discussion, than you can *in preparation* for the negotiation, while reading a document you find boring. If you notice yourself reaching for your ICTs before your designated break time, the interval is probably too long.

Taking technology breaks balances the benefits of minimizing distractions and the challenges posed by turning off ICTs altogether, including the fact that ICTs can be useful in a negotiation. (You may need to check your calendar to schedule the next meeting or contact your client to discuss a proposed settlement.) Having designated technology breaks in a negotiation means you can still do all these necessary things without having to half-listen to the conversation while trying to type a message on your phone underneath the table. Additionally, technology breaks may help to minimize your internal distractions. Knowing that a break is coming makes it easier to focus on the current task for the specified amount of time. Your attention should improve during the time in between breaks.

If you are a non-Digital Generation negotiator, your action plan starts with thinking through how you want to approach a negotiation with a Digital Generation negotiator. During your preparation for the negotiation, keep in mind the ways in which Digital Generation negotiators may differ from you (then again, they may not—if you use your ICTs as much as they do, you may be suffering from the same attentional deficits). If you anticipate generational differences and understand the reason for them, you may find them less frustrating.

Meditation can be part of your action plan as well. You can reap all the same cognitive benefits of meditation practice as the Digital Generation can. Moreover, learning how to meditate can help you accept any generational differences between you and your Digital Generation negotiation counterparts in a nonjudgmental way.

Once you get to the negotiation table, you can propose the technology break idea, employing the same strategy as above. Try to notice when your Digital Generation counterparts seem to lose focus.

If the time between technology breaks appears to be too long, revise your plan and try shorter intervals. You might find that ICTs pose just as much of a problem for you as they do for Digital Generation negotiators, and that *you* are the one whose attention is wandering before the scheduled technology break(!). Adapt your strategy accordingly.

Modifiers, Caveats, and No-Go Areas—When This Advice Just Won't Apply

A few caveats: First, improving attention through meditation requires time and effort—both initially, in learning to meditate, and continuously, to maintain a meditation practice. It may be challenging to find time to sit quietly and meditate. It may also be difficult to set your ICTs aside long enough to establish a regular meditation practice—especially if you are using a meditation app, listening to a podcast, or otherwise involving ICTs in your meditation.

Second, designating specific times for technology breaks does not prevent you from checking your ICTs between scheduled break times. You still need willpower. If you take breaks with a certain frequency when you are on your own, it may be hard to focus for longer if your counterpart wants less frequent breaks. Technology breaks are also inherently disruptive. A technology break may cut a productive conversation short; frequent breaks may prolong the negotiation unnecessarily, and may be a waste of time if you remain distracted throughout the negotiation. Also, technology breaks make the most sense for face-to-face negotiations, rather than for negotiations held via telephone or videoconference.

Third, these broad generalities about the Digital Generation do not apply to every individual member of the generation, no more than broad generalities about Baby Boomers apply to every Boomer. If you know your counterparts are members of the Digital Generation, prepare yourself for the *possibility* that they will have diminished powers of attention and work on your action plan. But interact with them as individuals, not as representatives of their generation.

Conclusion

ICTs are tools—only as "good" or "bad" as the ways we use them. They are a fact of today's life. Negotiators of all generations should use techniques that improve their attention—but that still make room for all of ICTs' benefits.

This Ties in With:

Schneider & McCarthy, Ch. 15, Hold the Phone; Ebner, Ch. 16, Email; Rabinovich et al., Ch. 17, Online

19

How to Listen for Persuasion

Brian A. Pappas[1]

Introduction

Competition and cooperation are commonly viewed as the two primary negotiation styles. Either you assume the role of a tough negotiator who uses tricks to manipulate, or you become a nice negotiator who rejects those tactics as unsavory. In reality, negotiation is far more complicated and nuanced.

The art of negotiation requires negotiators to determine what to do from moment to moment. In order to maximize your negotiation skills, listen for persuasion. Listening for persuasion requires abandoning the binary options of compete versus cooperate and learning how to use communications skills for a range of negotiation styles and situations. A disciplined approach to active listening is the key to unlocking your latent ability to perform under pressure. This chapter is based on B.A. Pappas, *Listening to Transcend Competition and Cooperation*, in 1 The Negotiator's Desk Reference 395–408

1. **Brian Pappas**, Ph.D., LL.M., J.D., is Assistant Vice President for Academic Affairs and Assistant Professor of Political Science at Eastern Michigan University. A mediator and mediation trainer, Brian has mediated hundreds of cases and trained thousands of mediators in court, community, business, and criminal justice contexts. Brian's research interests lie at the intersection of law, dispute resolution, and public administration, and examine how formal and informal processes interrelate. His writings on dispute resolution have been published in the *Journal of Legal Education*, the *Harvard Negotiation Law Review*, and the *Denver Law Review*.

(Honeyman & Schneider eds, 2017). The full references in that chapter can be found at www.ndrweb.com/chapter-29--public.html.

Why This Concept Might Change Your Thinking

Lawyers tend to be risk-averse and resistant to change. This results in overreliance on our strengths and a default to whatever style is most comfortable. In doing so, we often neglect our underlying weaknesses. As every negotiation is different, using the same style or strategies will not be effective in all instances. Listening is not only an essential skill for effective negotiation, it is also the most common barrier to resolution. Once one side sees the other as hostile, intractable, or difficult, every action or statement made by the other is viewed through a negative prism. Each subsequent statement or action is responded to in kind, further harming the communication and prospects for mutual understanding and agreement. Additionally, negotiators (almost) always have some bargaining authority at their disposal. The question is always the extent to which concessions and opportunities are offered. How can lawyers maximize what the other side might offer? How can lawyers navigate hostile negotiations, or better yet, prevent them from becoming hostile in the first place? The secret to dramatically improving negotiated outcomes is moving past "compete or collaborate" to underlying skills and taking the necessary risks to improve areas of weaknesses. Most negotiators neglect communication as a fundamental skill and, as a result, do not listen for persuasion. Through active listening, negotiators can learn how to both compete and cooperate with maximum persuasiveness.

Action Plan—What You Can Do Differently Tomorrow

Listening is not easy, requiring the negotiator to analyze information even while preparing a response. Negotiators commonly miss important details, interrupt the other side, or misinterpret what is being said. The best place to start is with a goal of making the other side feel heard. Nonverbal communication is not enough—the only way someone knows that you heard them is if you tell them directly what was said. Avoid "I understand" or "I hear you," as those phrases typically precede a "but"—and then statements of disagreement.

Reflection is the easiest way for someone to know that you heard what was said. Reflection is the act of repeating what someone says back to them by paraphrasing or directly stating the words spoken. And being *prepared* to reflect (even if we do not actually reflect, in the event) provides our minds with something to do, and quiets the impulse to interrupt. In fact, being prepared to reflect is the secret to effective active listening. Here are the five key steps to reflective listening:

1. ***Quiet your mind*** and focus on what they are saying, with the intent of reflecting it back accurately.
2. ***Use an introductory phrase*** like "it sounds like," "from your perspective," "what I'm hearing" so it sounds like less of an assertion and more of a question. If you are wrong, it was your perception and not something you were stating as fact.
3. ***Reflect both the words and the way they were expressed.*** The more important the words being stated, the more likely you should be to reflect the specific words. Additionally, the less trust you feel, the more likely you need to reflect more closely in order to build trust.
4. ***Be careful not to twist the meaning.*** If the other person suspects you are attempting to alter the message, or use it for your advantage, the reflection will result in lower trust and will further complicate the communication dynamics.
5. ***Practice to know how and when to reflect.*** People do not like feeling parroted, but they love being heard and acknowledged, whether they are the attorneys in a matter or the parties themselves. As normal conversation does not proceed in this way, the key is altering the introductory phrase (#2 above) and sometimes reflecting more and sometimes reflecting less (or not at all) to vary the pattern.

As an example, consider the statement "My client deserves to be paid an amount that reflects his value. Your salary offer is insulting and is nowhere close to a fair number!" Instead of becoming angry, reflect: "I'm hearing your client wants to be compensated for his skills and abilities, and that you feel our offer is disrespectful and unfair."

What are the advantages to reflection in this situation?

1. Reflective listening is a habit that will stop you from immediately launching a counterattack.
2. Reflection allows the other person to hear his or her own statement, allowing the other side to potentially hear where they are being overly aggressive. The act of labeling and acknowledging resistance often defuses its power and lowers its influence.
3. You are able to hear the information again a second time, and this provides a useful extra moment for you to process the information. Doing this allows you to see details you might otherwise miss. You also will be able to see questions ("Tell us more about your client's skills and why you feel our valuation is off?") and define potential interests ("Tell me more about what you would consider to be fair?").
4. Many people are unable to hear you unless *they* feel heard. Once you recognize the other person is not listening, seek to first understand their perspective. It will reduce tension in the room and make it more likely the other side will listen to your points *after* knowing you understand their perspective.

Reflection, when used in this way, can be used both competitively and cooperatively, and for a variety of styles and strategies in between. Listening is persuasive!

If someone likes you, if they think you are respectful and listening, they will do more for you. People tend to ascribe good qualities to people they have determined they like, and fundamentally people tend to like those who treat them better. Speakers who reflect another's viewpoint before their own are deemed to be more persuasive, even when not including a counter-argument or where there is resistance from the other side. Negotiators who can demonstrate the perspective of others thus can receive more concessions. More specifically, reflective listening builds rapport and trust, allowing the negotiator to be more competitive in other ways (e.g., through tougher questions and greater demands) without being viewed as unreasonable.

Reflective listening is also a skill that can be used for cooperation. Reflection allows time and space to identify interests, which is key for collaborating and crafting solutions that expand the pie.

Emphasizing the advantages that the other side stands to gain makes your proposal more likely to be accepted—but doing so requires understanding the other side's perspective. Your use of reflection also will impact how the other side acts: negotiators who feel positively toward your side are more likely to be flexible, more likely to try to develop cooperative agreements, and are more likely to decrease hostile behaviors and provide concessions.

Using reflective listening take practice. But there are endless opportunities to practice in everyday life. (Knowing how all the equipment works at the gym does not mean someone is in shape!) It takes practice to know how often to use it, to be able to reflect at the right depth, and to make it sound natural.

Conclusion

Reflective listening can be used to compete, to cooperate, or to do a variety of other strategy and style maneuvers. It is time to stop thinking about listening as something that only happens for conflicts involving ongoing relationships. Negotiators need to establish trust and some sort of a relationship in order to reach resolution. The best negotiators are extremely persuasive and the best deals are the ones in which both sides believe they got a good deal. By listening for persuasion, negotiators can help both sides find a good deal, whether in reality or merely in terms of perception.

This Ties in With:

Abramson, Ch. 3, Fashioning Styles; Itzchakov & Kluger, Ch. 20, Changing Attitudes

20

Changing the Other Party's Attitude with High Quality Listening

Guy Itzchakov[1] *and Avraham N. Kluger*[2]

Introduction

People who are involved in a conflict often complain that the other side is not listening. Even when the counterpart does listen, it is usually to debate, argue, convince, or discount, rather than to understand. Based on our research, we argue that people will be more

1. **Guy Itzchakov** is currently a postdoctoral fellow at the University of Toronto and Assistant Professor at University of Haifa. He completed his B.A in psychology and economics at the Open University of Israel, and received his M.A in public policy at Tel Aviv University in 2011. Guy received his Ph.D. at the Jerusalem School of Business Administration. Guy's research draws on Carl Rogers' theory and focus on how attentive and nonjudgmental listening facilitates an appeal to the speaker's emotions and cognitions. His research has appeared in *Personality and Social Psychology Bulletin*, *European Journal of Social Psychology*, and *International Journal of Listening*. Guy can be reached at guy.itzchakov@mail.huji.ac.il.

2. **Avraham N. (Avi) Kluger** is Professor of Organizational Behavior at the Hebrew University of Jerusalem. He has studied for more than twenty years the destructive effects of performance feedback (telling people something about their performance with the often-false hope that it will improve performance). Recently, he began researching what happens if instead of telling people things, people are given the opportunity to be listened to. In his ongoing meta-analyses of listening, Avi found that good listeners are good performers, are perceived as good leaders, generate satisfaction among their spouses, subordinates, and patients, reduce depression, and are liked by their interlocutors. For updates about his listening research, visit http://avikluger .wixsite.com /avi-kluger.

effective in negotiations when they practice high quality listening. The benefits of experiencing high quality listening include reduced anxiety, increased open-mindedness, better awareness of alternative perspectives, including those contrary to one's initial attitude, and moderation of extremism, to name only a few.

This chapter is based on G. ITZCHAKOV & A.N. KLUGER, *Listening with Understanding in Negotiation and Conflict Resolution*, in 1 THE NEGOTIATOR'S DESK REFERENCE 409–420 (Honeyman & Schneider eds, 2017). The full references in that chapter can be found at www.ndrweb.com/chapter-30--public.html.

Why This Concept Might Change Your Thinking

Good listeners lay aside their views and values when they try to enter the speaker's world without making judgments. Withholding judgments to become a good listener is not an easy task. It requires time, effort, and practice. However, by making a decision to become a good listener, negotiators gain numerous benefits.

Among the benefits of good listening, according to our empirical findings, high-quality listening makes speakers expose the complexity of their attitude. In so doing, they are likely to share with the listeners additional interests that may be in conflict with the interests they identified initially. This happens because experiencing high-quality listening brings to awareness solutions that are not accessible when poor listening instigates a defensive and competing approach. Therefore, high-quality listening can help shift the conflicting parties from positions (a particular viewpoint or requirement) to uncover interests (the needs and desires that people want to achieve in a conflict situation) and thus elicit an integrative solution to the conflict.

Second, negotiators who exhibit high-quality listening gain trust. For example, mediators who were perceived as good listeners by their disputants were also perceived as more trustworthy. These disputants also reported higher satisfaction with the process, a willingness to recommend that mediator, and perception of fairness from the decision. Carl Rogers, one of the noted fathers of modern psychology, recommended using a mediator who is skilled in listening in order to overcome failures in interpersonal communication. These failures, according to Rogers, are largely caused by people's tendency to judge and evaluate what they hear. A mediator who demonstrates good listening should be able to lay aside their own personal feelings and evaluations, listen with understanding to each party, and clarify the views and attitudes each holds. The same applies to negotiators.

Finally, high-quality listening has the potential to resolve conflicts that initially seemed nonnegotiable. Many conflicts become intractable because parties project their own inadequacies, difficulties, and problems on each other in order to avoid the necessity of changing themselves. Notwithstanding, when the parties listen to each other, ask good questions, try to empathize, and understand each other's feelings and perspectives, the "nonnegotiable" conflict could become solvable. Sometimes, a solution may emerge with mere listening to the other side without interrupting, even when the other side contradicts one's point. The safe space created by high-quality listening will make the parties share information, ask diagnostic questions, and seek to understand the needs and interests of the other side, which underlie their declared positions.

Action Plan—What You Can Do Differently Tomorrow

Recommendations for Becoming A Better Listener

Listening resembles a muscle. It requires training, persistence, effort, and most important, the *intention* to become a good listener. It requires clearing your mind from internal and external noise—and if this is not possible, postponing the conversation for when you can truly listen without being distracted. Here are some best practices:

1. ***Give 100% of your attention and maintain eye contact.*** Put aside your smartphone, iPad, or laptop, and look at the speaker, even if he or she does not look back at you. In an ordinary conversation, a speaker looks at you occasionally to see that you are still listening. Constant eye contact lets the speaker feel that you are listening.
2. ***Do not interrupt.*** Resist the urge to interrupt before the speaker indicates that he or she is done for the moment. Go to a fellow negotiator who makes listening very hard on you. Let her know that you are learning and practicing listening, and that today, for *X* minutes you will only listen (where *X* could be 3, 7, or even 15 minutes), and delay responding until the predetermined listening time is up, or even until the following day.

3. ***Do not judge or evaluate.*** Listen without jumping to conclusions and interpreting what you hear. You may notice your judgmental thoughts but put them gently aside. If you notice that you lost track of the conversation due to your judgments, apologize to the speaker that your mind was distracted and ask them to repeat. Do not *pretend* to listen.
4. ***Look for nonverbal cues and name them.*** High-quality listening is more than hearing words and nodding your head. Much of the meaning in the conversation passes through the nonverbal channel. You may want to indicate that you read the attempted meaning of your conversation partner by acknowledging their point of view: "It seems that you are excited about this opportunity," or "I guess that this was a painful experience for you."
5. ***Do not impose your solutions.*** The role of the listener is to help speakers draw up a solution themselves. Therefore, when listening to a client or a colleague, wait before you suggest your professional solutions. If you believe you have a good solution and feel an urge to share it, use a question, such as "I wonder what would happen if you chose to do *X*?" or "How would you feel if we choose to do *X*"?
6. ***Ask more (good) questions.*** Listeners shape conversations by asking questions that benefit the speaker. Good listening requires being thoughtful about the most urgent need of the speaker and crafting a question that would lead the speaker to search for an answer. Ask questions to help someone delve deeper into their thoughts and experiences.

   Before you ask a question, ask yourself, "Is this question intended to benefit the speaker or to satisfy my curiosity?" Of course, there is room for both, but a good listener prioritizes the needs of the other. One of the best questions you can ask is "Is there anything else?" followed by silence, allowing the speaker to ponder before responding. This often exposes novel information and unexpected opportunities.
7. ***Reflect.*** When you finish a conversation, reflect on your listening and think about missed opportunities—moments you ignored potential leads or remained silent versus asking questions. When you feel that you were an excellent listener, consider

what you gained, and how you can apply this type of listening in more challenging circumstances.

8. *Invite stories.* People like to listen to stories more than informative disclosure. Hence, invite your interlocutors to share their stories with you. Ask for the specifics to help the speaker move from abstract generalizations to meaningful narratives.

Modifiers, Caveats, and No-Go Areas—When This Advice Just Won't Apply

The Enemies of Listening

If high-quality listening is as beneficial as we suggested thus far, why is it not more prevalent? Why are most people not listened to in the way they want? A few barriers often stand in the way:

1. *Costs.* Listening consumes time and effort. In many instances, lawyers listen to clients under time pressure or while distracted by other thoughts or work. So, listening is an investment decision: lawyers must put in the time to listen in order to see the future benefits.
2. *Fear of change.* High-quality listening can be risky because it entails entering a speaker's perspective without trying to make judgments. This process could potentially change the listener's attitudes and perceptions. We observed several times that when we trained managers to listen, they gained crucial insights about their employees—they were stunned to learn how little they knew about the lives of people they'd worked with for many years. This realization threatened managers' self-view—an experience called cognitive dissonance, which can be difficult.
3. *Power disparity.* By dominating conversations, most people signal competence and consequently enjoy greater influence. Good listeners, on the other hand, can be perceived as submissive. However, at the same time, good listeners gain prestige and create *mutual* empowerment for both listener and speaker. This process can shed light on the importance of understanding the driving force behind common practices such as conversation domination. These types of destructive behaviors are familiar in conflict situations and may be motivated by the fundamental

drive for social status. Recognizing this need, however, may enable lawyers to gain status through building prestige while also creating psychological value for their counterparts.

Conclusion

Throughout this chapter, we illuminated the importance of high-quality listening for influencing a speaker's attitudes and negotiation outcomes. High-quality listening creates awareness of conflicting cognitions and enlarges the scope of potentially integrative solutions for a negotiation. We hope that our readers test our suggestions by expanding their practice of listening according to our recommendation and reflect on whether and how improvement in listening affects their effectiveness as lawyers, negotiators, and mediators.

"Listening is a rare happening among human beings. You cannot listen to the word another is speaking if you are preoccupied with your appearance or impressing the other, or if you are trying to decide what you are going to say when the other stops talking, or if you are debating about whether the word being spoken is true or relevant or agreeable. Such matters may have their place, but only after listening to the word as the word is being uttered. Listening, in other words, is a primitive act of love, in which a person gives self to another's word, making self accessible and vulnerable to that word."—William Stringfellow

This Ties in With:

Heen & Stone, Ch. 12, Your Story & Mine; Pappas, Ch. 19, Listening

21

Negotiating without Words

Jeff Thompson,[1] Noam Ebner,[2] and Jeff Giddings[3]

Introduction

While the field of negotiation (in writing and in training) does not place much emphasis on nonverbal communication (NVC), it is, in some ways, of even greater importance than the verbal elements of conversation. This chapter introduces the METTA model for conducting effective NVC. Mastering its use—in your own communication, and for understanding your counterpart—will make you a more effective negotiator, and also improve your performance in

1. **Jeff Thompson**, Ph.D., is a professor at the Institute for Conflict Management at Lipscomb University. His work in crisis and conflict includes detective, hostage negotiator, mediator, crisis communication trainer, and researcher. He conducts research and training in crisis communication in a variety of contexts, including policing, hostage negotiation, terrorism, international kidnapping, and mental health. As a practitioner, he has been engaged in a variety of crisis incidents ranging from barricaded perpetrators, large-scale incidents, and terrorist incidents. He can be reached at mediator.jeff@gmail.com.
2. **Noam Ebner** is a professor in the Negotiation and Conflict Resolution program at Creighton University's Department of Interdisciplinary Studies. An attorney and mediator, he has taught mediation and negotiation around the world. He was among the first teachers to engage in online teaching of negotiation and conflict studies. Noam's research interests include online negotiation and dispute resolution, trust, and negotiation pedagogy. Noam can be contacted at NoamEbner@creighton.edu; his work can be found at ssrn.com/author=425153.
3. **Dr. Jeff Giddings** is a Professor of Law at Monash University, Melbourne, Australia. He convened the Graduate Program in Dispute Resolution at Griffith University, Brisbane, Australia, from 2005 to 2015. He has practiced, taught, and researched in the fields of negotiation and dispute resolution for thirty years.

other legal activities such as client counseling, reading a jury's mood, or examining witnesses.

This chapter is based on J. Thompson, N. Ebner, & J. Giddings, *Nonverbal Communication in Negotiation*, in 1 The Negotiator's Desk Reference 449–468 (Honeyman & Schneider eds, 2017). The full references in that chapter can be found at www.ndrweb.com/chapter-33--public.html.

Why This Concept Might Change Your Thinking

During negotiation, words spoken are only the tip of the informational iceberg. In reality, our decision-making processes and behavior are affected by a much larger set of information. Expert negotiators require an ability to effectively use NVC, as well as the ability to decode another's, to maintain a truly robust communication toolbox—one that enables them to be more effective in negotiation and in other aspects of legal practice.

NVC is not confined to body language; rather, it comprises a wide range of cues and elements, some relating to the human body and many that do not. When clustered, micro-cues, along with nonverbal elements, affect significant aspects of negotiation, including developing trust, building rapport, demonstrating empathy, and more.

Efforts to remain aware of the multitude of subtle cues—individually and in clusters—can create cognitive overload, particularly when you consider the need to be equally mindful of our own nonverbal cues and those of the other negotiator. We need to do this in the stressful environment of negotiation, and while still minding the verbal elements of negotiation! The METTA model names and structures this information, to allow us to absorb and process it without suffering the effects of data overload. We will use it to name the components of NVC and to offer best practices for conducting your own NVC and decoding that of your counterpart.

Action Plan—What You Can Do Differently Tomorrow

The METTA Model of Nonverbal Communication

METTA represents *movement*, *environment*, *touch*, *tone*, and *appearance* (see Table 1). Together, these five dimensions comprise all the potential cues (kinesics, or body movement) and elements (environmental factors, clothing, and accessories) of NVC in any

Table 1 Introducing METTA, Demonstrating the Issues

Movement	Gestures, posture, body orientation, eye contact, facial expressions, head nodding, head shaking, and head angling
Environment	Location, distance between people, time (spent speaking; time of day), layout of the room
Touch	Handshaking, leakage (self-adaptors and object-adaptors)
Tone	Clarity, pauses, "ums" and "ahs," volume, tone, pitch, rises and falls (and other near-musical cues used to convey punctuation, turn-taking, etc.)
Appearance	Clothing, accessories, and adornments

given interaction. Using METTA, negotiators can be more aware of their NVC as well as that of the other participants in their negotiation, increasing their effectiveness in achieving their goals.

Movement

A key aspect of movement is body orientation and pose. The direction in which a negotiator aims his or her body (for example, facing a counterpart directly or facing at an angle), and the vertical positioning of the body (sitting up straight, leaning forward, or leaning back) can play a pivotal role in creating a sense of immediacy, contributing to the creation of trust and rapport. Negotiators should consider having an appropriately relaxed body posture and facing toward your counterpart.

Other powerful movement-related tools include nonverbal mirroring and mimicry—similar and complementary movement and actions between interactants. These can signal empathy, positive affect, and rapport—all important for influencing your counterpart.

Appropriate eye contact (think "gaze"—not a cold or blank stare) can engender trust and rapport and create positive perceptions of competence and pleasantness. Conversely, lack of eye contact is commonly associated with disinterest as well as with lying and evasion (even though, scientifically, this is incorrect.)

Additional specific nonverbal micro-cues that a negotiator will want to consider utilizing during a negotiation session include smiling appropriately, having your hands visible and using open-handed gestures, demonstrating listening through head-nodding (see minimal encouragers below), and using facial expressions to display engagement.

Environment

The design of the negotiation room and the seating arrangements impact negotiations through their effects on people's emotions, behaviors, interpretations, and negotiating styles.

Sitting in close proximity might create unease; too much distance might thwart efforts to generate immediacy. Where possible, adjust the distance to the context (paying attention to the local culture) prior to beginning the negotiation.

The shape of the table also matters; across various contexts, conflict resolution professionals prefer circular tables.

Use of space is another important element of NVC. For example, territorial displays, such as spreading out one's negotiation papers across the table, could be interpreted as wanting to portray dominance.

Negotiations can be emotionally charged, and this can reduce a person's ability to listen. Spending more time listening during the early stages can help reduce your counterpart's negative emotions. Utilizing active listening skills (involving both verbal and nonverbal aspects) can also help you build trust and rapport. This demonstrates the close links between different aspects of METTA.

Additional considerations include having writing materials and refreshments available, removing or reducing distractions and interruptions, and having appropriate and comfortable furniture.

Touch

Touch is often a sensitive subject (pun or no pun). Different habits, comfort zones, and preferences can be compounded by differing cultural norms. Two areas in which touch is particularly salient to negotiation are the initial greeting and "leakage" throughout the process.

First impressions greatly impact how people judge others. In Western cultures, shaking hands conveys a first impression in business and professional settings. In the absence of a specific reason to avoid shaking hands, you should certainly do so (as it tends to increase interparty cooperation)—and even initiate the contact. While being aware of cultural concerns, if you shake one person's hand, offer to shake everyone's hand.

"Leakage" is another element of touch. It has been characterized as physical movements that we make unknowingly; they are uncontrollable and unintentional and could be perceived as a sign of anxiety or as an expression of boredom. Either way, allowing leakage can have a detrimental effect on your efforts to build rapport with your counterparty—and also diminish your perceived confidence and professional presence. Leakage can be in the form of self-adaptors (touching your neck, face, or fingers) or object-adapters (touching jewelry, clothing, or a pen).

Tone

How we deliver our thoughts gives significance to the words we use, revealing our current emotional state. It affects the impression others form of us, as being assertive, polite, attractive, or dominant.

Tailor your tone and volume to your desired effect. Tone can reveal your true emotional state, either supporting or discrediting the messages you convey.

The more fluent your speech (lacking speech disfluencies such as "umms" and "ahhs"), the more powerful and professional you will be perceived.

Use minimal encouragers (such as "and?" or "ok" and "mmm") to demonstrate to your counterpart that you are listening and to contribute to building rapport and trust.

Additional considerations related to tone include using a calm, professional voice, alongside a strategically assertive (not aggressive) tone to demonstrate confidence or stress an important point.

Appearance

A person's appearance plays a significant role in the impression they make—and, thereby, their influence on others before a negotiation or dialogue begins. Appearance includes facial features, clothing, adornments, and accessories. It follows that negotiators should adapt their clothing and accessories to the context of the negotiation session.

In addition to matching your outfit to the context, wear comfortable, well-fitting clothes, and ensure that your accessories give the impression intended. For example, consider your impact if you were to enter a high-stakes negotiation with a Spiderman backpack, as compared to a briefcase.

Additional Considerations

Above all, your NVC must be done genuinely. This quality will allow you to impact the negotiation dynamics naturally, without appearing artificial, robotic, or out-of-sync with what is said—helping to ensure your NVC is decoded the way you intend. At the same time, being aware of your negotiation opposite's NVC can give you deeper understanding of their apparent perspective, motives, and current emotions. This allows you to further develop, and adapt, if necessary, your strategies and tactics.

Modifiers, Caveats, and No-Go Areas—When This Advice Just Won't Apply

Most research on NVC—particularly on body language—was conducted in Western cultures, and findings should not be generalized to other cultures without caution.

Conclusion

Both your own nonverbal cues and those of your counterpart require constant awareness. Understanding and effectively using your own nonverbal cues and elements can reinforce your trustworthiness and build rapport with the other person. This increases your chances for influencing them, advancing you toward your goal. Remember: it is not a singular cue or element that accomplishes this; nonverbal cues are most effective in clusters that make contextual sense and are congruent with verbal messages.

This Ties in With:

Schneider & Ebner, Ch. 7, Social Intuition; Newell, Ch. 18, Attention

Section V

Working with Them

Section V addresses a multitude of concepts around relationships with your negotiation counterpart. Chapter 22 begins with a brief account of how trust and distrust work, and moves on to an analysis of how trust, after it is broken, can be repaired. This, however, is not always possible, and Chapter 23 is a trenchant analysis of what you can do in an environment where trust is impossible.

Trust, of course, is related to reputation. How a reputation is formed and why a trustworthy reputation is important, in far more settings than is commonly believed, are the subjects of Chapter 24. Closely linked to reputation, in turn, is the negotiator's ethical behavior. Chapter 25 moves to an analysis that shows how morals, rules, and law might all treat the same situation, but in vastly different ways. Understanding how they differ can give you a better sense of how your counterpart thinks. This discussion is followed by Chapter 26, which is about how fairness is perceived, particularly with an eye to fair processes and outcomes. Naturally, human beings being what they are, the effort to maintain a good reputation is sometimes going to involve making an apology, which is the subject of Chapter 27. And perhaps, if the apology is effective, forgiveness and reconciliation will follow, as they do in our book, in Chapter 28.

22

Trust and Trust Repair

Roy J. Lewicki[1]

Introduction

Trust is critical to all effective interpersonal relationships—and by derivation, to attorneys in their relationships with clients, with each other, and with the broader legal system in which they operate. I will offer a definition of trust, and its related perspective, trustworthiness, and point out why attorneys need to fully understand the drivers of each concept. Finally, I will offer suggestions as to ways that attorneys may be able to repair broken trust. This chapter is based on R.J. Lewicki, *Trust and Distrust*, in 1 The Negotiator's Desk Reference 201–216 (Honeyman & Schneider eds, 2017) and R.J. Lewicki, *Repairing Trust*, in 1 The Negotiator's Desk Reference 217–229 (Honeyman & Schneider eds, 2017). The full references in those chapters can be found respectively at www.ndrweb.com/chapter-15--public.html and www.ndrweb.com/chapter-16--public.html.

1. **Roy J. Lewicki** is the Abramowitz Professor of Management and Human Resources (Emeritus) at the Fisher College of Business, The Ohio State University. He received his Ph.D. in social psychology from Teachers College, Columbia University, in 1969, and has held faculty positions at Yale, Dartmouth, and Duke. He is the author or editor of many research articles and books, including *Negotiation*; *Negotiation: Readings, Exercises and Cases*; *Essentials of Negotiation*; *Making Sense of Intractable Environmental Conflicts*; and *Research on Negotiation in Organizations*. He teaches and consults extensively in the fields of negotiation, conflict management, and executive leadership.

Why This Concept Might Change Your Thinking

Trust indicates a willingness to become vulnerable to another based on confident positive expectations of the other's conduct. In short, trusting another allows you to be more honest, more straightforward, and more candid, and to reveal your weaknesses as well as your strengths. Trust reduces uncertainty over future outcomes, simplifies decision-making, and provides us with peace of mind. But the very vulnerability created by trust can also be highly disconcerting, because trusting another creates opportunities for them to exploit that vulnerability. Thus, the decision to trust should not be made blindly or glibly; the other must earn and deserve trust, and the validity of that trust should be frequently tested. The best prescriptive advice comes from the Russian proverb (also frequently attributed to President Ronald Reagan): "trust, but verify."

It should also be clear that trust is essential to effective negotiation. First, at the outset of any negotiation, the level of trust will determine how much and what kind of information we share with the other side. If we have prior knowledge of the other party—through direct experience or their reputation—that prior knowledge will guide our trust and willingness to be honest and transparent with the other. If we cannot trust the other, we will be less candid and transparent and not believe what they are telling us. Negotiators make these judgments at the outset of a negotiation and should also regularly monitor whether the initial judgment continues to be validated by the other's conduct and by the situational circumstances.

Second, trust enables parties to construct agreements that can be reached quickly and verbally, sealed with a handshake, perhaps affirmed by a follow-up email or memorandum of understanding.

Finally, even when parties do need to prepare a formal agreement, that agreement cannot stipulate every possible contingency; at some point, the negotiator must believe that the other party will be willing to act in the "spirit" as well as the letter of the agreement. Research has shown us that formal agreements do not build trust; instead, they are often aimed at controlling the distrust between the parties, which is not the same thing as building trust.

Equally important, negotiators must be sensitive to the other's behaviors that shape our trust of them. Research has shown that there are three critical factors by which we judge another's trustworthiness:

1. ***Ability or competence.*** For example, is the other skilled in the workings of the profession, in the substantive topics of the negotiation, and in the commonly accepted procedures of legal negotiation? Is the other able to construct logical and compelling arguments? Is the other well prepared and clearly capable of engaging in effective give-and-take?
2. ***Benevolence.*** Does the other treat us with courtesy and respect? Does the other listen, remain calm, and follow accepted protocols for legal conversations? Is the other clearly working toward a positive agreement for both sides or only driven by self-interest?
3. ***Integrity.*** Is the other speaking honestly and straightforwardly? Does the other speak with conviction? Does the other refrain from using deceptive and emotionally manipulating tactics? Does the other demonstrate that he or she will endorse and follow the agreements that we reach?

These are the qualities on which we judge another's trustworthiness, and also the factors by which they judge our trustworthiness. Since judgmental biases often cloud our perceptions of how trustworthy others may appear to us, we continually need to monitor what the other may be doing to either bolster or diminish our trust—and vice versa. Trust judgments are not necessarily fully rational, but often self-fulfilling; our own trustworthiness affects how much others trust us.

Action Plan—What You Can Do Differently Tomorrow

Build Trust

There are a number of things a negotiator can do to build trust with another party:

1. Create and meet the other party's expectations.
2. Treat the other with respect and courtesy.
3. Stress the benefits of creating mutual trust to the other party.

4. Establish credibility.
5. Build your arguments well. Demonstrate that you have done your homework and know what you are talking about.
6. Keep promises.
7. If you expect the relationship with the other to be long term, work to strengthen that relationship by being reliable and dependable, acting in the best interest of both parties, and by being transparent about your actions and intentions.

Monitor Your Own—and the Other's—Trustworthiness

Implicit in the mechanisms of building trust is a requirement to pay attention to how you are behaving, and to how you are being perceived by others. Your reputation for honesty and trustworthiness as a negotiator is likely to be one of your most valuable assets in your profession! You will periodically need to test *on yourself* the criteria by which you are judging them:

1. Test whether others see you as competent and "know what you are doing." Be open to feedback from others that you may not be well prepared or knowledgeable of the protocols for effective negotiation.
2. Test whether others judge you as treating them with courtesy and respect. Carefully listen to others, acknowledge that you have been listening and paying attention, and are genuinely seeking an agreement that acknowledges the legitimacy of their arguments (even if you don't agree with them).
3. Test whether others see you as honest and credible. Do not consistently lie, bluff, and distort information, which can hurt your credibility. Do not be tempted to use some of the traditionally competitive negotiation tactics that might be effective in the short turn but damaging to your reputation.

Learn to Repair Trust if Necessary

Being consistently perfect in building and maintaining trust is impossible. Miscommunication, misinterpretation, manipulation of information, poor coordination, and not treating the other with respect are only a few of the many ways that trust can get broken.

Here are several major strategies that a negotiator can use to repair trust:

1. ***Verbal explanations and apologies.*** The most common strategy for repairing trust is to offer the other party an explanation for why the violation occurred and offer an apology for causing that violation. Research has shown that there are multiple components to an effective apology. First, the negotiator should express regret for the violation, indicating that the negotiator is aware of what happened. Next, the negotiator should offer an explanation for why and how the trust violation occurred and directly acknowledge personal responsibility for whatever role the negotiator may have had in causing the violation. The negotiator should clearly indicate that the violation will not reoccur, and offer the other compensation for damages that may have resulted from the violation. Finally, the negotiator should request forgiveness and give the other an opportunity to express both residual thoughts and feelings about the incident.
2. ***Compensation and reparations.*** A second strategy can be to offer the other party some penance, reparations, or "compensatory damages" for the trust violation. The form of this compensation is likely to vary significantly depending on the context in which the violation occurred; compensation can also be token or symbolic, since the gesture is likely to be more significant than the actual value of the payment.
3. ***Structural changes in the ways the parties interact.*** Broadly, this refers to approaches, such as rules or procedure, that minimize or regulate the way the parties can interact. This might include using third-party intermediaries, brokered communications, formalized contracts, court orders, etc. As we indicated earlier, the structural solutions, when effective, are likely to reduce distrust, but other actions will also be necessary to rebuild broken trust.

Modifiers, Caveats, and No-Go Areas—When This Advice Just Won't Apply

If the relationship has been seriously damaged in the past, or your own reputation is widely suspect, simple trust repair tools are not likely to work. Similarly, if the other party continues to be adversarial and is unresponsive to trust-building measures, you should abandon efforts to build trust and properly defend yourself. Finally, differences in the substantive issues, the performance expectations placed on you and the other negotiator, and the cultural context in which the dispute occurs—to name only a few—can all make trust easier or more difficult to build and repair.

Conclusion

Trust is perhaps the single most effective tool a negotiator has. If one trusts others, and enjoys trust from others, negotiation is easier and more straightforward. In contrast, if one does not trust the other, or is not trustworthy, negotiation is more guarded, tedious, and in need of extreme caution and frequent verification. The adversarial nature of much legal practice often fuels the forces that diminish trust, making trust a more fragile—but nonetheless critical—part of effective negotiation.

This Ties in With:

Pappas, Ch. 19, Listening; Itzchakov & Kluger, Ch. 20, Changing Attitudes; Cristal, Ch. 23, No Trust; Schneider et al., Ch. 24, Reputation; Brown & Robbennolt, Ch. 27, Apology

23

When There's No Trust

Moty Cristal[1]

Introduction

We all want trust and would all like to be trusted. Yet, although the classic interest-based negotiation paradigm argues that establishing trust is essential for success in negotiation, this chapter will provide you with an alternative view and clear prescriptive advice on how to handle the hardest negotiations with people whom you don't trust. Indeed, you can negotiate, and you can reach an agreement with people whom you consider to be your enemies, as long as you will legitimize the hostile feelings; respect the counterpart as a human being; and build a carefully designed process that both sides will own. This chapter is based on M. CRISTAL, *Negotiating in a Low-to-No Trust Environment,* in 1 THE NEGOTIATOR'S DESK REFERENCE 231–248 (Honeyman & Schneider eds, 2017). The full references in that chapter can be found at https://www.ndrweb.com/chapter-17--public.html.

1. Lt. Colonel (R.) **Moty Cristal** is CEO of NEST, Negotiation Strategies Ltd. A graduate of Bar-Ilan Law School (1994), and Harvard's Kennedy School (1998), he has served on Israeli peace negotiation teams and gained extensive operational experience in complex and crisis negotiations, which he has since applied to business and governmental crises, including in the cybersphere. Cristal is a Professor for Negotiation Dynamics at the Skolkovo business school in Russia and adjunct professor at the Coller School of Management, Tel Aviv University, and at Arison Business School at the Interdisciplinary Center in Israel. He developed the Negosystem™ model to apply system thinking to complex negotiations.

Why This Concept Might Change Your Thinking

Researchers have conducted a number of influential studies investigating the role that trust plays in negotiation and conflict management, and they have formulated more than one definition. I will argue that regardless of the definitions, however, trust can be considered neither a prerequisite nor a foundation for a successful conflict negotiation process. "Low-to-no trust" environments are not uncommon, and any lawyer who must negotiate in one might consider ignoring the traditional prescriptive advice to develop "trust-building measures" in favor of a quite different strategy, outlined below.

Low-to-no trust represents a reality where a party has no alternate counterpart to negotiate with rather than the one whom he or she does not trust. This can be where two or more parties are negotiating in order to come to an agreement, either because they were forced to by a third party (court decision or political power) or because they face a "mutually hurting stalemate." This often means negotiating with someone who has hurt you, damaged you, or with whom you have already declared war. A low-to-no trust environment represents a reality that extends beyond the absence of trust: it's the existence of a strong, solid, and deep-rooted distrust. Consequently, both sides can see no other valid alternative that satisfies their own interests other than negotiating an agreement.

Action Plan—What You Can Do Differently Tomorrow

Negotiating in a low-to-no trust environment can be defined as a system that exhibits a complex interaction of three time dimensions, across different levels of the conflict (personal, structural, and procedural), which together create an extreme state of untrustworthiness.

Past is represented by grievances, mutual damages caused by the negotiating counterparts, plus their constant need to articulate these, refer to them, seek compensation, and most important, allow these past events to dictate not only their current *behavior*, but also their individual or collective *identity*. *Present* is represented by a series of behaviors that focus on impasse, reluctance to come to the negotiating table, inflammatory statements, coalition building with third parties in order to elevate one's bargaining power, long ranting sessions once sitting at the mediation table, and adopting an all-or-nothing strategy. *Future* is implicated when the physical, emotional, and financial well-being of the parties are tied together.

In other words, despite the hostility, their future lives or quality of life, and often those of other individuals, organizations, or societies, depend on the negotiated outcome they will achieve with someone they do not trust. In the face of all this, it may be surprising that as a lead negotiator or process designer, the steps you should follow are essentially just three:

Freedom to Hate

Psychological research shows the strong necessity of individuals, as well as groups (trade unions, communities in conflict), to define their own selves through distinguishing from others, identifying the other as an enemy. Demonizing the other is a strong catalyst for building personal as well as group (national or organizational) identity.

Negotiations face the gap between the fundamental psychological need to demonize the other and the traditional call to show empathy to your untrustworthy counterpart. In difficult negotiations, people are flooded with emotions, can hardly talk logically, and, most of the time, will reject any attempt to show empathy. Therefore, they ought to be *allowed* to hate the other side, meaning to maintain their negative emotions toward the other party. This is not suggested as an obstacle, in fact, it's quite the opposite—it's an enabling mechanism for parallel rational thinking.

By its nature, negotiation in a low-to-no trust environment seeks conflict management, rather than resolution, since the deep level of mutual distrust does not allow true *resolution,* let alone *reconciliation.* However, if the process is led in the right direction, stable conflict *management* might eventually be achieved. Allowing parties to hate each other, and to maintain reciprocal negative feelings on the *emotional* level, will enable parties to take certain tangible and feasible steps on a *rational* level: for example, cessation of hostilities, a mutually agreed withdrawal of lawsuits, or visitation rights for their kids.

By legitimizing the parties' negative emotions toward the other side, a lawyer or a mediator assists a party to overcome a dissonance between "How can I make peace with the person who hurt me so much?" and a rational understanding that this fight must ultimately be stopped. By emphasizing to the conflicting parties that they are not seeking peace, that they are not engaged in a process of turning their enemy into a friend, that they need neither forget nor forgive, the lawyer reconciles their internal emotional and psychological dissonance. This increases the likelihood of accepting practical arguments regarding the high cost of no deal.

Shifting from Trust to Respect

You can *trust* someone you do not respect, and you can *respect* someone you do not trust.

Negotiating in a low-to-no trust environment calls for replacing trust with respect as a foundation for these negotiations. When trusting your negotiating partner, there is an imaginary shift in responsibility from you to the other side: the latter is now put in a position to prove that she is indeed trustworthy. But when you respect the other, you do this independently: the *responsibility* lies on *your* shoulders.

Such respect has nothing to do with actions, behaviors, or attitudes of the other side. It has nothing to do with the level of risk in the negotiation. It could mean simply showing up on time to meetings, respecting religious holidays, lowering your tone of voice, or adhering to mutually agreed-on process rules. When you choose to *respect* your counterpart, you will quite likely be respected in turn, because showing respect is not as demanding as trusting.

Another practical point to note is that while trust is a culturally sensitive concept, respect is defined as a universal moral value.

Trust in the Process, Rather Than Trusting the Other Side

The third component is replacing trusting the other side with trusting a negotiation *process* that both sides build together.

Negotiating in a low-to-no trust environment is mostly a distributive process, and, in particular, one that uses concession exchange. When law enforcement negotiators face a hostage taker, they enter into a delicate though structured process, whose foundation is *quid quo pro. You give something only if you get something in return.* No gestures, no "pay in advance." Thus, when you carefully build a quid pro quo process, even with your most despised adversary, both sides feel that they own the process. The two sides, despite the fact that they do not trust each other, still care about the process that was jointly built: the respected dynamics, the invested time, the efforts, credits, and commitments made. Because in this context, parties mostly have no best alternative to a negotiated agreement (BATNA), they will likely stick to the process until it yields an agreement. Putting the process at the center of attention, and referring to it as a joint achievement, provides another opportunity to overcome the absence of trust.

If and when possible, creating *trust in the process*, rather than building trust and confidence with another whom you will never ultimately trust, could benefit from an effective mediation.

Modifiers, Caveats, and No-Go Areas—When This Advice Just Won't Apply

Nothing here is intended to suggest that low-trust/no-trust environments should be eagerly sought or multiplied. If it is possible to create and build on trust, that is, of course, better all round.

Conclusion

If you are compelled to negotiate with someone whom you don't trust—whether in a divorce or with a former partner, trade union leader, or angry neighbor—the "low-to-no trust" paradigm gives you a practical alternative to seeking peace, repairing the world, or trying to generate a win-win outcome. The more limited goals become to cease active hostilities and reduce tension to a level that will allow a satisfactory outcome. In these negotiations, you should follow three steps that constantly intertwine. First, feel free to *hate* your counterparts. Second, show them *respect*, rather than trust. And third, build a quid quo pro *process* that both can trust.

This Ties in With:

Lewicki, Ch. 22, Trust; Volpe et al., Ch. 37, Unknown; Wade, Ch. 50, Dobermans

24

Reputation Matters

Andrea Kupfer Schneider,[1] *Catherine H. Tinsley,*[2] *and Jack Cambria*[3]

Introduction

In this chapter, we draw from both academic research and professional experiences to argue why reputations are critical for negotiators. We explain how reputations influence the negotiation process and subsequent outcomes. Moreover, we use theory developed in

1. **Andrea Kupfer Schneider** is a Professor of Law at Marquette University Law School, where she teaches dispute resolution, negotiation, ethics, and international conflict resolution and is the director of Marquette's nationally ranked dispute resolution program. Andrea has written numerous books, book chapters, and articles on negotiation skills and styles, dispute system design, international conflict, and gender and negotiation. She was given the American Bar Association (ABA) Section of Dispute Resolution Award for Outstanding Scholarly Work for 2017. Andrea received her A.B. *cum laude* from the Woodrow Wilson School of Public & International Affairs at Princeton University and her J.D. *cum laude* from Harvard Law School.
2. **Catherine H. Tinsley** is a Professor at the McDonough School of Business at Georgetown University, and is Faculty Director of the Georgetown University Women's Leadership Institute. She studies how factors such as culture, reputations, and gender influence negotiations, and how near-miss events bias people's decisions under risk. She has served on three committees for the National Academy of Sciences, has published more than fifty peer-reviewed articles and book chapters, and has been on the editorial boards of *The Academy of Management Journal*, *Organizational Behavior and Human Decision Processes*, and *International Journal of Conflict Management*.
3. **Jack Cambria** retired from the New York City Police Department (NYPD) in 2015 after nearly thirty-four years of dedicated service. For over sixteen years, he served in the Emergency Service Unit (ESU), whose primary focus is to provide rescue, SWAT, and counterterrorism services to the City of New York. He ended his NYPD career as the longest-standing commander of the Hostage Negotiation Team, serving in that capacity for over fourteen years.

other domains (game theory and social and cognitive psychology), as well as studies from the legal and business domains, to help us reason why reputations should influence the negotiation process. This chapter is based on C. Tinsley, J. Cambria, & A.K. Schneider, *Reputation in Negotiation*, in 1 The Negotiator's Desk Reference 249–264 (Honeyman & Schneider eds, 2017). The full references in that chapter can be found at www.ndrweb.com/chapter-18--public.html.

Why This Concept Might Change Your Thinking

What is a reputation? A reputation is a coherent image of the nature of another party's character. This image suggests to people how that other party will behave, and why, in any particular context. In other words, reputations not only offer information about another party's future actions, but also about the intent underlying such action.

An important characteristic of reputations is that they emerge over time. Often, this time spans across different transactions, so that reputations are a way of linking transactions across time. For example, although one may be currently negotiating a more discrete deal (for example, a single contract or settling a case), these discrete transactions are often embedded within a series of prior negotiated transactions (as a repeat player working with the same attorneys), or future ones. It is in these repeat-play situations that parties have been advised to be concerned with their reputations, and that the parties themselves appear to have an intuitive sense that reputations are important. For lawyers where repeat play is the norm, reputation is particularly crucial. But experience with high-stakes hostage negotiations shows that developing a trustworthy reputation *over the course of a single negotiation* can be essential, even when "this is a one-shot deal."

Action Plan—What You Can Do Differently Tomorrow

If reputations are perceptual mechanisms that develop over time and help us characterize the other party, how do they influence the negotiation process? Although negotiators typically try to maximize their final outcomes, the process by which final outcomes are maximized is "mixed motive" in nature: for negotiators to maximize their own individual outcomes, they must also try to cooperate with the other side to create joint value. Given that there are at least two strategic orientations embedded in any negotiated exchange, negotiations are marked by high degrees of uncertainty. This uncertainty is where reputations become important.

What Reputation Should One Establish?

Most research in negotiation has assumed that there are two general strategic orientations one can take in a negotiation—integrative/cooperative or distributive/competitive, and that there are likewise two general reputations a negotiator can develop—integrative/cooperative or tough/competitive. An "integrative" negotiator is someone known for trying to cooperate, problem-solve, be trustworthy and compassionate, create joint value, or generally get a deal that works for both (or all) parties. A "distributive" negotiator is someone known for trying to be tough, use power, extract concessions, claim value, and ensure they get a good deal personally. Which is the more desirable reputation?

One argument is that a distributive reputation is most desirable, helping a negotiator by intimidating the other party. For example, a negotiator might purposely delay a negotiation in order to build a reputation for toughness which she plans to use to extract concessions from a counterpart. Alternatively, a party might threaten negative consequences to force concessions from her counterpart. In these cases, a negotiator's reputation for being a tough value claimer might reinforce the belief that her threats are credible and, therefore, make the threats more effective. A tough reputation can also act as a deterrent. Hence, when negotiations are more distributive than integrative in nature, parties with a distributive reputation could reap significant rewards regardless of whether they actually employ these tactics.

However, when negotiations have a significant integrative potential, as most do, then having a reputation as a skilled distributive negotiator might be a handicap. To achieve a negotiation's integrative potential, negotiators must, among other things, make tradeoffs among issues and add elements that might address the other party's interests. The success of these integrative behaviors depends on sharing information to develop an accurate understanding of the parties' interests and priorities. For example, if a party understands what her counterpart cares about, she can propose trades that will meet her counterpart's interests, or she can offer other resources that may not otherwise be considered. An accurate understanding of each other's interests requires negotiators to build rapport and create an environment of trust at the table. Shared trust encourages parties to share specific information about their interests, preferences, and priorities.

How We Know Integrative Reputations Matter

Results of a variety of studies showed that when negotiators were given information that their counterpart had a distributive reputation, the negotiators shared significantly less information about their specific interests, needs, and priorities—which is exactly the kind of information necessary to expand joint gain. Moreover, they were significantly more likely to just make small talk—sharing general information about the negotiation, and essentially wasting time. Overall, negotiators that were labeled as having a distributive reputation did significantly worse than other negotiators.

Results from a controlled study on integrative reputations were consistent, showing that when negotiators were given information that their counterpart had an integrative reputation, the negotiators opened up and freely shared what might be sensitive information. They shared significantly more information about their specific interests, needs, and priorities—which, again, is exactly the kind of information necessary to expand joint gain. Moreover, they were significantly less likely to just beat around the bush. As a result, negotiation pairs in the "integrative reputation" condition achieved economically better outcomes than negotiators in the "control" condition. Also, both negotiators in the integrative reputation condition did equally well economically, suggesting that an integrative reputation of *one* negotiator was all that was necessary to set the negotiation on an integrative course. Crucially, and contrary to some lay theories, the cooperative negotiator with the integrative reputation did *not* suffer exploitation attempts from the other party. Finally, in this study, the researchers tested negotiators' satisfaction with the process and willingness to negotiate in the future, and found that both sides in the integrative condition were more satisfied and more willing to negotiate in the future than the negotiators in the control condition, thus adding more potential future value to both negotiators.

Results from Surveys of Lawyers about the Real World

How do lawyers' reputations get measured in reality? If lawyers value an integrative approach in their colleagues, we would expect them to perceive that as a more effective negotiation approach. Similarly, if lawyers do not find a distributive approach valuable, lawyers would tend to describe this approach as relatively ineffective in negotiations. Therefore, to measure lawyers' reputations, we need to ask lawyers about other lawyers' behaviors.

In a study of lawyers asked about a previous negotiation, it appeared that attorneys actually do value an integrative reputation, as measured by its perceived effectiveness. For example, 72% of those attorneys described as "true problem-solvers" were perceived as effective by their peers (and only 1% of these attorneys were seen as ineffective). In contrast, only 3% of "unethical adversarial" attorneys were perceived as effective, while 75% of unethical adversarial attorneys were perceived as ineffective.

Modifiers, Caveats, and No-Go Areas—When This Advice Just Won't Apply

Some would argue that, in one-shot negotiations, reputation might not matter. The hostage negotiation context, however, provides an interesting counterexample to the business and legal examples above. In crisis negotiations where a criminal or psychopath has isolated himself, issuing threats and demands, and perhaps even holding hostages, might the threat or the use of force be more appropriate? The answer is partly yes: the *threat* of force (on the part of law enforcement) is important to motivate a dialogue between the perpetrator and the crisis negotiator. But within the negotiation itself, having a reputation for being cooperative, trustworthy, and honest turns out to be critical for successful resolution without *using* force, averting the danger of hurting innocents.

What the NYPD Hostage Negotiation Training teaches is that each discrete negotiation *can* be seen as a repeat-play situation. A negotiator's behavior at the beginning of the negotiation has critical implications for a hostage taker's responses to the negotiator at later stages of the negotiation. Indeed, the rule of thumb stipulates that the first 15–45 minutes (of what might be a protracted, multi-day negotiation) are the most critical. In this early window, a negotiator must try to begin establishing his or her reputation for trustworthiness, problem-solving, compassion, and cooperation. If a crisis negotiator demonstrates a strong and sincere desire to resolve the crisis in a compassionate and cooperative way, then the chances of successful resolution are enhanced.

And while we might not readily think that this type of situation applies to lawyers, many lawyers have actually been in high-stakes, emotional negotiations. The lessons of thinking about setting the tone and the type of reputation you want to establish at the outset of negotiation should not be lost.

Conclusion

Reputation is too important to be left to chance. Negotiators need to understand the impact of their reputations. We have argued that an integrative reputation leads to better rapport and information sharing, leading to more satisfying outcomes. This integrative behavior is perceived as more effective by one's negotiation counterpart. Finally, even under conditions in which repeated interactions are highly unlikely, the ability to create a trustworthy reputation has value.

This Ties in With:

Lewicki, Ch. 22, Trust; Welsh, Ch. 26, Fairness; Volpe et al., Ch. 37, Unknown

25

Negotiation Ethics

Art Hinshaw[1]

Introduction

Norms, rules, or law—to which are we referring when making claims of unethical negotiation conduct? The answer is important because what may be an acceptable norm in some quarters may be problematic under rules of professional conduct for lawyers. To make things more difficult, different norms present differences in acceptable conduct, the rules of professional conduct are easily misconstrued, and the law of misrepresentation, especially in the omission context, can be tricky. Understanding these differences is critical to making the right choice when facing pointed questioning and in defending against the use of questionable tactics. This chapter is based on A. Hinshaw, *Negotiation Ethics*, in 1 The Negotiator's Desk Reference 481–492 (Honeyman & Schneider eds, 2017). The full references in that chapter can be found at www.ndrweb.com/chapter-35--public.html.

1. **Art Hinshaw** is the John J. Bouma Fellow in Alternative Dispute Resolution, the Founding Director of the Lodestar Dispute Resolution Center, and a Clinical Professor of Law at the Sandra Day O'Connor College of Law at Arizona State University. His research bridges dispute resolution theory and practice, focusing primarily on mediation and negotiation. Professor Hinshaw is active in the dispute resolution community having served on several academic and professional committees at the state and national levels, including the ABA's Standing Committee on Mediator Ethical Guidance. He is a regular contributor to *Indisputably*, the ADR law professor blog, and has served on the Arizona Commission of Judicial Conduct.

Why This Concept Might Change Your Thinking

Ethical questions are simply questions of fairness, yet unlike in other settings, some deception is acceptable and even expected in negotiation. Yet not everyone accepts duplicity as the prevailing norm. Idealists view negotiation as any other interaction and follow the golden rule: treat others as you would have them treat you. Pragmatists weigh deceit's short-term benefits against its reputational costs and harm to current and future relationships to determine whether it's worthwhile. Aggressive negotiators view dishonesty as an essential element of negotiation and expect others to engage in cunning deceit, as well. It is important for lawyers to understand these norms, and attorneys must also abide by the bargaining rules promulgated in their state's professional rules of conduct.

With regard to statements, Rule 4.1(a) of the ABA Model Rules of Professional Conduct requires lawyers to speak the truth as they understand it about "material facts and law" but not about non-material facts or law. A statement is material if it is reasonable to view it as important to a fair understanding of what is being given up and gained in the transaction. Thus, the standard of care is that of a reasonable listener. Therefore, to identify the material facts in a negotiation, a lawyer should look at the negotiation from the counterpart's point of view. With regard to omissions, lawyers have no general duty to inform others of relevant facts when negotiating, but if silence makes the attorney knowingly complicit in a client's fraud, Rule 4.1(b) creates a duty to disclose material facts in order to avoid assisting in the criminal or fraudulent act. Furthermore, Rule 8.4(c) specifically defines "dishonesty, fraud, deceit, or misrepresentation" as professional misconduct. Statutory interpretation gives Rule 4.1's specific analysis precedence over Rule 8.4(c)'s general prohibitions, but Rule 8.4(c)'s exhortation augments Rule 4.1's prescriptions.

Finally, Rule 3.3 prohibits lawyers from "making false statements of fact or law" to a tribunal. Note that this is any statement of fact or law, not just material facts. Additionally, it requires attorneys to correct any false statements of material fact or law. Thus, lawyers need to be extra careful with what they say to judges when in judicial settlement conferences.

Action Plan—What You Can Do Differently Tomorrow

While there are several items attorneys can do with regard to negotiation ethics, three are paramount: learning to defend against deception, understanding fraud, and recognizing the negotiation's context.

Learning to defend against deception first requires identifying where an attorney sees herself in ethical terms: does she operate primarily through the idealist, pragmatist, or aggressive mode. But that is only part of the equation; she also needs to be able to defend against those using questionable tactics. This is particularly true where the deal is more important than any present or potential relationship. Although there is not enough space to get deep into defensive tactics, there are some basic defensive strategies that all negotiators should know. The first tactic is to conduct thorough background research on their counterpart's reputation. This can be done in a number of ways, most notably by contacting former colleagues and prior negotiation counterparts. If the person has a reputation for deceit, the negotiator will know to be cautious or defensive throughout, and to nail down every commitment.

Negotiators should also probe relentlessly for information to get counterparts to elaborate on their statements. Research has shown that most people lie through omissions and half-answers, so further questions may cause some counterparts to walk back from earlier statements. Careful listening is the best method to thwart evasive negotiators. If a question has not been addressed in full, continued questioning should focus on the issue until the information is either revealed or protected in a very direct manner. Asking for confirmable objective standards is a classic method of justifying the reasonability of offers, and "come clean" questions (i.e., "is there anything unknown to me that could materially impact this deal?") should be used strategically.

If a counterpart deflects such questions or changes the topic, negotiators should use them more than once. And finally, negotiators should make sure to observe their counterparts' nonverbal signals to make sure that they match what is being said. Inconsistency between verbal and nonverbal messages is a signal of deception.

With regard to fraud, attorneys should understand that the Model Rules' approach to negotiation ethics mirrors the law of fraudulent misrepresentation. Thus, understanding fraud is important, which simply is a knowing misrepresentation of a material fact resulting in justifiable reliance and damages. These elements are fairly straightforward, but a few explanations are necessary. First, the knowledge requirement is met if the person making the statement knows or believes that the matter is not as represented, does not have confidence in the accuracy of the statement, or does not have the basis for the representation. Whether one is aware that the conduct in question is fraudulent is irrelevant. And, consistent with Rule 4.1, the term *material fact* is defined as a fact a reasonable person would find important in determining whether to go forward with the transaction.

As with Rule 4.1, an omission can be an affirmative misrepresentation, but only when a duty to disclose the matter exists. Such duties arise in fiduciary relationships (e.g., trustee to a trust, directors and shareholders, guardian and ward) and when necessary to prevent partial or ambiguous statements from being misleading. Situations applicable to lawyers include when subsequently discovered information makes untrue a previous representation thought to be true, or circumstances such as when the parties' relationship or regular business practices would lead to a reasonable expectation of disclosure. What might those trade customs be? For litigators, they would include Rule 26 of the Rules of Civil Procedure, requiring periodic updates to initial disclosures.

The final key ethical consideration is the negotiation's context. While the setting may be business, legal, or something else, the importance of the negotiators' relationship going forward is critical. Do these negotiators need to work together with respect to this transaction down the road, or will they be negotiating with each other in different circumstances? Or, is this a one-time negotiation? Associated with these variables is the importance placed upon one's reputation as a negotiator. Not surprisingly, a negotiator's reputation has a direct correlation with both the amount of information that negotiator receives and the negotiation's outcome.

Modifiers, Caveats, and No-Go Areas—When This Advice Just Won't Apply

Labeling deceptive tactics just short of fraud as "ethical" is doublespeak, and the resulting confusion creates difficulty for those attempting to apply ordinary ethical notions of truthfulness to negotiation. Moreover, the inherent contradiction represents a refusal to incorporate any true systemic notions of ethics into the bargaining process, which means that abiding by typical ethical norms may lead to being exploited in a negotiation. As a result, rather than preparing for answering a pointed question, many negotiators simply make in-the-moment choices of being truthful, evasive, or deceitful. Unfortunately, when preparing to negotiate, most people gravitate to what they believe to be most important—the substantive issues—while leaving other important matters to chance, including ethics.

Most lawyers do not have the luxury to engage in an analytical look at the rules of professional conduct during a negotiation. Therefore, the best advice for negotiators is to listen to your own sense of personal ethics. It will provide more guidance in the heat of the moment than any other decision-making method. That said, a surprisingly high number of lawyer negotiators have a poor understanding of how the rules of professional conduct regulate negotiation behavior. Thus, legal negotiators should endeavor to improve their ethical instincts, and the best way to do that is (a) to study the ethical limitations to bargaining, and (b) to prepare for difficult questions to avoid making in-the-moment choices of being truthful, evasive, or deceitful. Doing so will help you become primed to spot ethical issues in the moment, and to act accordingly.

Conclusion

Ethical dilemmas are said to be at the heart of many bargaining encounters. Without a fundamental understanding of negotiation ethics, negotiators have little outside of unreliable instincts to guide their way through these situations. Lawyers who take negotiation ethics for granted do so at their peril.

This Ties in With:

Welsh, Ch. 26, Fairness; Amsler, Ch. 45, DSD

26

Distributive and Procedural Fairness Perceptions in Negotiation

Nancy A. Welsh[1]

Introduction

Negotiators use their perceptions of fairness to make all sorts of decisions during negotiation: What offer shall we make? How should we respond to the other side's demand? Is the other side being so ridiculous that it is time to call an impasse? However, negotiators' perceptions of distributive (substantive) fairness are far from objective. They depend upon the allocation principle that a negotiator has chosen to apply, and that choice is influenced by social, psychological, and cognitive variables. Finally, and rather surprisingly, perceptions of the procedural fairness of the negotiation process can play a powerful role in negotiators' perceptions of distributive fairness.

1. **Nancy A. Welsh** is Professor of Law and Director of the Dispute Resolution Program at Texas A&M University School of Law. Her research focuses on the procedural justice provided by court- and agency-connected mediation, as well as the effect of institutionalized "alternative" processes on the legitimacy and mission of the courts. Professor Welsh mediates for the U.S. District Court of the Middle District of Pennsylvania and previously was a member of the Minnesota ADR Review Board, which developed and implemented rules governing the innovative alternative dispute resolution (ADR) program adopted by that state's courts. For 2016–17, she served as Chair of the American Bar Association (ABA) Section of Dispute Resolution.

This chapter is based on N.A. WELSH, *Perceptions of Fairness in Negotiation*, in 1 THE NEGOTIATOR'S DESK REFERENCE 515–531 (Honeyman & Schneider eds, 2017). The full references in that chapter can be found at www.ndrweb.com/chapter-38--public.html.

Why This Concept Might Change Your Thinking

To assess distributive fairness, negotiators choose from among four allocation principles—equality, need, generosity, and equity. The *equality principle* provides that everyone in a group should share its benefits equally. According to the *need principle*, those who need more of a particular benefit should receive more than those who need less. The *generosity principle* decrees that one person's outcome should not exceed the outcomes achieved by others. Finally, according to the *equity principle*, those who contributed more should receive more than those who contributed less. The closer that a negotiation outcome is to the outcome anticipated by a negotiator, the greater the likelihood that the negotiator will perceive the outcome as fair.

Negotiators' relationships with each other significantly influence their selections among these allocation principles. A negotiator who has *no* relationship with the other person will use whatever principle produces the best result for her. When a negotiator has a *negative* relationship with her counterpart, she will define her desired outcome in relative terms and will choose the principle that enables her to do *better* than the other negotiator. She will even undertake a risky strategy to achieve this goal. On the other hand, a *positive* relationship makes the attainment of a mutually fair outcome desirable, and the negotiator who expects future, positive interactions with the other person will tend to use the equality principle to define distributive fairness.

Even when negotiators share a desire to use the equity principle to arrive at a fair result, their definitions of an "equitable outcome" are affected by both self-interest and perceptions of the other negotiator. People—including lawyers—value their own contributions (and losses) more highly than they value the identical contributions (or losses) of others. This is called the "egocentric bias."

Meanwhile, negotiators who have been harmed by the other person are likely to assume that this was due to the other person's general disposition, intentions, or character rather than situational circumstances. Thus, they fall victim to the "fundamental attribution error."

A significant body of research has found that people's perceptions of distributive fairness also can be influenced by how they felt they were treated during a dispute resolution or decision-making process, and this research is being applied to negotiation. If people perceive themselves as treated in a "procedurally fair" manner during the dispute resolution or decision-making process, they are more likely to judge the outcome of the process as fair, even if it is unfavorable. They also are more likely to share information, discover integrative potential, and comply with the outcome.

Action Plan—What You Can Do Differently Tomorrow

As lawyers prepare for negotiations, they should think carefully about how the quality of their interactions with each other can affect how much information they will share, their assessments of each other's character, and their relationship—all of which influence how they will judge distributive fairness. In other words, lawyers should consider how to behave in a procedurally fair manner. They should also consider whether their clients would benefit from being involved in a procedurally fair negotiation process.

Researchers have discovered a striking consistency in the criteria that people use to judge whether a dispute resolution or decision-making process was fair. First, people are more likely to judge a process as fair if they were given a meaningful opportunity to tell their story (i.e., an opportunity for *voice*). Second, in a process that people feel was fair, they had received assurance that the decision maker *listened* to them and understood and cared about what they had to say (i.e., trustworthy consideration). Third, people watch for signs that the forum was neutral, and the decision maker was trying to treat them and their claims in an evenhanded manner. Finally, people value a process that accorded them dignity and respect. If people perceive that they were treated in a procedurally fair manner, they are more likely to perceive the outcome as fair, even if it is unfavorable. They are also more likely to comply with that outcome.

In two studies involving law students as negotiators, Tom Tyler and Rebecca Hollander-Blumoff tested the application of these findings to negotiation. They found that these negotiators were indeed more likely to perceive an outcome as fair—even if relatively unfavorable—when their counterparts had treated them in a procedurally fair manner. In the first study, with a bargaining situation that permitted only distributive outcomes, perceptions of procedurally fair treatment were highly correlated with perceptions that the other negotiator: listened; behaved in a courteous manner; respected the rights of the responding negotiator's client; demonstrated concern about that client's satisfaction; was trustworthy; and shared information. Tyler and Hollander-Blumoff found that behaving in a procedurally fair manner neither helped nor hurt the individual negotiator's bottom line. However, when negotiators behaved in a procedurally fair manner, their counterparts were more likely to accept (or recommend that their clients accept) the negotiated outcomes.

In the second study, with a bargaining situation that permitted the development of integrative outcomes, Tyler and Hollander-Blumoff found that a procedurally fair negotiation process was positively correlated with the maximization of joint gains. They concluded that the disclosures necessary to achieve integrative solutions were more likely in a procedurally fair negotiation process.

Thus, lawyers can benefit from behaving in a procedurally fair manner in negotiation. Of course, this includes treating each other courteously and not interrupting each other. Furthermore, it suggests the value of being respectful of each other's clients and of using reflective or active listening to demonstrate understanding (though not necessarily agreement) and to encourage additional disclosures that may unlock integrative potential.

Lawyers also should consider whether their clients would benefit from being involved in a procedurally fair negotiation process. Such a process would allow clients to express what is important to them and witness the other negotiator or lawyer demonstrating an understanding of what was said. In a procedurally fair negotiation process, clients also would gain the benefit of experiencing respectful treatment.

Modifiers, Caveats, and No-Go Areas—When This Advice Just Won't Apply

Procedurally fair behavior in a negotiation will not have the same effect on all negotiators. Negotiators who define and evaluate themselves based on their relationships with others, or who believe that social interactions should affirm basic moral values, will react more strongly to the procedural fairness (or unfairness) exhibited by their negotiating counterparts. Individualistic negotiators' attitudes and behaviors are less affected by process fairness.

Negotiators' relative status also appears to influence how procedural fairness affects their attitudes and behaviors. In a negotiation between two individuals who perceive themselves to be of uneven status, the lower-status negotiator is more likely to be satisfied with an unfavorable outcome, as long as she is treated in a procedurally fair manner by the higher-status negotiator. The higher-status negotiator, in contrast, is less likely to allow process fairness to soften the blow of an unfavorable outcome. In fact, for the higher-status negotiator, procedural fairness tends to contribute significantly to her satisfaction only if the outcome is also favorable.

Unfortunately, something called "sham" procedural fairness also exists. A negotiator may engage in all of the behaviors described above and thus signal that her counterpart's voice has the potential to affect the outcome. However, the negotiator may have absolutely no intention of allowing herself to be affected by what she has heard or seen. This situation is most likely to occur when a person has a vested interest in the outcome—exactly the situation in negotiation. Under these circumstances, the negotiator may be using the lessons of procedural fairness simply to seduce the other negotiator's disclosure and compliance.

Conclusion

Ultimately, lawyers involved in negotiation should understand that their assessments of distributive fairness (as well as their clients' assessments) are subjective. They are very likely to be affected by the tenor of the negotiators' relationship, their assessments of each other's character, and the quality of their interactions during the negotiation process. Thus, lawyers need to consider *how* they (and their clients) will communicate with each other just as seriously as *what* they will communicate.

This Ties in With:

Hinshaw, Ch. 25, Ethics; Robbennolt & Sternlight, Ch. 40, Psychology & Ethics

27

When It's Wise to Apologize

Jennifer Gerarda Brown[1] *and Jennifer K. Robbennolt*[2]

Introduction

Lawyers, their clients, and other negotiators are increasingly considering apology as a potential element in the resolution of disputes. In order to script an effective apology, one must first identify the purpose of making one. In addition, legal negotiators should consider who should make an apology, who should receive it, the optimal time for making an apology, and the apology's content. This chapter is based on J.G. BROWN & J.K. ROBBENNOLT, *Apology in Negotiation*, in 1 THE NEGOTIATOR'S DESK REFERENCE 265–277 (Honeyman &

1. **Jennifer Gerarda Brown** is Dean and Professor of Law at Quinnipiac University. She has an A.B. from Bryn Mawr College and a J.D. from the University of Illinois College of Law. Brown clerked for the Hon. Harold A. Baker, U.S. District Court (C.D. Ill.) and litigated at Winston & Strawn in Chicago before turning to academe. In 1994, she joined the Quinnipiac faculty. From 1997 until 2013, when she became dean, Brown served as Director of Quinnipiac's Center on Dispute Resolution. She has also served as a visiting lecturer and senior research scholar at Yale Law School. Her teaching and scholarship focus on alternative dispute resolution (ADR), LGBT rights, and lawyers' professional responsibility.
2. **Jennifer Robbennolt** (J.D., Ph.D.) is Associate Dean for Research; Alice Curtis Campbell Professor of Law and Professor of Psychology; and Co-Director of the Program on Law, Behavior, and Social Science at the University of Illinois. A leading scholar in psychology and law, torts, and dispute resolution, her research integrates psychology and empirical research methodology into the study of law and legal institutions. She is coauthor of several books, including *The Psychology of Tort Law; Psychology for Lawyers;* a textbook on *Empirical Methods in Law*; and the influential casebook, *Dispute Resolution and Lawyers*.

Schneider eds, 2017). The full references in that chapter can be found at www.ndrweb.com/chapter-19--public.html.

Why This Concept Might Change Your Thinking

Apologies might serve a variety of purposes in legal negotiation. They may be essentially self-regarding, in that the offender's moral rehabilitation is paramount. An instrumental and self-serving focus of apologies might be seen when criminal defendants apologize to their victims in the hope of reducing their criminal sentences, or when defendants in civil cases seek to reduce expected liability by apologizing in mediation or settlement negotiations. A conception of apology more focused on the recipient is one that strives to console, restore dignity, or provide assurance that it was the offender (or some other entity), and not the victim, who bore responsibility for the harm that occurred.

Sometimes the primary audience for the apology is not so much the victim of the wrongdoing as it is a third party, often an authority figure. In this case, the obligation to apologize is externally imposed rather than internally driven. We have seen the possibility for such externally focused apologies in the context of apologies offered for the purpose of reducing criminal sentences. But in the broadest sense, the third-party audience for an apology is also the larger community of which both the offender and the victim are a part. The offender's apology may seek to address the loss of dignity that the offense has caused the victim in front of the witnessing community and to convince the witnessing community that the offender's moral integrity has been restored.

In addition to thinking about the purposes of an apology, it is also useful to acknowledge the potential benefits of *not* apologizing, along with the potential risks of apology. Refusing to apologize can result in greater feelings of control and can have effects on self-esteem and value integrity that are similar to those that result from apologizing. Defendants also worry that apologizing will have negative effects on insurance coverage or the potential for legal liability. Theoretical and policy debates have focused on this final category: state statutes, federal rules of evidence, and other forms of privilege aim to create "safe space" in which apologies can be made without giving rise to admissions of fault or liability. Scholarly debate has raged, however, about whether apologies made in this safe space can be effective or morally authentic.

Action Plan—What You Can Do Differently Tomorrow

Choose Legitimate Agents to Deliver and Receive Apologies

There are important questions about legitimacy for those who deliver and receive apologies. When the offense is specific, short-running, or has occurred within the context of a single relationship (or small set of relationships), the answers to these questions will be fairly straightforward. It will not be difficult to identify an offender who might apologize and a victim who might receive the apology. This is not to say that it is always easy to identify victim and offender; in some relationships, each person will play both roles. But if the harm has occurred on a small scale or in an interpersonal context, we can usually identify people who, if willing, could legitimately apologize or receive an apology on their own behalf.

At times, however, there may be interest in having an intermediary—perhaps an attorney—offer an apology to the victim. While many are skeptical that such intermediated apologies can be effective, there is some evidence that apologies given by attorneys can have positive effects, though these effects tend not to be as positive as they might have been had the same apology been offered directly by the offender. Apologies offered by attorneys may also be perceived as being more likely motivated by the desire to avoid a lawsuit and less motivated by a focus on the victim.

When the offense is more complex, more historical, or has occurred on a grander scale, the situation becomes even more difficult. For example, perhaps it is clear that the Pope can legitimately speak for the Roman Catholic Church and apologize for a predecessor's failure to denounce the Holocaust, and any living Holocaust survivors are the clear recipients of that apology. But are they the only ones? Can the victims' descendants also be recipients of the apology? Are current-day Roman Catholics, while not perhaps the intended recipients, nonetheless an important audience for this apology? Consider groups that lack a central and authoritative leader such as the Pope, or groups whose leader is disinclined to apologize. Is it possible for such groups or institutions to apologize authentically? "National Sorry Day," for example, was started in 1998 by community groups frustrated with the Australian government's failure to apologize to the "Stolen Generations"—Aboriginal and Torres Strait Islander children forcibly taken from their families over decades, into the early 1970s. In 2008, Kevin Rudd became the first Australian Prime Minister to publicly apologize to the Stolen Generations on behalf of the federal government, and this official apology bore great weight despite the intervening decade of decentralized, unofficial engagement.

Engage in Introspection

Almost everyone seems to agree that an apology should be the result of some analysis and introspection on the part of the offender: if it comes too spontaneously or off-the-cuff, an apology loses power and legitimacy. This can create a tension. The offender may need time in order to reflect upon the harm done, form true remorse for the offense, and prepare a heartfelt apology; but the more an apology is delayed, the more profound the offense may seem in the eyes of the victim. Empirical research has found that allowing time for the victim to express his or her concerns and to feel that the offender understands those concerns is central to an effective apology. The central value here is a guided process of moral inventory—taking stock of one's behavior and the harm that it might have caused.

Determine Whether to Take Responsibility

Social scientists distinguish apologies from other types of remedial accounts, such as denials, excuses, or justifications, in that apologies specifically admit responsibility for one's actions. Moreover, many have argued that in order to be effective, an apology must articulate the norm that has been violated. Sometimes the offended standard is a personal one—a sense of oneself that has been compromised by errant behavior. In other cases, it will be a rule, policy, or social norm of the organization or group of which the offender is a part. In potential lawsuits, it is the violation of a legal standard or rule that may give rise to liability. Some contend that a statement that falls short of a responsibility-accepting apology (one that admits fault and expresses regret) can still be effective and helpful to the recipient. However, empirical research has found the effects of apologies that merely express sympathy for the victim's injuries to be variable and dependent on the context. In contrast, people who receive apologies that *accept responsibility* make more positive attributions about the offender and the offense, are more likely to accept particular settlement offers, and have lower settlement levers (for example, aspirations) than those who did not receive a responsibility-accepting apology.

Consider Forbearance and Repair

Harm repair and promises of forbearance are crucial components of apologies. Forbearance from future offense, in particular, appears to be important to recipients of apologies, and may be inferred even in the absence of an explicit promise. Research has found that promises of forbearance and offers of repair each improve the effectiveness of the apology, and that offenders who express remorse are expected to be less likely to repeat their transgression in the future. We might expect victims who hold such expectations to settle on more favorable terms as a result.

For lawyer-negotiators, the precise wording, timing, and delivery of the apology will depend upon client preferences, the legal context, and the needs of the opposing party. Legal scholars have enriched our thinking about client counseling, however, by highlighting the importance of apology.

Conclusion

In many legal disputes, the moments for apology come and go without notice or action, either because lawyers do not think to advise their clients on this point, or because aversion to vulnerability (emotional or legal) makes people overly cautious about pursuing this avenue toward resolution. But the better we understand the potential purposes and formulations of effective apologies, the richer our understanding of negotiation will be.

This Ties in With:

Schneider & Ebner, Ch. 7, Social Intuition; Itzchakov & Kluger, Ch. 20, Changing Attitudes; Lewicki, Ch. 22, Trust; Toussaint & Waldman, Ch. 28, Forgiveness

28

How to Support Forgiveness in the Negotiation Process

Loren Toussaint[1] *and Ellen Waldman*[2]

Introduction

Attorneys and other third parties involved in heated negotiations regularly work with clients who are deeply angry with those they believe have "done them wrong." Although legal professionals focus on curing the legal problem, frequently this hard-fought cure is not sufficient to make clients "feel whole." Clients need an emotional solution as much as a legal one, and the emotional solution frequently calls for forgiveness. Unfortunately, attorneys and other dispute resolution

1. **Loren Toussaint** is a professor of psychology at Luther College in Decorah, Iowa. He is a consultant to the Mayo Clinic, Cancer Treatment Centers of America, and Boise State University, and is the associate director of the Sierra Leone Forgiveness Project. Dr. Toussaint's research examines religious and spiritual virtues, especially forgiveness, and how they are related to health and well-being. He and colleagues recently published a compendium of research titled *Forgiveness and Health: Scientific Evidence and Theories Relating Forgiveness to Better Health* (Springer). Dr. Toussaint directs the Laboratory for the Investigation of Mind, Body, and Spirit at Luther College (https://www.luther.edu/touslo01/).

2. **Ellen Waldman** has been a member of the Thomas Jefferson Law School faculty since 1992. Professor Waldman founded and supervises the school's mediation program, which affords students and alumni an opportunity to mediate small claims and probate disputes. She is active on ethics committees in both the health-care and mediation realm, and has taught conflict resolution and bioethics-related courses nationally and internationally. She has published over twenty-five articles and book chapters in the areas of alternative dispute resolution and bioethics, as well as the first book-length treatment of ethical dilemmas in mediation practice.

professionals are rarely able to help clients recognize or address that need. This chapter is based on L. Toussaint & E. Waldman, *Forgiveness and Reconciliation: Processes and Outcomes*, 1 The Negotiator's Desk Reference 279–293 (Honeyman & Schneider eds, 2017). The full references in that chapter can be found at www.ndrweb.com/chapter-20--public.html.

Why This Concept Might Change Your Thinking

As the world's philosophical, religious, and spiritual literature makes clear, forgiveness is a practice that leads to both emotional healing and spiritual growth. Arguably, learning to forgive is one of life's most demanding and meaningful tasks, because forgiveness asks the offended person to reappraise both the hurt and its source. This is a significant challenge and, in our adversarial legal system, too often ignored. In their role as guardian of a client's long-term best interests, attorneys should be alert to the benefits of forgiveness, and be equipped to help their clients walk down that path. In the last twenty years, scientific study has uncovered a link between forgiveness and enhanced physical and mental well-being. The research shows associations between forgiveness and lower levels of stress hormones, improved cardiovascular functioning, reduced pain among those suffering from a variety of medical conditions, and enhanced activity in the areas of the brain involved in high level thought and emotion. Unfortunately, even cooperative and settlement-minded disputants seeking to eschew the polarizing rituals of the courtroom are woefully ignorant about how to gain emotional release from their grievances. If the scientific research is to be believed, aggrieved disputants, even if they want to forgive, do not know how. The good news is that forgiveness can be learned, and lawyers *can* help teach their clients.

Action Plan—What You Can Do Differently Tomorrow

There are several action items for improving negotiation outcomes by being aware of the desire to forgive and appropriately supporting forgiveness as part of a negotiation process.

Recognize the Need for Forgiveness

Forgiveness often begins when a disputant recognizes that whatever happened to them, while difficult, often is not what the offending party intended or imagined would occur. In addition, forgiveness comes from an understanding that being hurt or wounded is a difficult but expected part of life. Forgiveness is only one of many possible responses to interpersonal offense—but one that rarely comes into play until other responses proved inadequate (often revenge or justice). Too often, suffering individuals focus repeatedly on their grievances and, as a result, trigger in themselves anger, self-pity, and resentment.

Forgiveness Is NOT Contingent on Justice

Forgiveness is independent of justice. That means that forgiveness does not depend on getting justice. Lawyers may have to help clients recognize when forgiveness is the goal. Sometimes forgiveness occurs with justice, sometimes it occurs following, and it might even occur before justice is achieved. No matter where someone is in the often long and arduous process of negotiation, forgiveness can be an important goal for clients. Some might even argue that forgiveness would best precede justice so that, freed of the blinding blaze of revenge, one might recognize a fair and just outcome when one sees it.

Guide the Process of Forgiveness

Fortunately, for clients willing to learn, lawyers can use several well-tested methods of supporting the motivation to forgive.

Lawyers can help clients:

1. **Understand what forgiveness is and is NOT:** Call clients' attention to the difference between forgiveness and forgetting, reconciliation, and justice. Clearly define forgiveness for clients, as most will not fully understand it. *Definition: Forgiveness implies emotional release of negative attitudes, behaviors, or feelings toward a wrongdoer.* Be clear with clients that rarely should we try to *forget* these occurrences, lest we be revictimized. Often, it may not be wise to reconcile with the offender, and justice may or may not be forthcoming; but the outcome of justice doesn't set the course for forgiveness.
2. **Be clear about what is being forgiven:** Help clients identify what exactly it is that needs to be forgiven. It may or may not be the same event that is being negotiated.

3. **Empathize with the offender:** Like it or not, and most people do not like it, helping clients see the offense from the offender's viewpoint can be a pivotal moment for forgiveness. If a client can see how someone might have hurt them, often they realize that they are also capable of hurting others. We all need forgiveness.
4. **Acknowledge their own wrongdoings:** Empathy tends to beget humility. If clients see things from their offenders' viewpoint, they will likely remember times when they have hurt others and needed to be forgiven. When clients understand that they need forgiveness, too, they realize they cannot logically withhold the very forgiveness they are likely to need in the future.

   The four keys above are critical, in-the-moment tools for helping a client forgive. Lawyers don't have to be masterful psychotherapists to use these tools: the mere discussion of these issues can sometimes be enough to change clients' view on forgiveness as a potential, achievable goal. If the four issues above can be successfully resolved, then the issues below might be worth discussing.
5. **Commit to forgiveness:** Forgiving is really hard, especially in the context of negotiation. For clients to succeed, they will need appropriate encouragement and support, perhaps even professional counseling. Lawyers should be cognizant of the likely challenges to forgiveness, be ready to support clients who truly desire to forgive—and be ready to refer clients in need of additional help to professional counselors.
6. **Maintain forgiveness and overcome "unforgiveness" when it reappears:** No matter how hard clients may try, feelings of unforgiveness will undoubtedly crop up along the process of negotiation. Lawyers should be prepared for vacillation on this issue, and discuss with clients their levels of commitment and intentions for moving forward in the forgiveness process. Reoccurring unforgiveness is natural and unavoidable; but for clients that decide that their decision or motivation to forgive was premature, lawyers should not become prescriptive in their conversations and should remain open to different approaches to coping with the offense, both legally and psychosocially.

Lawyers will likely not feel equipped to address these issues in a structured fashion. But if these topics can even be casually considered and time can be spent processing these issues, even in brief conversation, this may open the door to some degree of personal healing. Research has shown that even brief consideration of forgiveness issues (3–5 minutes) through personal reflection, prayer, or meditation can immediately bring some small gains in forgiveness. Perhaps most important, the research suggests that the method employed in promoting forgiveness is not nearly as important as the amount of time that individuals spend *focused* on forgiving. Time invested, not the specific technique, returns the rewards of forgiveness. Having the conversation with clients truly matters.

Modifiers, Caveats, and No-Go Areas— When This Advice Just Won't Apply

There are several qualifiers on the forgiveness process. First, socio-demographic variables are important. Women are slightly more forgiving than men, and blacks tend to be slightly more forgiving than other racial groups. Moreover, socio-cultural factors are also important, as a person's individualistic-collectivistic perspective may have important influences on forgiveness. Second, the offense itself is important to consider, as well as the relationship of the offender to the offended. Not surprisingly, less severe offenses and those perpetrated by individuals who are closer to the victim (e.g., immediate family members) are more easily forgiven. Third, individual differences are important to consider, as some individuals who are more anxious and distressed are less likely to forgive, while others who are more agreeable and outgoing might be more inclined to forgive.

Forgiveness offered by a victim to an offender is complicated by the presence of third parties, especially when these parties are family members or close friends of the victim. Offenses are experienced by the victim but they are felt by the victim *and* close family and friends. Third parties are *less* likely to forgive an offender, even though they were not directly victimized. This can complicate the forgiveness process, make the victim second-guess a decision to forgive, and potentially delay negotiations as a result.

A final qualifier applying to the entire forgiveness process is that forgiveness cannot and should not be prescriptive. Victims should be empowered to forgive—but not expected to. Victims should feel supported in deciding to forgive (using action items outlined in this chapter) but they should feel equally supported in a decision not to.

Conclusion

The motive to forgive in the context of negotiation is an issue that requires the attention of a deft negotiator. Forgiveness can facilitate the negotiation process by lifting emotional burdens and improving perspective and quality of life. Lawyers should recognize the value of forgiveness, support it when the motivation arises, and remain open to clients' wishes regarding revenge and forgiveness as they navigate the process of negotiation in seeking justice.

This Ties in With:

Brown & Robbennolt, Ch. 27, Apology; Love & Stulberg, Ch. 46, Mediation

Part II

Complications, Groups, and Firms

Section VI

Complexity and Culture

Section VI starts off Part II by diving straight in to more complicated situations. Chapter 29 addresses whether mental illness might be affecting someone at the bargaining table. The authors lay out information about the surprising frequency of mental illness in our society and the varied ways that we might need to respond to it in a negotiation.

Then, we turn to a triad of chapters about cultural differences, starting with Chapter 30 on how negotiating style integrates with culture—except for when it doesn't. Chapter 31 analyzes how Westerners tend to misread Chinese culture when they negotiate there—and "there," of course, includes the Chinese communities in many American cities. Chapter 32 assesses the often-unfortunate experiences of western or northern negotiators and mediators when they have taken their (implicit, and often unrecognized) cultural codes with them. . . . to an *extremely* different culture.

Chapter 33 combines a classic analysis of how even a major negotiation in an international setting has some predictable stages, in a somewhat predictable process, with an equally classic discussion of timing and ripeness.

29

Mental Health in Negotiations: Challenges at the Table

Elizabeth L. Jeglic[1] *and Alexander A. Jeglic*[2]

Introduction

During negotiations, it is typically assumed that counterparties are rational and capable of making logical decisions. However, approximately 20 percent of Americans suffer from a diagnosable mental disorder. Disorders such as depression and anxiety can cause distortions of fact and impair information processing. Other mental disorders, like psychopathy or psychosis, can result in callous, manipulative, or delusional behavior. This chapter is based on E. Jeglic & A. Jeglic, *Mental Health Challenges at the Table*, in 1 The Negotiator's Desk Reference 187–198 (Honeyman & Schneider eds, 2017). The full references in that chapter can be found at www.ndrweb.com/chapter-14--public.html.

---

1. **Elizabeth L. Jeglic**, Ph.D., is a Professor of Psychology at John Jay College of Criminal Justice, CUNY in New York City, and a licensed clinical psychologist. Her research interests include the interface of psychology and the criminal justice system. Dr. Jeglic has published over eighty journal articles and book chapters and sits on the editorial board of several leading psychology and criminal justice journals. She is the coeditor of the book *Sexual Violence: Evidence Based Policy and Prevention*.

2. **Alexander A. Jeglic** is Procurement Ombudsman at the Office of the Procurement Ombudsman, Government of Canada. Alexander is also a leader in the American Bar Association, Section of International Law, and teaches procurement law at Carleton University. Alexander's legal background is in procurement, contracting, and alternative dispute resolution.

Why This Concept Might Change Your Thinking

Given the prevalence of mental disorders in the American population, it is likely that some of the individuals with whom you are negotiating will have a mental illness. As there is still a significant stigma in our society about discussing mental health issues, it is unlikely that your counterparty will disclose their mental illness. Further, they may be unaware of the degree to which the disorder is impacting their performance. If you become aware that a counterparty may have a mental illness that is impacting their performance, your job is to ensure the integrity of your negotiation such that all parties are of sound mind to make rational and informed decisions and agreements. If a negotiation is compromised by poor judgement or decision caused by a mental illness, it may invalidate the work you are doing. Further, the safety of all those involved should be prioritized. While some psychological disorders such as depression and anxiety may cause issues with focus, attention, and information processing, other disorders like bipolar disorder and schizophrenia may impact behavior and logical thinking, and may result in distortions of reality. Moreover, those with psychopathic traits may be manipulative and deceitful and may seek to maliciously undermine the negotiation process. Thus, it is important to enter into a negotiation knowing that it is possible that one or more parties may be affected by a mental illness that may impact the integrity of the negotiation.

Action Plan—What You Can Do Differently Tomorrow

Negotiating with those who have a mental illness is relatively uncharted territory, as there are no protocols about a negotiator's responsibilities in such situations. Given that negotiators are generally not trained mental health professionals, their obligation lies in the integrity of the negotiation process and not in assessing the mental health of their counterparty. However, if during the course of a negotiation you suspect that one of the parties involved is impacted by mental illness, there are several steps that you can take to ensure a positive outcome and the safety of all involved. When negotiating with someone you suspect of having a mental illness, the following strategies may be employed:

1. First assess whether anyone is in danger. While it should be noted that the vast majority of individuals with mental illness pose no danger to themselves or others, negotiations can often

result in strong emotions. Those who have difficulty controlling their emotions or who are having problems with reality testing (determining what is real from what is delusional) may respond to these stressful situations poorly. If it should become evident that the counterparty in the negotiation is a threat to themselves (suicidal) or others (homicidal), remain calm and notify the appropriate authorities immediately (911, police, security). These trained individuals will be able to deescalate the situation and get the individual the care they require.

2. If the mental illness is severe and is hindering the negotiation to the point where it is unproductive but the individual poses no threat to themselves or others, then it is best to discontinue the negotiation until such time that the individual is more mentally stable or another counterparty can be brought in to assume the negotiator role.
3. In some instances where there is a milder degree of impairment—such as cases where individuals are suffering from mild to moderate mood or anxiety disorders—some degree of cognitive impairment may be evident. The individual may have difficulty focusing or remembering, may be easily distracted, or may lose track of what is being said. If this is the case, you have the power to help: you can slow the pace of oral discussions, repeat key statements, and include visual aids and written documents to keep the individual focused.
4. Depression and anxiety can also result in cognitive distortions, resulting in neutral statements being perceived as negative. In such cases, you can attempt to help the counterparty reframe issues by providing evidence that disproves their negative beliefs. For example, those who are depressed take criticism very personally and may view disagreement on a tenet of the negotiation as a personal attack against them. In such instances, you can provide concrete reasons for your disagreement and emphasize that the disagreement is not personal in nature but pertains to the material being discussed.
5. Individuals with psychopathic traits can be deceitful, manipulative, and aggressive, and might engage in unethical conduct when negotiating in an effort to attain their desired outcome. Should such a situation arise, it should be considered that this individual wants to win at all costs. In these cases, using strategies

of principled negotiations can be helpful in keeping the counterparty focused on the negotiation. Strategies include separating the person from the problem being discussed, negotiating based on interests and not positions, creating opportunities for mutual gain, and insisting on objective criteria. In addition, having written documentation of any agreements and bringing in a neutral third party can help to minimize the potential for deceit.

6. Symptoms of mental illness may be exacerbated by stress, substance abuse, and lack of sleep. Thus, trying to make sure that discussions are calm, are in places where alcohol is not served, and don't start too early or run too late can help to minimize impairment.

Modifiers, Caveats, and No-Go Areas—When This Advice Just Won't Apply

Mental illness affects everyone differently, yet no one is immune. While it may be assumed that individuals in positions of authority are psychologically healthier than those who did not achieve such career success, that is not always the case. They may mask an appearance of normality rather than seek help. Just because someone doesn't "look mentally ill" doesn't mean that they are not impacted by mental illness. If someone is indeed not disclosing their mental illness, it is not something that is always evident or that can be addressed, as negotiators are not mental health professionals. It may be the case that negotiations that have been conducted will need to be renegotiated or reviewed after the fact, when it has been revealed that they were impacted by mental illness. If, however, you find that the individual with whom you have entered into negotiations is indeed mentally ill, then adopting some of the strategies noted in the previous sections can lead to better outcomes for all.

Conclusion

It is perhaps most logical to enter into a negotiation prepared to face a counterparty that is not rational—with the hope that the evidence will suggest otherwise as the negotiation progresses.

This Ties in With:

Volpe et al., Ch. 37, Unknown; Lee & Shanahan, Ch. 39, Martial Arts

30

Negotiation Styles Inspired by Chinese Wisdom

Eko Y. Liao[1] *and Cheryl Q. Zhang*[2]

Introduction

Negotiation styles that are inspired by ancient Chinese wisdom, especially from *The Art of War* by Sun Tzu, are highly interactive, are sensitive to change, and focus on flexibility. These characteristics have much in common with the agile methods adopted in the software development field. Agile methods introduce a reflective and evolving process in which problems are solved in a dynamic manner. While traditional negotiation strategy emphasizes getting to know one's own style, Sun Tzu told us to be mindful of the style of our negotiation opponent, and to keep up with the power dynamics: "When

1. **Eko Yi Liao** is an Assistant Professor at the Hang Seng University of Hong Kong. She earned a Ph.D. in management from the University of Hong Kong. Apart from her research and teaching experiences in Hong Kong, she is a coeditor of *Tan Pan: The Chinese-English Journal of Negotiation*. She has also been invited to teach in MBA programs in Shanghai University. Eko's research interests include negotiation styles and strategies, organizational leadership, and employee attitudes and behaviors. Her research has been published in leading journals in the management field, such as the *Journal of Organizational Behavior*.
2. **Cheryl Qianru Zhang** is an Assistant Professor at the School of Business in Macau University of Science and Technology. She earned a Ph.D. in law from Macau University of Science and Technology. She also holds the Legal Professional Qualification Certificate in the People's Republic of China. Cheryl's teaching areas include commercial law, corporate governance, and the legal environment of business.

the enemy advances, we retreat; when they retreat, we pursue." This chapter is based on E. Liao, *Styles and Culture in Negotiation*, in 1 The Negotiator's Desk Reference, 43–57 (Honeyman & Schneider eds, 2017). The full references in that chapter can be found at www.ndrweb.com/chapter-4--public.html.

Why This Concept Might Change Your Thinking

"Knowing yourself and your enemy, you can fight a hundred battles with no danger of defeat." This strategy and the citation from *Introduction* are perhaps the most classic tactics from *The Art of War*. Both point to one major theme—negotiation is always about style dynamics.

Many describe a lawyer's daily tasks, especially for litigation specialists, as warfare, full of conflicts among interests, confrontations, and defenses. With the purpose of gaining the most bargaining power with the best timing in scheduling, Sun Tzu told us at least two lessons. First, never underestimate the importance of adequate pre-trial preparation. In order to reach a better outcome for the client, lawyers must have clear knowledge of their own style and learn as much as possible about any potential situations that might happen at the negotiation table. There are times where preparation is more crucial than any other stage of negotiation. This approach also encourages lawyers to develop an estimation of what may happen during the process or the negotiation, as it allows one to be more agile and flexible. Second, the importance of "knowing yourself and your enemy" indicates a classic Chinese perspective of never engaging in a negotiation without sufficient understanding of both parties. Negotiators are often overly focused on their own arguments and evidence, while neglecting the fact that negotiation is by nature a dynamic process. Sun Tzu developed his philosophy of military strategy—which was followed and used constantly in various fields, including negotiation—with the concern that one has to form a full-picture perspective toward any negotiation.

These ancient Chinese war tactics promote the notion of staying mindful of the changes that attend any negotiation over time, such as keeping up with the power dynamics, and also responding to the changes in unpredictable litigation processes. Being change-sensitive is not an easy job. It would be a natural thing to fight back against those who are powerful, yet it would also be wise to take a step back to reevaluate the situation. The essence of negotiation with a mindful perspective is to develop a set of flexible skills to keep up with the changing dynamics; that is, "when the enemy advances, we retreat; when they retreat, we pursue."

Action Plan—What You Can Do Differently Tomorrow

In *The Art of War*, Sun Tzu elaborated on fundamental elements for military preparation. These ancient Chinese military tactics have been proven helpful in numerous situations, and they can shed light on lawyers' negotiation activities. While the original tactics include five essential elements, one of them—*Di*, taking advantage of territory—is not applicable in this case. To that end, the following are four things you can do differently tomorrow:

Focus on the Long-Term Outcomes/Tao

The wisdom from Taoists is always inspiring—"Heaven follows Tao, Tao follows nature." Generally, *Tao* refers to a typical Taoist philosophical perspective that focuses on sticking to the most basic and natural forms of conduct, and living and working toward harmony; it emphasizes the natural sequence. Although the fast pace of contemporary negotiations does not always allow lawyers time and energy to think far ahead, Taoism suggests that long-term outcomes should not be sacrificed.

Specifically, lawyers should always ensure that their conduct is consistent with legal justice (i.e., substantive justice, procedural justice) in order to address their long-term goals. For example, in an environment pollution lawsuit, if the lawyer is able to incorporate the "living in harmony with nature" principle into his or her practices, it would be easier to gain bargaining power and favorable public recognition because these follow the way of nature. If lawyers violate the laws of nature, they will probably encounter failure in the end.

Grasp the Best Timing/Tian

Chinese philosophy always highlights the importance of timing, or *Tian*. From the perspective of subjective judgment, this means exploring and making use of favorable time conditions.

The best litigation timing usually depends on the client's litigation purpose. Clients' requirements for deterrence, injunction, and compensation would suggest rather different timing of negotiation *or* litigation. While lawyers need to pay particular attention to satisfying clients' needs, choosing a favorable element of timing can be an unexpected strategy in gaining bargaining power. Lawyers using the essence of the Tian principle would have relatively high power in negotiation, in the way that they are more aware of what argument is most suitable to be brought up in what timing and circumstances. Simply regarding the usage of critical information based on how powerful it is may not be sufficient; an effective lawyer also needs to consider the best situation and timing to put forth the idea.

Art of Leadership/Jiang

Negotiations, in their various forms and styles, require teamwork. Mastering effective leadership skills in leading and managing a high-performing team is thus a necessity. Teamwork contributes to the success of negotiation in legal agency affairs.

Two specific characteristics cannot be ignored in developing inspiring leadership styles, one of which is fostering moral character. The most trustworthy leaders are often the most moral. Integrity is one of the three critical elements in team members' trust in leaders. Once the leading lawyer is regarded as a moral leader, the team's overall effectiveness is enhanced. The second characteristic is competence. Competent team leaders are able to demonstrate that they possess the professional skills, experience, and knowledge necessary for a large-scale case. For example, in class actions relating to business mergers and acquisitions, a negotiation team is often formed with members in charge of different aspects of the case. Leaders who can effectively motivate the team to work collaboratively toward the common goal need to show that they are reliable in terms of morality and competent in terms of expertise.

Follow the System/Fa

Nothing can be accomplished without a consistent system of norms and regulations. Yet such accomplishments require individuals to follow these norms and regulations. Both in ancient and modern times, military forces must strictly follow military law, which is the bottom line of military action. Similarly, lawyers' negotiation conduct should follow certain legal norms and requirements.

There is no question that lawyers need to stay familiar with statutes and case law and pay attention to the most recent information. As a client's representative, a lawyer negotiates to seek results that comply with the client's requests, while following social and professional codes. For example, in economic disputes, a lawyer should never compromise on basic legal requirements in order to satisfy the client's needs. During the process of negotiating a case, properly using references to the law is also facilitative to favorable outcomes.

Modifiers, Caveats, and No-Go Areas—When This Advice Just Won't Apply

Guided by the Tao, Tian, Jiang, and Fa elements from ancient Chinese philosophy, lawyers need to stay flexible and mindful of style dynamics before and during negotiations. The power dynamics between two parties often require sufficient preparation and wise reaction. These action tips would be particularly useful when your counterpart is from a Chinese background. Then, the lesson would be not only getting your own strategy ready, but also staying alert to your counterpart's actions continuously during the negotiation process. For example, while lawyers may decide on the best timing for litigation, they should not ignore the fact that their counterparts may also have settled on a favorable timing from *their* perspective. Sufficient investigation into the potential tactics used by their Chinese counterparts is thus necessary.

Conclusion

Although agile methods are primarily a Western concept, ancient Chinese philosophy offers similar wisdom that can guide a negotiator's actions. Conducting comprehensive due diligence before every case and staying alert to every subtle move and change of power dynamics during the negotiation are two of the most important lessons from Sun Tzu. The Tao, Tian, Jiang, and Fa elements provide practical tips for keeping one's mind on negotiation details. From the Chinese cultural perspective, negotiation is never a one-man or one-party task; it is always a dynamic process, as parties keep changing their tactics, styles, and strategies. As Sun Tzu pointed out, "The highest form of generalship is to attack one's strategy." Negotiators should never be satisfied with only developing a perfect negotiating plan; it is more important that one should always pay attention to the other party, and to master the dynamics.

This Ties in With:

Abramson, Ch. 3, Fashioning Styles; Goh, Ch. 31, Mistakes; Kaufman & Blanchot, Ch. 32, International

31

Forewarned Is Forearmed: Sino-Western Negotiation Pitfalls and Tactics

Bee Chen Goh[1]

Introduction

Globalization has become a buzzword, and as we witness the rise of China in the Asian Century, it is imperative that one acquires cultural literacy in negotiating with the Chinese. Here, the reference to the "Chinese" is ethnological: specifically noting a collectivistic Chinese person professing the Confucian heritage who may be resident in mainland China or elsewhere. More than likely, the Chinese cultural values described below will guide their negotiating behavior in a cross-cultural setting. The Western negotiator in this context is one probably leaning toward being individualistic with an Anglo-Saxon background. This chapter is based on B.C. Goh, *Typical*

1. A former Malaysian Rhodes Scholar, **Bee Chen Goh** is Professor of Law and Director of the Centre for Peace and Social Justice, School of Law and Justice, Southern Cross University, Australia. She is a director and Fellow of the Australian Academy of Law, Fellow of the Cambridge Commonwealth Society, and Fellow of the Society for Advanced Legal Studies in London. Her scholarly interests include mediation and alternative dispute resolution (ADR), especially cross-cultural dispute resolution. Her publications include *Negotiating with the Chinese* (Dartmouth 1996) and *Law Without Lawyers, Justice Without Courts: On Traditional Chinese Mediation* (Ashgate 2002).

Errors in Chinese-Western Negotiation, in 1 THE NEGOTIATOR'S DESK REFERENCE 583–593 (Honeyman & Schneider eds, 2017). The full references in that chapter can be found at www.ndrweb.com/chapter-42--public.html.

Why This Concept Might Change Your Thinking

Engaging in Sino-Western negotiation calls forth a shift in mindset. This is because the Chinese way is predominantly relational, whereas the Western approach is fundamentally transactional. The former focuses on values embedded in relationship-building, and the latter emphasizes efficiency (as demonstrated notably by annually set corporate key performance indicators, popularly known as KPIs). The Chinese way is quite similar to marriages and business partnerships, as ideally, both are for the long term. On the other hand, transactional negotiation concentrates on successful outcomes for immediate deals, and any resulting friendship is pure bonus.

If one can grasp the above difference right at the outset, one can avoid unnecessary misunderstanding and frustration in any untrained Sino-Western negotiation setting.

Action Plan—What You Can Do Differently Tomorrow

The following outlines some of the major Sino-Western negotiation pitfalls and tactics. It would be prudent to be forewarned and forearmed.

Build Trust and Friendship

The Chinese are generally uncomfortable with the idea of negotiation in the Western sense. Western-style negotiation is seen as confrontational, direct, and assertive (bordering on aggressive). The Chinese prefer to talk things through, meander around the subject if necessary, accompanied by a low tone of voice. Negotiation in the Chinese sense is more of a dialogue, give-and-take discussions, than open debate.

Therefore, rule number one is to seek to form friendship and gain interpersonal trust. This emotional investment is definitely worthwhile. In the longer term, one is cultivating *guanxi*, a priceless network of obligatory connections. One often sees Chinese business partners indulging in lengthy meals and continuous toasts—such behavior enhances the negotiation process in building relationships and getting to know one another better. Do not be alarmed if one is taken on plenty of sightseeing tours (if visiting foreign places, especially for the first time) and sitting down for endless meals. Relax and enjoy these social interchanges, and learn to create a bank of goodwill that will come in handy in traversing Sino-Western negotiation waters.

Gift-giving becomes a normal habit, as long as the intention is expressive and not instrumental (amounting to bribery), for gifts enhance relationship-building. There is an art to gift-giving. Because Mandarin is a tonal language, one has to be made aware of homophones through advance research and checking with those who know local customs. For instance, "clock" is homophonic with "termination." As such, it is to be avoided as a gift for a birthday, especially for one senior in age, as it is interpreted as wishing death upon that recipient. There are other taboos associated with gifts, as gifts carry cultural symbolism. To avoid causing inadvertent offence, most Chinese gifts among close friends and families take the form of little red packets, which are monetary gifts.

The Chinese attitude toward contracts, generally, is opposite to the Westerner who worships the written word. Bear in mind that it is the foundation of the interpersonal relationship that counts; a contract is nothing more than a piece of paper to be locked away, and differences arising ought to be amicably ironed out between the parties, who are in it for the long haul. This may explain why the Chinese tend to favor memoranda of understanding over formal contracts.

Cultivate Abiding Patience

It has been observed that negotiating with the Chinese requires the utmost patience. This is more so as examined from the Western perspective of efficiency, whereby time is money and there is no point in small talk. Following on from the above-said cardinal value of interpersonal trust, it indeed takes considerable time to build relationships. It is, therefore, necessary to cultivate patience when dealing with the Chinese.

Additionally, originating from a collectivist culture, the Chinese are accustomed to polychronic time management, which is simultaneous or concurrent, permitting interruptions. It can be exasperating for the uninitiated Westerner who sticks to appointments and schedules to find their Chinese party is engaged elsewhere, or to combine unexpected meetings. Westerners tend to be monochronic and adhere to clockwork, and manage things and people one at a time. In contrast, the Chinese enjoy multitasking and have no problem accommodating unscheduled appointments as necessary. This is because the Chinese negotiator places primacy on people over things (a trait in relational negotiation). Therefore, where possible, if someone is requesting urgent assistance, that request needs immediate attention.

Embrace Face-Saving Behavior

One cannot emphasize enough how important it is for the Chinese to save face. Face here is both self-related and other-related, and it is the latter that is significant—a cultural trait all too familiar for collectivists. In Mandarin, "face" is described as *mien-tze* and *lien*: the former indicates one's reputation or social standing (which can be increased or decreased) and the latter can incur the idea of shame (which can entail forfeiture of one's social regard).

Relational cultures like the Chinese are more concerned with the precept of harmony than the idea of justice. Compromises and meeting in the middle are often expected. With long-range views in mind, eventually things are likely to balance out and there is no need to claim all of the benefit in any single deal.

Beware of Ambiguity in Communication

Similar to face-saving behavior is the tendency for the Chinese to engage in high-context communication, as opposed to the Western-style of low-context communication. High-context cultures thrive on indirect means of communication, and ambiguity is the high point. Low-context cultures are direct, assertive, and confrontational. Popular social injunctions like "say what you mean" or "don't beat about the bush" bear testimony to low-context communication. However, it can be quite frustrating for the upfront Westerner to have to deal with a situation of "yes-no-and-maybe-so." It is also considered rude, and sometimes offensive, to ask the Chinese counterpart directly when one is unsure of the exact meaning of a given communication. The tactic is to find an interlocutor for assistance. This intermediary may be the Chinese counterpart's secretary, business partner, family member, or other trusted associate. In this way, one can avoid unintentionally causing the Chinese party to lose face, especially if the response is negative—for the Chinese loathe saying a direct no.

Be Formalistic and Respectful

The Chinese tend to be hierarchically ordered. An awareness of title and rank is important around the negotiating table. In the Confucian tradition, knowing one's own place in society is critical, reflective of the Confucian teaching of Five Cardinal Relations. In this regard, formal addresses like "President Tan" demonstrate respect and good upbringing. Social relations are vertically structured and should be so observed. First names ought not to be used at the acquaintance stage, and may be encouraged as friendship deepens. When in doubt, always stick to the tried and true of formal addresses. The exchange of business cards is an important ritual: business cards are not only informative (giving contact details, and so on) but are communicative, providing background and professional standing, thereby slotting people appropriately in their social order.

Modifiers, Caveats, and No-Go Areas—When This Advice Just Won't Apply

A crucial thing to remember in every negotiation is that one must take one's negotiator as one finds him or her, without making cultural assumptions. The above statement is also true in the context of Sino-Western negotiation. Just because your negotiating counterparts are ethnically Chinese does not mean that they will fit into the above "model"—the caveat is the *Confucian* Chinese. A Westerner is likely to find the predominantly Western-educated Chinese, with little inclination toward the Confucian heritage, behaving in ways and indulging in habits resembling the Western negotiator. In such an instance, the Westerner and the Chinese may be on a culturally level playing field or even a merged cultural norm, and what is called into question is one's negotiation prowess. In light of this, it is essential for Westerners to do a background check of their Chinese counterparts to gauge their cultural thermometers and consequently, act suitably: as Sun Tzu advises, "know yourself, know your enemy, all the hundred battles will be won."

Conclusion

The global negotiator in what China clearly sees as the Asian Century will undoubtedly need to manage cross-cultural, especially Sino-Western, challenges in communication. Therefore, a willingness and preparedness to embrace cultural literacy to become more self-aware will stand one in good stead. As always, "the journey of a thousand miles begins with the first step."

This Ties in With:

Green, Ch. 5, Negotiating While Black; Liao & Zhang, Ch. 30, Chinese Wisdom & Your Style; Kaufman & Blanchot, Ch. 32, International

32

Insights for Lawyers from International Negotiation

Sanda Kaufman[1] *and Eric Blanchot*[2]

Introduction

International negotiation needs lawyers' expertise. However, lawyers trained in Western practices are sometimes unprepared for the issues, decision-making processes, laws or their absence, and formal or informal engagement rules in other contexts—or for the perils of making mistakes when among armed disputants.

1. **Sanda Kaufman** is Professor of Planning, Public Policy and Administration at Cleveland State University's Levin College of Urban Affairs. Her research spans negotiations and intervention in environmental and other public conflicts; social-environmental systems resilience; decision analysis; program evaluation; and negotiation pedagogy. Her articles have appeared in the *Journal for Conflict Resolution*, the *Negotiation Journal*, *Conflict Resolution Quarterly*, *International Journal for Conflict Management*, *Negotiation and Conflict Management Research*, *Revue Négociations*; and others. B. Arch. and M. S. in Planning, Technion; Ph.D. in Public Policy Analysis, Carnegie Mellon University.

2. **Eric Blanchot** is Director of Operations at Promédiation, a Paris-based mediation organization. His missions for Promediation focus on the crises in Mali and Libya. Since 2013, he has also served as a mediator in Chad, on behalf of the World Bank's Compliance Advisor Ombudsman. He has done mediation and training work for the United Nations (UNDP and UNITAR) and other international organizations (including HD Centre, the Crisis Management Initiative, and the WorldWide Immigration Consultancy Services), working with officials of many countries. He has also taught negotiation, business communication, conflict analysis, and crisis management at the École Nationale d'Administration, the Sorbonne, and other institutions of higher learning.

We examined typical negotiation theory prescriptions in the context of repeated violent confrontations between Mali's government and ethnic groups with serious grievances. We identified prescriptions valid even for places completely different from the Western context where most negotiation theory evolved. We also found prescriptions that (predictably) cannot be implemented or fail due to these differences. This chapter is based on S. Kaufman & E. Blanchot, *Theory Meets Reality: Negotiation and Mediation in Mali*, in 1 The Negotiator's Desk Reference 621–643 (Honeyman & Schneider eds, 2017). Full references for this chapter can be found at www.ndrweb.com/chapter-45--public.html.

Why These Ideas Might Change Your Thinking

The Mali case illustrates why we need to know *which* negotiation theories and prescriptions rely heavily on the Western context, behaviors, and attitudes that do not exist elsewhere. Like fish unaware of water until they are pulled onto dry land, we are rarely conscious of the extent to which our strategies rely on the stability and predictability of our context, and on our knowledge of how it works. Adaptation to other contexts is beyond necessary: sometimes it is a matter of life and death in international negotiations.

For example, access to legal remedies for breach of agreements reduces reliance on trust during implementation. Absent such remedies, those unhappy with how agreements are implemented default on them, and even resort to violence. Among leaders guarding their reputations for trustworthiness or for fierce retaliation against double-crossers, verbal promises and handshakes are more meaningful and reliable than signed documents. Systems lacking written rules or institutional enforcement of verbal agreements function if everyone knows how they work; everyone *inside* such a system does. Western helpers often don't, or disapprove of these in other ways, on Western moral or ethical grounds that have little currency in places like Mali. While the prescription to craft agreements that foster compliance remains valid, we have to rethink how to accomplish that when parties prize trust and reputation instead of signed documents.

Mali (and other countries in which coauthor Blanchot has mediated and consulted) also surfaced the need to bring humility to intervention in unfamiliar contexts. We may misinterpret speech and garb, and make wrong assumptions about disputants' social status, level of understanding, and sophistication. Indeed, they may not fully get *our* ways, but neither do we fully get theirs. And we don't understand their language, while they often understand ours. They have seen many like us, and use our negotiation jargon to obtain resources, information, and assistance, while we misunderstand their circumstances. Hubris puts us at disadvantage in trying to contribute to lasting peace agreements.

Mali teaches us to be more patient and humble than we might like, to be realistic about the difference we can expect to make, to respect those with whom we work, and to earn their trust in our good intentions and fairness.

Action Plan—What You Can Do Differently Tomorrow

The key advice for lawyers considering intervention in international disputes is to *refrain* from starting tomorrow. Even if you have prepared heavily, assume you know less than you think about a specific conflict. Shadowing an old hand first helps understand local intricacies, power dynamics, and the conflict's history.

In non-Western contexts, we need to know about: the politics, culture, and institutional specifics; sources of complexity; the perverse incentives for all; the meaning of "preparing" in an ever-shifting environment; and the stakeholders' differential ability to engage in the negotiation process, and to devise mutually satisfying agreements. Mediation challenges include convening inclusively and genuine representation of stake-holding constituencies. These difficulties are also present in Western contexts, though perhaps not all at once, and not combining to generate perfect storms.

In theory, to craft durable, mutually satisfactory agreements, negotiators require information, incentives to settle, process transparency, mutual trust, and recourse for failure to uphold agreements. Not least, a stable context (e.g., courts that work) gives meaning to best alternatives to negotiated agreements (BATNAs), and to the notion that concessions now lead reliably to future benefits. Non-Western disputants tend to be resource- and information-deprived. They operate in unstable, quickly changing sociopolitical spaces fraught with corruption, barely existent rule of law, coalitions forming and dissolving rapidly, resources and support moving quickly from one group to another, and high risks, including prison or loss of life for those who "get it wrong." Today's BATNA may no longer be there tomorrow. Trust—in other parties, governments, or international actors—is also sorely lacking (wisely so) and life-endangering. To survive in the long run (measured at times in months) disputants develop survival strategies that can thwart agreement implementation.

Parties, interveners, and sponsors sometimes give in to perverse incentives to prolong rather than conclude negotiations. Participating in recurrent negotiation rounds yields valuable rewards for some disputants, ranging from per-diem coverage, to training, being seen in the company of powerful people, networking, and the appearance of legitimacy; all these dry up when negotiations conclude. Interveners, especially career professionals, work for Western countries and organizations. Prolonged negotiations yield employment and enhanced résumés from claiming (temporary) success as long as parties negotiate, especially in cases of high risk for violent outbreaks. Sponsors, too, sometimes value prolonged negotiations, especially when some of the warring groups are their clients, whom they support with costly weaponry and troops when the fighting resumes. For such incentives to become less consequential in everyone's calculus, the parties need expectations of even larger gains from peace, coupled with good examples of such gains in the past or elsewhere.

Other practical deviations from theoretical prescriptions include principal-agent issues, as well as behind-the-table and away-from-the-table events. For example, armed groups prefer negotiation representatives who are educated. Some of these skillfully favor their own political and financial interests; or, they misrepresent themselves and their constituencies. With little or no control over their agents, or recourse when misrepresented, parties realizing they have been wronged lose faith in the process and refuse to participate in new negotiation rounds.

In theory, agreements that address the parties' interests enhance implementation chances and longevity. Best intervener practices include helping disputants co-create their information base and generate mutually acceptable alternatives. Given sufficient time and resources, such practices are feasible in stable, mostly nonviolent environments, among stakeholders who can either fend for themselves or can be trained to negotiate effectively on their own behalf. These conditions are often absent in the international field. Worse yet, options the disputants favor are sometimes unacceptable *to the interveners*, whether due to value frames or their sponsors' direct interests in the outcomes. Consequently, interveners entirely driven by the norms and values of their international sponsors may eliminate from consideration options thwarting their sponsors' interests. Besides limiting everyone's creativity and incentives to find solutions, this is a recipe for engendering parties' dissatisfaction. In addition, some interveners form unrealistic expectations about how things work, the time it takes for anything to get done, the extent to which real communication occurs, parties' motivations, and the incentives that make them tick.

Those still considering international intervention given the challenges should avoid stereotypes and generalizations (Mali is not the same as Libya or Chad, just as California is different from Oklahoma). Interveners should certainly get out of the way if parties are headed for violent interactions—but also when they seem able to handle their conflict without assistance. Not least, interveners should spend time developing authentic relationships, since disputants have phoniness radars. The key lessons from Mali, surprisingly generalizable, are that context matters, and that investing time and resources in preparing is critical to success. These, however, are among the *few* generally valid negotiation theory prescriptions for any context, location, or nature of a conflict.

Modifiers, Caveats, and No-Go Areas—When This Advice Just Won't Apply

While not every Western prescription fails everywhere outside the West, each situation is unique in stakes and dynamics; what worked in one place may fail elsewhere. If the ultimate goal is to reach agreements that spare innocent lives now and establish future nonviolent conflict management practices, then we should pursue this goal doggedly, even if it requires renouncing for the moment Western criteria that contravene local norms and practices. But despite scholars' and practitioners' hopes, not all conflicts can be resolved peacefully through negotiations. This suggests caution when deciding to assist in an international conflict or when weighing whether to withdraw from it.

Conclusion

The Mali case suggests that we should be honest with ourselves regarding our own motives and avoid prolonging the conflict for self-serving reasons. Intervention in international conflicts takes more time to prepare and implement than we might expect. Rewards are commensurate with investments: limited, rapid efforts yield at best short-lived results. Long-term efforts that build relationships may make a meaningful difference in disputants' lives, even if we only manage, rather than resolve, a conflict.

This Ties in With:

Goh, Ch. 31, Mistakes

33

Timing, Process, and Stages

I. William Zartman[1]

Introduction

Negotiation has its rhythms—steps through which it passes—and knowing them makes mastery easier. Knowing when you need to begin negotiating (and how to play on the other party's need), what the successive phases of negotiation and the modes of crafting an agreement are (and how to use them effectively), and how parties behave in the endgame (and what to do about it) is important. This chapter is based on I.W. ZARTMAN, *Process and Stages* and *Timing and Ripeness* in 1 THE NEGOTIATOR'S DESK REFERENCE 645–652 and 653–666 (Honeyman & Schneider eds, 2017). The full references in those chapters can be found respectively at www.ndrweb.com/chapter-46--public.html and www.ndrweb.com/chapter-47--public.html.

1. **I. William Zartman** is Jacob Blaustein Distinguished Professor of International Organization and Conflict Resolution (Emeritus) at the School of Advanced International Studies of Johns Hopkins University. He is author of *The Practical Negotiator* (Yale 1982), *Ripe for Resolution* (Oxford 1989), *Preventing Deadly Conflict* (Polity 2015), and *Cowardly Lions* (Rienner 2005), and editor of numerous works, including *Escalation and Negotiation in International Conflicts* (Cambridge 2005), *Peace vs Justice* (Rowman and Littlefield 2005), *Peacemaking in International Conflict* (USIP 1993; 2006), *Arab Spring: Negotiating in the Shadow of the Intifadat* (University of Georgia Press 2015), and *How Negotiation Ends: Behavior in the Endgame* (Cambridge 2016). He is a member of the Processes of International Negotiation (PIN) Group of the Clingendael Institute for International Relations in The Hague, Netherlands.

Why These Concepts Might Change Your Thinking

Thinking about phases and stages of negotiation can determine your most effective strategies. First, we tend to think of negotiation as beginning with fixed positions and proceeding on a straight trajectory until the two lines meet or one party caves in. To act thus is to miss the dynamics of the encounter and increase the chances of incurring losses and losing chances of gains. Conflicts and problems are ripe for resolution only when *each* party realizes that it cannot resolve the situation by itself, when this stalemate is *painful* to each of them, and when both then sense that there is a common outcome that can be attained. To come to that realization, parties must look at their security point (reservation price) to see what their best alternative to a negotiated agreement (BATNA) can be. But all these calculations are part of just the first phase, diagnosis—which includes other questions, such as precedents, real interests, issues, personalities, and others.

The next phase of the negotiation is formulation: a search for a common understanding of the nature of the problem or conflict, the notion of distribution that should govern the solution, and the appropriate terms of trade. This understanding may be tacit or explicit, but if not engaged, its absence will return to trouble communications and lead to an incoherent agreement.

In a third phase, negotiation can then turn to details that translate the understood formula, using three different modes of distribution: division or concession, in which the outcome is simply allocated between the parties; compensation or exchange, in which allocation of one item is "paid for" by the allocation of a different item; and construction or reframing, in which the problem or conflict is reconsidered in a new formula that benefits all parties.

Finally, sensing they are close to an agreement, parties can adopt one of several behaviors: dueling, driving, dragging, mixed, or mismatched. Dueling parties take public stands to lock themselves into their positions; driving parties sense that a mutually satisfactory agreement is in view and move each other toward it; dragging parties sense that an impending agreement is not where they want to go, and slow down or even terminate the process as gently as possible; mixed behavior can involve any of these behaviors on different parts of the conflict or problem as long as the approach is shared; and mismatched behavior is when parties do not reciprocate behavior, adding damage to disagreement. But the key is for a party to understand *what phase they are actually in*. Any or all of the above strategies will fail if applied at the wrong time.

Action Plan—What You Can Do Differently Tomorrow

First Phase—Diagnosis

Negotiators say that diagnosis should take 75 percent of the negotiating time, yet this phase contains matters that are often left unaddressed. The availability of alternatives or fallback positions is a principal key to the power of a party in negotiation. As parties consider their own alternatives, they should also look at the other party's best fallback, both for comparison and to see if they might possibly worsen it: negotiations take place on the level of alternatives and expectations, as well as offers.

As negotiators move into preparation, they should not only consider their case and the arguments behind their position, but also look for precedents, analyzing both similarities and lessons, but also differences. They need to look behind stated positions to find the real interests these positions express, and to see if other positions are more attractive; finding real interests can often be a joint creative effort. Not all issues on the table need to make up the final package of the agreement, and other issues can sometimes be added to make the package more acceptable. Not only agreed allocations, but also implementation and further measures to ensure that the problem or conflict does not reemerge, bring the parties into forward-looking cooperation, as well as backward-looking distributions. Although diagnosis is essentially a job for each party on its own, each of these elements helps the parties prepare to develop a formula for their agreement.

Second and Third Phases—Formulation and Distribution

Armed with their diagnoses, parties need to work out a common understanding of what they are negotiating *about*. Explicitly or implicitly, they need to agree on the nature of the problem, the relevant terms of trade, and a sense of justice that will govern the outcome.

Once in negotiations, with a joint understanding of the nature of the problem or conflict they are addressing and of at least a concept of distribution in the outcome, parties can turn to allocating detail, *but not before*. Thus, jumping into distribution of pieces of the outcome without all the preliminaries is an impetuous step into incoherence.

Among the possible modes of negotiation, it is simplest to look for a distributive way of allocating outcomes. The notion of "split the difference" should be reserved for the very end, yet its spirit, with a poverty of imagination, is often used to guide allocation. (Except for the added value of resolving the conflict or problem, 50 percent is a zero-sum solution where we all lose half of whatever pie is at stake.) More creative is to look for positive-sum solutions, in which one side's preferred items can be won in exchange for some of the other side's preferred items. Yet with the best will in the world, not all items will fall into those two piles. There is usually something left over that both sides want and that has to be split, shared, or bought. Buying goes back to concepts of compensation, splitting to concession, and sharing to some sort of construction or reframing, so that both sides *can* share the item's value. Creativity and innovation center on the use of compensation and creation.

Final Phase—Closing

In the end game, the chosen approach depends on how parties have gotten along so far and what sort of relations they have built up. Driving is the most positive, with the parties working together—without losing sight of their own interests—to come to a mutually satisfactory agreement. It is important to realize that leaving the other party satisfied is the key to your own long-range satisfaction; if *they* are satisfied, the other party will keep to an agreement that leaves you satisfied. Driving does not prevent either party from hanging firm on an important matter; in fact, it makes firmness on a special point more possible, because of the robust relationship that has been fashioned together up to that point. (In that sort of negotiation, it's best to keep the press out and keep things private.)

However, if the other party is set on dueling, duel in turn; seeking to drive with a dueler makes the other party think the "driver" is a weakling. Dueling involves a very public debate. Parties lock themselves publicly into their positions and publicly show the other party how they can't possibly live with their own proposed solution, each putting its own feet into concrete before its public and undercutting the other side's offered alternative.

When it appears that negotiations are heading in the wrong direction, on the whole outcome or on one issue, dragging remains a possible strategy. It's best done when done by both sides so as to disengage gracefully. But on a subtler level, one must also sense when it's possible to shift modes on a particular thorny issue without destroying the productive reciprocity; this can actually preserve the ability to work out an overall deal. Otherwise, the parties are simply dancing different steps and walking on each other's feet.

Modifiers, Caveats, and No-Go Areas—When This Advice Just Won't Apply

All counsel is a guide to perfection; all models are ideal types. Probably the most important caveat concerns the formula. Not always do parties sit down to negotiate a joint view of the problem or share a sense of justice that will govern their allocation of items in the outcome. If they do not set out specific guidelines explicitly, they may still do so within the opening discussions or alongside them, even in op-eds or speeches. But sometimes they do not reach such an understanding, and formulas have to be cobbled together inductively, from the pieces of agreement as they are (probably painfully) put together. The result is a coherent agreement only by accident, and more often, a messy outcome that risks long-term instability.

The other caveat, already noted, is to be sure of the approach each party chooses for the endgame; mismatching undoes the process of agreeing, even if the substance of the negotiation would have lent itself to agreement. Also, if one is dueling, always retain the ability to step out of the concrete and compromise with the other party in any agreement.

Conclusion

These observations are about how negotiations are done when they are done best. There are plenty of instances to the contrary, which fail or succeed nonetheless, human nature being what it is. But it is best to observe "best practice" whenever even remotely possible.

This Ties in With:

Abramson, Ch. 3, Fashioning Style; Kaufman & Blanchot, Ch. 32, International

Section VII

Context and Other Constraints

Section VII addresses some deliberately varied contexts, each of which poses particular limitations. Chapter 34 describes the common situation in which you, as an individual, must face off with a huge organization that has boiled down all its negotiation moves to a script. (When you read this chapter, you might find that you have more leverage than you think.) This is followed by Chapter 35, which discusses another common setting, arbitration, in which only one side suffers the major constraints—and unless you happen to be a major corporation, this means *you*. In turn, Chapter 36 discusses a very common setting in which the constraints are major for both sides: plea-bargaining.

Some readers might be surprised when we assert that they can also learn negotiation lessons from some seemingly unrelated—not to mention, dangerous—contexts: hostage negotiation and martial arts. Yet, we have three chapters (Chapters 37 to 39) that demonstrate how lessons from hostage negotiation and martial arts really can be adapted into a lawyer's more typical negotiation settings.

36 How to Negotiate with Constraints: Lessons from Plea Bargaining

Cynthia Alkon

37 Negotiating with the Unknown: More Common than Not?

Maria R. Volpe, Jack Cambria, Hugh McGowan, and Chris Honeyman

38 What Lawyers Can Learn from Hostage Negotiators

William Donohue

39 Dealing with Amygdala Hijack: Lessons from the Martial Arts

Joel Lee and James Shanahan

34

Negotiating against a Script

Robert Dingwall[1] *and Carrie Menkel-Meadow*[2]

Introduction

Scripts or playbooks created by corporate managers to handle consumer and other claims reduce the discretion for negotiators to resolve individual disputes. How can one possibly "get to yes" by offering creative options to solve problems when the other party won't even engage in basic negotiation behaviors (questioning and responses, information exchange, agenda setting, offers, brainstorming, arguments, proposed solutions, counterarguments, or even counteroffers)? How can we negotiate successfully in these predetermined and limited negotiation settings? This chapter is based on

1. **Robert Dingwall** is a consulting sociologist in private practice and part-time Professor of Sociology at Nottingham Trent University. He has wide international experience in teaching and research, particularly in the interdisciplinary study of law, medicine, science, and technology. This has included extensive studies of mediation, particularly in family disputes, and civil justice, particularly in relation to personal injury and medical negligence. He is also interested in the application of ideas from conflict resolution to issues of public engagement and the interactions between science and society.
2. **Carrie Menkel-Meadow** is Chancellor's Professor of Law and Political Science, University of California, Irvine and A.B. Chettle Professor of Law, Dispute Resolution, and Civil Procedure at Georgetown University Law Center. She has published over 10 books and 200 articles in the fields of conflict and dispute resolution. She has received three honorary doctorates, and has taught and practiced mediation, restorative justice, negotiation, conflict resolution, and ethics in twenty-six countries, and on all seven continents. She has been a conflict consultant to the World Bank, United Nations, International Red Cross, and the U.S. Federal Judicial Center, as well as to many court systems and public and private organizations.

C. Menkel-Meadow & R. Dingwall, *Scripts: What to Do When Big Bad Companies Won't Negotiate*, in 1 The Negotiator's Desk Reference 711–724 (Honeyman & Schneider eds, 2017). The full references in that chapter can be found at www.ndrweb.com/chapter-51--public.html.

Why This Concept Might Change Your Thinking

A natural experiment many years ago alerted us to a new line of thinking. The authors were both stranded, by the same airline and along with many colleagues, at Denver airport on the way to a conference. But the passengers did not receive equal treatment: our handling of the airline's rote responses differed, and mattered. Since then, more and more companies have adopted scripts for handling consumer complaints (and lawyers who represent, e.g., insurance claimants, add non-consumer issues to this list). It has become increasingly common to face a faceless entity, much more powerful than ourselves, that does not care about losing one or two, or even many, dissatisfied customers.

In our longer essay, we considered the issues in mass scripted negotiations; explored some success stories and failures; and offered some thoughts and advice about how to continue to try to "get to yes," despite very difficult circumstances. Even the most experienced negotiation theorists and practitioners struggle to find clear patterns in this brave new world. But we can offer some practical tips.

Action Plan—What You Can Do Differently Tomorrow

First, are you in an arena where the other side faces competition? Not all big companies have the luxury of indifference. Where there is some customer choice, a business that acts like the "customer is (almost) always right" can gain a loyal following. Amazon, for example, is widely credited with providing good customer service (possibly at the expense of employees and suppliers). Where there is less choice or a more captive audience, as in government services or monopoly businesses (cable TV), the contrary may more often be true. The moral is to deal, when possible, with a provider that does not see itself as a monopoly, or that cares about its reputation.

When that's *not* possible, you are in a different world from the high-intensity, question-asking, interest-seeking, information-sharing, creative problem-solving, idealized negotiation environment. That doesn't mean nothing can be done. It is important to at least begin with some well-tried elements of our canon. First, what might *the other side need or want or have interests in*? To what extent *is there a reason, method, or plan behind the script*—efficiency, profit, simplicity of policy application, equity for all customers, inventory control, quality assessment? Can this be appealed to in any direct or indirect way? To what extent can one use our usual methods of *asking questions* before making arguments to *learn what the other's side's interests might be? What are the incentives or disincentives for the front line negotiator*? (Commissions, quality control, norming by numbers, cases completed, etc.?) Is there any effective way to make the script or playbook work for what we need or want by appealing to its underlying purposes? If not, is there any way to use the script, playbook, or policy to get what we need? If not, is there any way to argue for or to obtain an exception or reinterpretation of the script so that it "won't apply here"?

This means using all the tools in our usual canon of negotiation strategies—appeals to the other party's needs and interests; having good reasons; making good arguments; being persuasive; being able to trade; and to appeal to emotional, moral, or other affective, as well as instrumental, concerns. Perhaps your particular issue for negotiation reveals concerns or needs of others, too. That may provide leverage.

There is also hope in aggregating consumers: your opponent's size may make it more powerful, but it is also a bigger target. The growth of ratings, reputations, and review sites (e.g., Amazon, Yelp, OpenTable, Angie's List, TripAdvisor), as well as regular social media sites like Facebook and Twitter has made it possible to use *publicity* and *reputation* (what used to be called *shaming*) to get results in both individual and mass consumer negotiations. Many consumers have reported both personalized and quick responses to even minor complaints when the claims of bad service or product have quickly gone viral. While such public claims raise a host of legal issues—libel, slander, false claims, possible business torts, etc.—they also often stimulate action. Public reputational resources can provide the "carrots and sticks" of positive incentives and negative shaming to equalize some negotiation power disparities.

Making a scene or making a fuss can still be an effective, if risky, tactic when dealing with scripted negotiators. Telephone customer agents may hang up (even if monitored)—or transfer a complainant to a supervisor, or sometimes, actually do something positive, just to avoid the ongoing conflict or scene (or noise on the telephone). An ability to signal familiarity with relevant law, and willingness to use it if not satisfied, can be a source of extra leverage, including simply moving a grievance upward to meet someone with enough discretion to resolve it.

It can also be effective—some would argue, more effective—to make the other side's job easier or more pleasant, even in playbook settings. Rather than making a scene or being threatening, being kind, helpful, engaging, charming, amusing, or instrumentally offering a particular solution can sometimes work even in routinized settings. *Start with nice*—as our scholarly literature has long demonstrated, it is far easier to escalate a conflict than to de-escalate it.

Online dispute resolution is another response to mass scale and seemingly inflexible negotiations with big companies. Both in the private sector (e.g., eBay) and the public (see Modria.com), more entities now use online platforms for complaints and redress. Some have automatic algorithms (e.g., "if this is a first-time complainant and dispute is for less than $50.00, just pay refund"); others provide access to live mediators, arbitrators, or even adjudicators.

Complaining to the government, perhaps after unsuccessful efforts at direct negotiation with a private company, demonstrates another important move in your playbook: *change the negotiator or climb the supervisory ladder.* Good negotiators know that, especially in hierarchical settings, the first responder may not be the best responder. Because of lack of discretion, cultural differences in offshore customer service departments, lack of authority or alienated working conditions, front-line negotiators are most likely to follow their scripts and not move off suggested responses or outcomes. "May I speak to your supervisor, please" is one way to move up the organization's negotiating ladder until one finds someone who has enough authority to exercise some discretion.

It is also possible, sometimes, to encounter *variation and flexibility or difference* in both negotiation behavior and outcome simply by changing partners and starting over. This may work better than getting caught up in unproductive arguments or time-wasting waits for higher-ups. This strategy, of course, is less successful when "big brother or sister" is keeping electronic or other files on you as you negotiate—but of course, you could also always do the same thing. *Always take notes, names, ranks, and serial numbers* of all those you negotiate with—and remember to get last names. (It is hard to make "Susan," "Jennifer," "John," "Nigel," or "Stephen" accountable for what was promised; big companies have too many agents with those names. Companies also sometimes assign false names to customer service agents, or even assign a certain name to a role filled by multiple people.)

Modifiers, Caveats, and No-Go Areas—When This Advice Just Won't Apply

Much of this advice won't work if customer service is separate (or off-shored) from the principal one is negotiating with; even government agencies are doing this now! Accountability, allocation to appropriate internal units, and assigned responsibility for dispute resolution all have great effects on what happens in negotiation. To the extent that one buys products or services from those with close to monopoly power (e.g., Amazon), such advice might fall on relatively deaf ears. Companies will decide whether they will respond to reputational postings and want to have a good image; some will clearly decide that some matters can simply be ignored. As is often the case in negotiation, power (on both sides, including both consumers and vendors) will still play a role in who is successful in negotiation.

Conclusion

Although we may seem to live in a disheartening time of inability to negotiate with many big, bad, and inflexible organizational negotiators, all is not lost. New technologies provide opportunities to aggregate claims, to use publicity, and to use reputational and shaming effects to move even big organizational negotiators to grant redress, or even to change policies. We do not naively believe that power imbalances among and between large economic and governmental organizations and individual consumers can all be corrected or realigned. But, as with all human development, innovation comes with some good as well as some bad. The magnification of our production and management units can be met by changes in negotiation strategies, using our traditional canon of skills and theories.

This Ties in With:

Gross, Ch. 35, Shadow Arbitration

35

Negotiating in the Shadow of Adhesive Arbitration

Jill I. Gross[1]

Introduction

Dispute resolution professionals have long understood that negotiators bargain in the shadow of the law, meaning that the alternative to settling a dispute is adjudication of the dispute by a judge or jury applying principles of law. However, due to the increasing prevalence of pre-dispute arbitration clauses in adhesive contracts, more and more disputants in those settings will end up in mandatory arbitration, not court, if they do not settle the dispute. This chapter is based on J. Gross, *Negotiating in the Shadow of Adhesive Arbitration*, in 1 The Negotiator's Desk Reference 701–709 (Honeyman & Schneider eds, 2017). The full references in that chapter can be found at www.ndrweb.com/chapter-50--public.html.

1. **Jill I. Gross** is Associate Dean for Academic Affairs and Professor of Law at the Elisabeth Haub School of Law, Pace University, teaching dispute resolution, securities law, ethics, and lawyering skills. She is an arbitrator for the American Arbitration Association (AAA) and Financial Industry Regulatory Authority (FINRA) Office of Dispute Resolution, a member of the Securities Experts Roundtable, former Chair of the AALS ADR Section, the Securities ADR Committee of the ABA Section of Dispute Resolution, and the Practising Law Institute's annual Securities Arbitration program. She has published prolifically in the area of securities arbitration and has been retained as an expert in securities arbitrations, litigations, and enforcement proceedings.

Why This Concept Might Change Your Thinking

In the dispute setting, each party's Best Alternative to a Negotiated Agreement (BATNA) typically is litigating the dispute in court and pursuing a favorable judgment for the full amount of relief requested. However, if the dispute arose out of a contractual relationship and the underlying contract included an arbitration clause, each party's BATNA is pursuing a win in arbitration, not court.

Arbitration—in which one or more third-party neutrals (arbitrators) provide the parties with an opportunity to be heard and resolve the dispute by issuing a binding award—is often considered a faster, cheaper, more party-driven, and more private dispute resolution mechanism than litigation. Many arbitration clauses designate a particular arbitration forum, such as the American Arbitration Association (AAA), JAMS, or Financial Industry Regulatory Authority (FINRA) Dispute Resolution, all of which have well-developed Codes of Procedure, to administer the case. Some of these forums have consumer due process protocols designed to protect consumers subject to a pre-dispute arbitration clause (e.g., AAA) or rules designed to protect investors (e.g., FINRA); others do not. In these commercial settings, arbitration's distinguishing characteristics (as compared to litigation) include party input in the selection of the arbitration panel, discovery limited to document exchange, few dispositive motions pre-hearing, a private hearing only very loosely following the rules of evidence, a short time from claim filing to outcome (award), awards without explanation, precedential value or public availability, and sharply limited grounds to appeal from those awards. Additionally, because arbitrators are less accountable for their awards and they can apply principles of equity to their deliberations, it can be harder for practitioners to predict outcomes in arbitration.

Negotiators must consider how these substantive and procedural differences between arbitration and litigation impact their negotiation plan.

Action Plan—What You Can Do Differently Tomorrow

When developing a negotiation strategy for a client whose dispute arose from an adhesive contract with an enforceable arbitration clause, lawyers must take into account three critical differences from disputes that would end up in court: differences in the dispute resolution process, differences in the negotiators themselves, and differences in substantive outcomes. First, practitioners should learn about the rules and procedures of the arbitration forum where the dispute has already been filed, or will be filed, absent a settlement. What are its procedural rules? What are the criteria to be an arbitration panelist at that forum? How much input can your client have in selecting the arbitrator? Is mediation a precondition either in the pre-dispute arbitration agreement or pursuant to forum rules? How much discovery is available to your client? Does the forum permit dispositive motions? Do arbitrators in that particular forum have a reputation for being accountable to the law? How long does it typically take to get a hearing? Are awards publicly available?

Knowing the answers to these questions might suggest to the advocate that the client has a greater chance than originally thought of prevailing in arbitration as opposed to in litigation or vice versa. For example, claims that might be subject to time-consuming and expensive dispositive motion practice in court might get to a hearing on the merits in arbitration before even motion papers would be filed in court. Thus, it is more likely that arbitrators (as compared to judges and juries) will actually hear those claims on their merits—and thus the parties will have to incur the costs of a full hearing. Conversely, not knowing the answers to these questions will give opposing counsel with more experience in arbitration an informational advantage to exploit.

Second, before attempting to negotiate a settlement of a dispute for a client who is subject to an adhesive arbitration agreement, practitioners must consider the counter-negotiator. Unlike in the balanced power setting, parties to an adhesive contract did not, by definition, negotiate to reach the underlying contract and thus likely have little to no prior sense of their wants, aspirations, behaviors, or even hidden interests. The parties have built no trust, exchanged no information, and observed no ethical leanings. Unfounded stereotypes abound: the big, bad corporation out to maximize profit; the gadfly consumer; the greedy broker; the investor with "sour grapes"; the exploitative employer; the lazy employee. To reach an integrative agreement, negotiators starting from a place of skepticism and mistrust must set aside these and other preconceptions before entering the bargaining phase. Moreover, some litigators have more experience in the courtroom than in the arbitration forum. They likely have less knowledge about the arbitration process and less ability to accurately assess the probabilities of a particular arbitration outcome (especially since most arbitration forums do not publish outcomes). You might have to educate such a counter-negotiator or consider whether the lack of arbitration experience influenced an offer or counteroffer.

Third, while the procedural rules of arbitration may be predictable, substantive outcomes in arbitration are not. In their deliberations, arbitrators often apply the law combined with principles of equity and custom and practice. Arbitrators are widely perceived to "split the baby," i.e., achieve a more equitable, compromised outcome, even if strict application of legal principles would dictate a different outcome. As a result, negotiators may find it difficult to identify the legal rules that would impact the outcome in arbitration. Unable to predict and thus manage the downside risk of arbitration, negotiators might be more tempted to settle a claim in arbitration as opposed to that same claim in court. Likewise, the very limited grounds of appeal increase the finality and thus consequences of an adverse award. The risk of not settling for both parties might be higher than for a claim pursued in court. Conversely, negotiators might incorrectly calculate the value of a case based on the likely outcome in court, rather than in arbitration, and not perceive a reasonable settlement offer as acceptable.

The negotiator should also consider whether a client's nonmonetary interests may be addressed differently in arbitration. For example, given the relative intimacy of the arbitration hearing room, relationships among parties might end up being more fractured than after a trial in a less intimate courtroom. In situations where an ongoing relationship between the parties is a paramount interest to the institution, negotiators should consider whether that relationship could survive an arbitration hearing where the parties are sitting at a conference room table across from each other accusing each other of misdeeds for several days. And arbitration will not address a party's interest in a public result that holds an opposing party accountable. On the other hand, arbitration better meets a party's interests in privacy, flexibility, and control over outcome.

Finally, if one party is reluctant to pay an award, the prevailing party will first have to convert an arbitration award into a court judgment to be able to collect on it. In those cases, a client's likelihood of recovering a monetary award is higher in court than in arbitration. If collection is at risk, then a negotiator seeking to collect may identify a "more realistic" zone of agreement than if negotiating in the shadow of court.

Modifiers, Caveats, and No-Go Areas—When This Advice Just Won't Apply

This advice would be slightly different in the non-adhesive setting. It would also be different if negotiating in the shadow of an international arbitration, a labor arbitration, or a noncommercial domestic arbitration.

Also, contrary to myth, arbitration is not necessarily confidential. Arbitrators and forum staff have an obligation of confidentiality, but absent a case-specific confidentiality order, the parties and their lawyers are free to discuss publicly any aspect of the arbitration. A client might be less willing to settle for a particular amount if the process is not confidential.

Conclusion

Practitioners trying to settle a dispute must adjust their negotiation strategies when mandatory arbitration is the process the parties will use in the absence of a settlement. Among other things, they must consider the impact of arbitration procedures on the settlement value, the impact on the negotiators themselves, and the impact on substantive outcomes.

This Ties in With:

Dingwall & Menkel-Meadow, Ch. 34, Scripts; Amsler, Ch. 45, DSD

36

How to Negotiate with Constraints: Lessons from Plea Bargaining

Cynthia Alkon[1]

Introduction

Plea bargaining is an example of negotiating with constraints: each of the parties in the negotiation is limited by a number of factors, including the existing law and extreme power imbalances. However, within these constraints, at times, skilled negotiators can accomplish creative results. This chapter will give you some examples of how strong negotiation skills can be used to your advantage within plea bargaining and how those skills could be useful in other highly constrained and restrictive environments. This chapter is based on C. ALKON, *Plea Bargaining: An Example of Negotiating with Constraints*, in 1 THE NEGOTIATOR'S DESK REFERENCE 683–699

1. **Cynthia Alkon** is a Professor of Law at Texas A&M University School of Law. Prior to joining academia, Professor Alkon was a Deputy Public Defender with the Los Angeles County Public Defender's Office. Professor Alkon also spent over seven years working in Eastern Europe and the former Soviet Union providing rule of law development assistance, primarily for criminal justice reform. Professor Alkon's scholarship focuses on plea bargaining, comparative criminal procedure, and rule of law development assistance efforts.

(Honeyman & Schneider eds, 2017). The full references in that chapter can be found at www.ndrweb.com/chapter-49--public.html.

Why This Concept Might Change Your Thinking

Constraints and limitations are not the full picture of what is possible in a negotiation. Lawyers who are better prepared and flexible can often get more out of the negotiation than might seem possible at first glance. The lesson of plea bargaining is that even those who have less power (such as criminal defense attorneys) may be able to negotiate better deals if they are prepared and look for common interests. For example, judges, prosecutors, and defense lawyers (not to mention defendants) all share a common interest in decreasing recidivism rates in the criminal justice system. This common interest may make it possible to negotiate a better deal for an individual defendant, such as participating in a problem-solving court or diversion, if it will help to address the underlying problem that is leading to criminal behavior for this particular defendant, and thereby reduce the chances of recidivism. Prosecutors may be more likely to accept such an outcome, even in cases where a "standard deal" would involve jail time—but only if they have enough information about why it makes sense in this particular case, with this particular defendant, at this particular time. It is more likely to get these kinds of outcomes in jurisdictions where these programs are already commonplace and where prosecutors have already seen the value of reduction in recidivism rates due to these alternative approaches.

Action Plan—What You Can Do Differently Tomorrow

There are three things you can do differently tomorrow: look for common interests, prepare for the negotiation, and don't accept constraints as immovable. The stereotypical view is that prosecutors and defense lawyers are adversaries whose interests are in constant conflict. It is true that prosecutors' ethical duty is to do justice, while defense lawyers' ethical duty is to zealously represent their client. But if you look below the surface, there are interests in common that can aid the plea negotiation process. For example, both prosecutors and defense lawyers rely on plea bargaining to manage their work loads. Neither side *can* do a jury trial for every case they handle. Experienced defense lawyers know that they can expect better deals in at least some of their cases on busy trial days, as prosecutors need to manage the number of cases going to trial and may give better deals to help make that happen. Prosecutors also know that defense lawyers want to get the best possible deal for their clients—so they may agree to reduce the sentence, within their existing policies, to resolve the case. Understanding the underlying interests of the other side is as important in these cases, in what may appear to be a highly constrained negotiating environment, as it would be in any negotiation.

The second thing that you can do differently is to be well prepared for the negotiation. You should never assume that because there are few options, it doesn't matter if you go in underprepared. Defense lawyers who investigate their case and who learn more about their clients have more of a chance of getting a better (and different) deal. For example, driving under the influence of alcohol tends to be a criminal case with little room for creativity in negotiation. But defense lawyers who fully prepare their cases may learn facts that can help. Was the breathalyzer in good working order on the day of the test? If the police officer claimed he pulled the defendant over for swerving in a lane, is there dashcam video that shows the swerving? If the defendant claims his friend was driving, do you have that friend as a witness? But even if there are no facts in favor of the defendant, it could be possible to negotiate a better deal due to the particular situation of your client. For example, a defendant in the military may also be punished *by* the military for their misdemeanor driving under the influence conviction. Depending on the laws in the individual state, and the local prosecutor's policies, some prosecutors will agree to waive some of the fines or not require alcohol classes through the court, knowing that the defendant will be doing a substance abuse course through the military. The more you know about your case and your client, the more likely you are to be in a position to work around existing constraints.

The third thing that you can do differently is not accept the existing constraints as immovable. The big example here is the development of drug courts in the United States. Drug courts began in the late 1980s at the height of the "War on Drugs" in Florida, a center of the war. The "war on drugs" rhetoric, and the accompanying policies and legislative changes, were focused on punishment and imprisoning people for longer periods of time. To most people both within and outside the criminal justice system, this would not have seemed the moment to convince judges or prosecutors to focus on rehabilitation and not punishment. Yet the courts were overwhelmed with drug cases and judges were tired of the revolving door, seeing the same drug-addicted defendants over and over again. The harsh sentences and the fact that these sentences were not preventing recidivism was frustrating to some judges who wanted to see themselves in more of a helping role, and to have more options than simply punishing every defendant who came into their courtrooms. Problem-solving courts seemed like a good option to give judges the opportunity to do something about the underlying problems that were leading to criminal behavior. (Critics do worry that these courts can be *harder* on defendants, and question whether defendants who are the most in need are being admitted into problem-solving courts.) Yet problem-solving courts were a clear departure from the "lock 'em up" mentality of the "war on drugs" and gave a creative new option to defendants.

This was possible because there are few laws or rules surrounding plea bargaining. Generally, the plea bargain does not have to fit into any particular standard sentence as long as the prosecutor, defendant, and judge agree to the deal and it doesn't violate the law. The laws in the United States do not prevent plea deals that include treatment for addiction instead of prison time. The lesson to take from this example is that it is possible to think creatively about other approaches—and that good negotiators do not accept the existing constraints as the only option. Lawyers who practice in the criminal justice system should understand that in plea bargaining, as long as the approach does not violate an existing law, there is room for great creativity.

Modifiers, Caveats, and No-Go Areas—When This Advice Just Won't Apply

Prosecutors enjoy significantly more power in plea negotiations. They can decide what charges to file and what enhancements apply. This means that defendants are regularly put in situations where they have few good options: they can accept a bad deal or go to trial and get a worse sentence. Finding common interests in, for example, managing workloads, may not counter the political pressure in a particular case or type of case. There are some cases that prosecutors will not plea-bargain and some cases where the offer is truly a "take it or leave it" one. In these situations, the structure of our penal codes may make it difficult if not impossible to get a better deal or to be creative in finding alternative solutions. Good preparation and negotiating skills cannot and do not level the playing field in plea bargaining. Unfortunately, there is no shortage of cases when the facts are bad, the law is inflexible, and there is no space for creativity.

Conclusion

The challenge when negotiating in what might seem a hopeless environment, due to the serious power imbalances and constraints, is to remain open to the *possibility* of negotiating a better deal. At the same time, you should recognize when you cannot expect to do better. Lawyers who are prepared, and who are flexible enough to be creative when the situation allows for it, and who look for common interests, may be able to negotiate better deals than they would have thought possible given the constraints in the negotiation.

This Ties in With:

Schneider, Ch. 9, Measuring Success; Amsler, Ch. 45, DSD

37

Negotiating with the Unknown: More Common than Not?

Maria R. Volpe,[1] *Jack Cambria,*[2] *Hugh McGowan,*[3] *and Chris Honeyman*[4]

Introduction

The skills used by police hostage negotiators could be particularly valuable for a variety of negotiations undertaken by lawyers and,

---

1. **Maria R. Volpe**, Ph.D. is Professor of Sociology, the director of the Dispute Resolution Program, and the director of the CUNY Dispute Resolution Center at John Jay College of Criminal Justice, City University of New York. An internationally known scholar, she has lectured, researched, and written extensively about dispute resolution processes, particularly mediation, and has been widely recognized for her distinguished career in the field of dispute resolution.
2. **Jack Cambria** retired from the New York City Police Department (NYPD) in 2015 after nearly thirty-four years of dedicated service. For over sixteen years, he served in the Emergency Service Unit (ESU), whose primary focus is to provide rescue, SWAT, and counterterrorism services to the City of New York. He ended his NYPD career as the longest-standing commander of the Hostage Negotiation Team, serving in that capacity for over fourteen years.
3. **Hugh McGowan** retired in 2001 from the NYPD after thirty-five years of service, serving for his last thirteen years as commanding officer and chief negotiator of the Hostage Negotiation Team (HNT). He has personally responded to and coordinated negotiations at over 1,500 hostage, barricade, and suicide incidents and has instructed crisis negotiators for the NYPD and many other agencies. McGowan has a Ph.D. in criminal justice from the CUNY Graduate School.
4. **Chris Honeyman** is managing partner of Convenor Conflict Management, a consulting firm based in Washington, DC. He is coeditor of *Negotiation Essentials for Lawyers*, *The Negotiator's Desk Reference,* and five other books, and author of over 100 published articles, book chapters, and monographs. He has directed a thirty-year series of research-and-development programs, advised many academic and practice organizations, and served as a mediator, arbitrator, and in other neutral capacities in more than 2,000 disputes.

arguably, essential to avoid malpractice. Like hostage negotiators, lawyers experience their share of unknowns in their routine, otherwise uneventful negotiations. On a regular basis, lawyers are faced with constant confrontations with other lawyers where win-lose is the norm, as well as interactions involving unrelenting, often highly stressed clients who hold unrealistic expectations. To manage their negotiations, police have refined how to engage hostage situations, where the unknowns are a given and often extreme. This chapter addresses how techniques used by hostage negotiators can be vital for lawyers to be prepared for their unknowns. It is based on M.R. Volpe, J. Cambria, H. McGowan, & C. Honeyman, *Negotiating with the Unknown*, in 2 The Negotiator's Desk Reference 297–310 (Honeyman & Schneider eds, 2017). The full references in that chapter can be found at www.ndrweb.com/chapter-72--public.html.

Why This Concept Might Change Your Thinking

For lawyers, even when they think that they know the context they are operating in, many unknown factors may transpire to completely surprise them. Central to understanding what it means to negotiate with the unknown is that interactions in real time are socially constructed. Even when one engages in recognizable and repetitive negotiations, circumstances can occur that cause an element of surprise. The key is finding ways to normalize how to manage the unknown since it is nearly impossible to prepare for all of the positions and needs presented by others. Inevitably, something that has worked in the past will not occur as experienced previously. Hence, it is crucial for lawyers to have a toolbox ready with easy-to-use tools when all else seems to be missing.

Action Plan—What You Can Do Differently Tomorrow

What can lawyers learn from hostage negotiators who, as a matter of routine training, are prepared to negotiate with the unknown?

There are parallels between negotiations undertaken by police hostage negotiators and negotiations undertaken by lawyers. At a moment's notice and often with little if any specific information about what is going on, when responding to a hostage situation, police hostage negotiators must engage hostage takers as well as a broad range of other essential parties, including hostages, significant others associated with the hostages and hostage takers, other police personnel, relevant experts, bystanders, and the media, among others. What the hostage negotiators bring to the table is an understanding of police policies and practices as well as their past experience demonstrating suitable temperament. Similarly, before individuals can practice law, they will have acquired legal knowledge in law school, passed the bar exams, and undergone character review to be admitted to the bar.

Since lawyers, like hostage negotiators, can't prepare for every possible unknown they will experience in their negotiations, what is crucial is having a default set of techniques that they can rely on and apply to all situations.

Greetings

At the outset, lawyers must figure out how to address the others. Politeness, here, is more than "just politeness." It gives everyone the dignity that she or he may not typically experience, especially from opposing counsel. The politeness may take them back a little bit, and the emotional level comes down. This initial interaction sets the tone for more respectful contact between the parties. Even if it is the only exchange between them, it will have primed them to move on with positive first impressions.

Schmoozing

A subtle and subjective way of connecting with the "unknown" other involves informal warm-up talk, often called *schmoozing*. For hostage negotiators, this is neither a waste of time nor a phony gambit just to get close to someone, or to buy time for setting up some other kind of action. It is, instead, recognition that the other person, regardless of what they have done, is a human being and needs some human interaction beyond initial greetings.

Ground Rules

Beginning a negotiation with an understanding of boundaries is invaluable. Hostage negotiators start a negotiation itself by establishing boundaries for the ensuing exchanges. They are trained to explain what they are going to do and explain again when they are doing it. Establishing credibility is a slow process when dealing with hostage takers; the same is true in any new relationship where the parties do not know each other. For the hostage negotiators, a key part of preparing the other party and to engage him or her in the negotiation process is to help him or her interact constructively with the officers. If this aspect of the interaction is skipped in the interest of saving time, the hostage taker is likely to get a wrong impression about what the officers intend—starting a slippery slope toward a true disaster. Similarly, lawyers need to establish an understanding with others about how they will proceed.

Clarifying Assumptions

Clarifying assumptions is an important aspect of negotiating with the unknown. The challenge is to avoid assuming that what one is doing is understood, by taking the time to explain one's actions even in the midst of a tremendous amount of activity and potential danger. As a result, hostage negotiators always talk about the "drill." This means that the hostage negotiators explain to all of the people involved what the hostage team's role is and what will be done. Part of the drill is to get the onsite negotiation team together in a football-like huddle, so that when others inevitably try to rush them in the negotiation process, the negotiators are ready to respond—by saying, for instance, "here's what we're going to do: we're not going to talk about the gun, we're not going to talk about the fact that the kids got slapped around. Here's what we're going to do: we're going to—."

In hostage negotiations, the negotiators will attempt to relay a premise that it's not so important how we got here, but rather how we can get out of this together. The hostage taker is thus given a theme. The theme is like a working paper that is not etched in stone, and can certainly change as the interactions unfold. Overall, it has a continuing function; it helps the hostage taker understand that no sudden action, such as a surprise attack, is contemplated, and it also demonstrates to others that the negotiators have a plan and that they have the situation under control.

Assumptions are commonly made by everyone and heuristics are not entirely avoidable by anyone who must act in the real world. Unlike police who have to have years of experience prior to being selected to serve as a hostage negotiator, lawyers can find themselves negotiating in uncharted waters with each new case, especially if they have an eclectic practice with little opportunity to anticipate all of their next steps. The key for them is to always be mindful that assumptions *are* being made and that they need to clarify their own assumptions, as well as those of their clients and of opposing counsel.

Establish Respect and Trust

For lawyers, what framework needs to be kept in mind for them to establish and maintain communication with unknown entities or where unknown situations arise? The simple answer is for them to constantly remember that they need to establish respect and trust. Hostage negotiators do so by taking the time to listen to what the hostage taker is saying and to explain what they are doing. They communicate that they are not going to operate solely from a position of winning at any cost. Simultaneously, they are mindful that they need to immediately demonstrate respect for the person they are talking to, as the beginning of establishing trust. Similarly, lawyers must respect not only their unrealistic clients, but the opposing counsel and others whom in legal battle they would like to crush. Treating all with respect becomes a very powerful tool in managing unknowns. Respect is demonstrated by incorporating the aforementioned greetings, the time to make small talk (i.e., schmoozing), articulation of ground rules, and clarification of assumptions into their playbook. Collectively, these techniques "warm up" the other side, make them feel more comfortable with continued discussion, and build trust.

Moreover, a hostage negotiator's efforts to establish respect and trust continue even when confronted with daunting interactions. The hostage negotiator is not easily rattled by rejection. More times than not, hostage takers and barricaded and suicidal subjects are extremely hostile toward the negotiator, who is there to interrupt their plans. The negotiator must demonstrate staying power and continuously modify his or her negotiation strategy in seeking a constructive outcome. This essential mind-set is applicable in lawyers' negotiations, too, particularly when opposing counsel injects surprise moves that can derail the best-laid plans.

Conclusion

Negotiating with the unknown is a common situation for lawyers. It is important to construct a creative toolbox with some basic tools that one can quickly rely on. Much like police agencies are increasingly teaching the techniques and skills used by hostage negotiators to patrol and community police officers, so should the legal field share the importance of having a default set of skills that can keep negotiation situations moving smoothly and evenly, even when stress is high.

This Ties in With:

Donohue, Ch. 38, Hostage Negotiation; Lee & Shanahan, Ch. 39, Martial Arts

38

What Lawyers Can Learn from Hostage Negotiators

William Donohue[1]

Introduction

How should professionals respond to extremely tense, emotional negotiations? Police negotiators facing a typical hostage negotiation situation answer this question by relying on a trusted process and recognizing that these kinds of negotiations are very different from ordinary economically-driven bargaining scenarios. Yet not all legal or business negotiations are ordinary. Some have many of the characteristics of hostage negotiations. This chapter is about those cases. This chapter is based on P.J. Taylor & W. Donohue, *Lessons from the Extreme: What Business Negotiators Can Learn from Hostage Negotiations*, in 2 The Negotiator's Desk Reference 311–325

1. **William A. Donohue** is a Distinguished Professor of Communication at Michigan State University. He received his Ph.D. from The Ohio State University in 1976. Dr. Donohue has published extensively in conflict, communication, negotiation, and mediation while also conducting workshops and other intervention activities focusing on communication, leadership development, and conflict management. His coauthored book *Framing Matters: Perspectives on Negotiation Research and Practice in Communication* provides a broad understanding of the role of framing in negotiation research. Dr. Donohue is a past president of the International Association for Conflict Management and is on the editorial board of several major journals. Dr. Donohue is also a Fellow of the International Communication Association.

(Honeyman & Schneider eds, 2017). The full references in that chapter can be found at www.ndrweb.com/chapter-73--public.html.

Why This Concept Might Change Your Thinking

First, what makes hostage negotiations different? The key differentiators are extreme emotions and high stakes. Peoples' lives are at stake! These high stakes cause hostage takers to get very emotional: they are afraid, aggressive, confrontational, and cornered. When you encounter another lawyer (or client) who seems in the grip of these emotions, that's a clue: she or he may be thinking like a hostage taker.

Hostage negotiators have learned to follow a specific process to engage the hostage takers and work through these emotions, to discover the substantive issues that can lead to problem-solving. The first step in the process is ensuring that the hostage takers are contained into a specific physical area before any negotiations begin. Containment ensures the hostage taker has to work through the negotiator to end the situation—escape is not an option. For a lawyer, the equivalent to containment is to evaluate whether your opponent is bargaining in good faith. (Do they have to go through you to get a deal, and know that?) If the answer is yes, then you can proceed to determine if emotions are going to play a big factor in the negotiations. The second step is engaging the hostage taker with active listening and low-power language, to reduce tensions, build a relationship, and open up communications. Time is always on the side of the police negotiator; hostage-taker behavior hints that time may be on your side, too. Take the time to expand the emotional pie and reflect and legitimize the emotions.

In police negotiations, the third step is slowing transitioning to, and then unpacking the substantive issues that serve as the cornerstone of the problem-solving. Are the issues primarily substantive, like money and freedom and personal rights? Or are they more identity driven, such as proving how in-charge or courageous the person is? The fourth step involves negotiating these issues as a package to determine how the police negotiator can wrap his or her concerns for hostage safety around the substantive or identity needs of the hostage taker. What is a deal going to take? The final step is the surrender, or nailing down the specific features of the agreement in great detail to ensure everyone's safety. All of these steps have their equivalents in legal and business settings.

Action Plan—What You Can Do Differently Tomorrow

The simple answer is, "Slow down and listen." Does your specific communication style allow you to do that?

Beyond this, several lessons about legal and business negotiation contexts can be derived from the crisis context. First and perhaps most important, the crisis approach to negotiation is very proactive and deliberative. One police negotiator termed it "dynamic inactivity." He meant that hostage negotiation is all about working aggressively behind the scenes to develop strategies and tactics aimed at solving the problem, while slowing down a process that might naturally turn frenetic. The goal is to move by "known successful" steps to achieve a successful resolution.

The second lesson focuses on the need to understand the foundational issues in the conflict. Police negotiators cannot deal with superficial treatment of issues because they may not be able to save lives until the hostage taker's deeper issues are at least acknowledged, and probably addressed overtly. The crisis orientation is always focused on uncovering the hostage taker's key drivers. Legal and business negotiators face a similar challenge. Thus in a business context, negotiators can get lost in such superficial issues as price and delivery dates, and ignore the larger identity issues that are really driving the deal. Again, the desire to be expedient and take shortcuts often compromises the outcome.

The third lesson is that hostage negotiators need to understand how their own biases about hostage takers (i.e., your counterpart), negotiation, and conflict impact their ability to work constructively with hostage takers. While it is difficult to understand the full range of cognitive biases that any given negotiator might face, it would be useful for any negotiator to explore one or two fundamental biases that are well understood, like framing the negotiation as a competition, for example. Certainly, negotiators don't want to handicap themselves with cognitive constraints that might hinder their ability to see settlement opportunities. Gaining feedback about these biases would be important.

A final lesson is the need to look at a negotiation comprehensively. Crisis negotiation is not a process that is reducible to focusing only on gain or loss frames, or negotiator style, or power differentials. A crisis negotiator has to understand the entire context, including constituent relations, events happening external to the scene, and certainly the process of interaction. Of course, the effective business negotiator facing hostage-taker behavior must take this same broad view.

Remember, emotions are about fear, anxiety, vulnerability, and personal identity. Emotions emerge when people perceive resistance to these specific needs. Once emotions have subsided, allowing parties to identify their substantive concerns, then the substantive negotiations can actually begin. The key is not to rush this process, either. Take the time to manage the emotions and build trust, making clear that you're there to help and not to punish the other person. This work involves untangling an always vast array of difficult issues that are driving the negotiations. What are the two or three most important substantive concerns? In a prison uprising, are the hostage takers mostly concerned about food, fair treatment, access to resources? Are there also identity concerns? Do they feel powerless? Do they want to prove they have a voice? Identify the substantive and identity issues and systematically move through them. Remember, relationship is everything! Continue active listening throughout.

Generally, once the parties enter at least a moderately collaborative mode, with key issues being exposed and substantive problem-solving holding its course, the parties craft the outline of a deal. At some point, a deal is struck and both parties say yes. However, at the point of surrender, the hostage taker has lost his leverage and is very sensitive to any suggestion that he has been tricked, duped, or generally led into a deal that appears different from what he envisaged. To deal with this problem, police negotiators stress the need to move slowly through the surrender sequence, in a very deliberate fashion. Each detail must be carefully orchestrated so that everyone's safety can be maximized. The lesson for other contexts here is a simple but important one: "Aftercare" is a big deal in negotiation.

The goal is not simply to "get to yes," but to close the deal after "yes" has been heard. This closing requires meticulous attention to detail about how the process will unfold, and specific markers of success. For example, once the buyer has said yes to the agent about the money part of the deal, then all the process issues kick in. How will the deal be consummated? Steps 1 through N must be laid out and clearly documented, leading toward the final delivery of the product. The post-yes steps might even include follow-up to ensure customer satisfaction. The key point is that clear steps make the deal work, just as they do in hostage negotiation.

Modifiers, Caveats, and No-Go Areas—When This Advice Just Won't Apply

Hostage situations are conducted between strangers. However, many negotiations are conducted between people who work together for years. When the relationships between the parties are well established, all the upfront work needed to create that relationship from scratch may not be needed.

Negotiations can still become heated among long-term colleagues and friends. When that occurs, the active listening and understanding become very important. Don't assume you know everything about the person and the issues simply because you have a long-term relationship with the person. Surprises still happen. If someone you thought you knew well starts to show fear and aggression and to act confrontationally, this chapter may apply after all.

Conclusion

Tough business negotiations, like hostage negotiations, can benefit from listening carefully, focusing on foundational issues, understanding your own biases, and maintaining a comprehensive perspective.

This Ties in With:

Schneider et al., Ch. 24, Reputation; Volpe et al., Ch. 37, Unknown

39

Dealing with Amygdala Hijack: Lessons from the Martial Arts

Joel Lee[1] *and James Shanahan*[2]

Introduction

At first blush, readers may be forgiven for thinking that the title of this piece is an oxymoron. The violence associated with the martial arts (especially in movies) seems incongruous with images of negotiators seeking the much vaunted win-win outcome. As they say, truth is often stranger than fiction, and the authors draw upon their extensive experience in the martial arts to surface uncanny parallels between martial arts and negotiation.

1. **Joel Lee** has been training in the martial arts for thirty years and is the chief instructor of the Singapore Wing Tsun Training Centre. Apart from being an exponent of Wing Tsun (詠春), he also has experience in Jeet Kune Do, Kali, and Aikido. By day, his secret identity is mild-mannered Professor at the Faculty of Law, National University of Singapore, where he teaches conflict resolution and furthers the development of mediation in Singapore. Joel has received the National University of Singapore's highest teaching award and an Honorable Mention by the International Institute for Conflict Prevention and Resolution.

2. **James T. Shanahan** recently retired as a detective with the Special Investigations Division of the New York Police Department (NYPD), following thirty-six years of dedicated service. He also served as an active member of the Hostage Negotiation Team, and as the senior instructor of the Crisis Intervention Team. He has taught on the adjunct faculty of John Jay College of Criminal Justice, CUNY, is a lifelong practitioner of traditional Japanese martial arts, and is an experienced stage, screen, and television actor.

This chapter will focus on one such parallel, the impact of the amygdala hijack on our ability to respond to crises and explore ways to manage the effects of the amygdala hijack. This chapter is based on J. LEE & J. SHANAHAN, *Martial Arts and Conflict Resolution*, in 2 THE NEGOTIATOR'S DESK REFERENCE 355–368 (Honeyman & Schneider eds, 2017). The full references in that chapter can be found at www.ndrweb.com/chapter-75--public.html.

Why This Concept Might Change Your Thinking

This piece is premised on the idea that we are already skillful and effective negotiators. We have many frameworks, strategies, and skills that we can deploy at any one point. However, we are not always able to deploy them and live happily ever after. Sometimes, we give in to our instinct to fight or to run away. Sometimes, we may even freeze, unable to say or do anything.

The reality is that, despite our best intentions, when under stress, our biology runs away with us. There is a part of our brain, the amygdala, which when triggered by a perceived threat, hijacks the rational part of our brain. It is the amygdala that puts us into the survival responses of fight, flight, or freeze. When in this state, our responses to external events are often disproportionate, and expecting anyone in this state to be able to use the frameworks, strategies, and skills they possess is unrealistic.

This is one area where insights and lessons from martial arts can be helpful. The notion of amygdala hijack is not new to martial arts. It explains why many practitioners of martial arts are not able to execute their training when faced with assailants. In essence, the amygdala hijack causes them to lose their balance, first mental and consequently physical. This is also the experience of soldiers and security forces when involved in a firefight for the first time and mentally unprepared for the effects of the amygdala hijack.

Martial arts discipline offers us three ways to manage the amygdala hijack and regain your balance in a negotiation.

Action Plan—What You Can Do Differently Tomorrow

There are three components to managing the amygdala hijack and regaining your mental balance: regaining physical stability, activating the peripheral vision response, and engaging in tactical breathing. We will consider each in turn.

The first component is physical stability. It is well known that how we physically hold our bodies affects how we feel. If we are physically not stable, this can affect our mental center of gravity. We might feel off-balance or literally "on the back foot." In times like this, sitting and standing with both feet firmly on the floor, about shoulder-width apart, can help you regain your physical stability and can contribute to being internally centered.

The second component is activating the peripheral vision response. The human eye is geared toward two types of vision. The first, foveal vision, is a function of the cone cells. This is central vision, which gives you clarity, accuracy, and detail of vision. The second, peripheral vision, is a function of rod cells. Peripheral vision detects context and movement. When we are stressed, we tend to fixate on foveal vision, often leading to what is referred to as tunnel vision.

Going into peripheral vision activates the parasympathetic nervous system which, among other things, lowers blood pressure and relieves stress. Peripheral vision can be activated by first fixing one's attention (foveal vision) on a distant point (though in the context of a stressful event, one is likely to be in foveal vision already), then paying attention to movement in the environment—without moving the eyes. It takes some practice, and can be assisted by having a friend stand to the side and make hand movements. Once you get used to being able to see your surroundings without having to look directly at them, this tactic will become easier to call into use. The key in activating peripheral vision is to not worry about detail but to look for movement.

The third component is to engage in tactical breathing. It is a truism that in times of stress, we hold our breath. What air we have is usually situated in our upper lungs (thereby raising our mental center of gravity) and our sympathetic nervous system is activated as our body prepares to fight, flee, or freeze. This stoppage of breathing is easiest to deal with by simply going back to breathing—but in a very specific way. Rapid breaths in the upper part of the chest will lead to hyperventilation and exacerbate the problem. The breath that helps us regain our balance is diaphragmatic or belly breathing. This means breathing using as much of the lungs as possible, by taking a slow, steady, and deep breath and sinking that breath to a point just below your navel. The breath is then held for a period before slowly and steadily being released. A simple formula to follow is a four-count.

- Breathe in (4 counts)
- Hold (4 counts)
- Exhale (4 counts)

This diaphragmatic breathing lowers your mental center of gravity and grounds you. It will also invoke what Dr. Herbert Benson refers to as the relaxation response.

Done correctly, these components activate one's parasympathetic nervous system. This correlates with the brain entering into an "alpha" state. This internal state is referred to by some as being in the state of mindfulness, which is in turn characterized as being "in the moment," paying attention to the present (both internally and externally), a subjective slowing down of perceptual time, and a sense of calm. Put simply, it allows one to be the eye of the hurricane; to be calm even though there may be a maelstrom around you. And with this calm, we can respond to what is actually happening, as opposed to what we anticipate, perceive, or create in our minds. This then provides us the ability to select and engage in the tools and frameworks that we have learned and practiced.

Each of these components can be done both before and during an interaction. For example, before an anticipated challenging encounter, you can engage in one or more of these components to put yourself in an optimal state for the interaction.

And if, during an interaction, you feel the onset of an amygdala hijack, you can subtly engage in one or more of these components. "Subtly" is, of course, the key word! If you notice that you are not seated in a way that feels stable, straighten your posture and plant your feet firmly on the floor. If you find yourself experiencing tunnel vision or obsessing about details, shift to peripheral vision and look at the bigger picture. If you find yourself breathing shallowly and if it might not be convenient to engage in the four-count breathing, then just simply take slow, deep breaths.

As the saying goes, the time to learn how to swim should not be when one is drowning. The analogy holds true with dealing with the amygdala hijack. Practice each of the three components above until you are familiar with them and they become part of your unconscious competence so that they will be ready to be deployed when you need them.

Conclusion

The challenge when facing a stressing event during a negotiation is not that a solution does not exist or that a deal cannot be made. It is that the amygdala hijack makes it difficult to see anything other than the perceived threat. The irony, of course, is that one's response to the perceived threat may in itself trigger an amygdala hijack response in one's counterpart. We cannot help our biology, or our circumstances, or the actions of our counterpart. What we can do, however, is manage our responses to achieve the best outcome we can.

This Ties in With:

Jeglic & Jeglic, Ch. 29, Mental Health; Donohue, Ch. 38, Hostage

Section VIII

Working with Your Client

Working with your client often might be the most challenging part of any negotiation—and four chapters in Section VIII address that particular challenge.

Chapter 40 focuses on how to use psychology to address ethical challenges with your client specifically, and inside their organization. This is followed by Chapter 41, a trenchant analysis of agents' frequent failure to ensure that their clients have given informed consent to the agent's actions. Then in Chapter 42, we turn to the challenge of herding cats—or when your client has a "tribe" behind them that might upend any decision they make. And finally, in Chapter 43, we address the unique circumstances of using an interpreter in negotiations: An interpreter is neither a true neutral nor a client—and he or she needs to be *managed*.

40

The Psychology of Ethics in Negotiation

Jennifer K. Robbennolt[1] *and Jean R. Sternlight*[2]

Introduction

Negotiation is replete with ethical challenges. Attorney negotiators must decide how forthright they ought to be about their goals, limits, alternatives, and the value or nature of any goods or services being discussed. Attorneys also face ethical questions about the duties they owe their clients and whether to use particular negotiation tactics.

Failure to follow appropriate ethical rules can lead to significant adverse consequences for attorneys or those they represent, including mistrials, invalidated contracts, allegations of fraud, disbarment or

1. **Jennifer Robbennolt** (J.D., Ph.D.) is associate dean for research; Alice Curtis Campbell Professor of Law and Professor of Psychology; and co-director of the program on Law, Behavior, and Social Science at the University of Illinois. A leading scholar in psychology and law, torts, and dispute resolution, her research integrates psychology and empirical research methodology into the study of law and legal institutions. She is coauthor of several books, including *The Psychology of Tort Law*; *Psychology for Lawyers*; the textbook *Empirical Methods in Law*; and the influential casebook *Dispute Resolution and Lawyers*.

2. **Jean R. Sternlight** is the Michael and Sonja Saltman Professor of Law and also founding director of the Saltman Center for Conflict Resolution at the University of Nevada, Las Vegas Boyd School of Law. Frequently cited by courts and the media, Sternlight has written numerous books and articles. She was named Outstanding Scholar by the American Bar Association (ABA) Section on Dispute Resolution in 2015, and also awarded the 2015 Lifetime Achievement Award by the American College of Civil Trial Mediators. Sternlight received her B.A. (High Honors) from Swarthmore College, and her J.D. (*cum laude*) from Harvard Law School.

other sanctions, and ruined reputations or relationships. It is, therefore, critically important to understand the cognitive, situational, and social influences known as "bounded ethicality" that can lead well-meaning people to behave unethically. This chapter is based on J.K. ROBBENNOLT & J.R. STERNLIGHT, *Drawing on Psychology to Negotiate Ethically*, in 1 THE NEGOTIATOR'S DESK REFERENCE 503–514 (Honeyman & Schneider eds, 2017.) The full references in that chapter can be found at www.ndrweb.com/chapter-37--public.html.

Why This Concept Might Change Your Thinking

While some ethical misconduct is intentional, good intentions are not always sufficient to prevent ethical missteps. Understanding the powerful psychological forces that may undermine good intentions is critically important for attorneys.

First, attorneys may fail to notice the ethical aspects of a decision, diminishing the influence of ethical constraints. Decision makers, for example, tend to act less ethically in negotiations framed as competitive compared to those framed as cooperative, and when a decision is characterized as a business or legal decision rather than as an ethical decision. Attorneys tend to perceive their own questionable tactics as more acceptable when they are responsive to similar tactics believed to have been employed by the other side. Euphemisms (like "puffing") can also push ethics to the background. And ethics tend to be discounted when the potential harm is unobservable, occurs to an unidentifiable victim, or is removed in time.

Second, attorneys are expert at rationalizing or justifying unethical behavior. Common excuses include "everybody does it," "the rules allow it," or "it's for a good cause." Believing that our perceptions of the world are objective; believing that we are more ethical than others; and paying particular attention to information that confirms our beliefs and preferences can make it easier to justify unethical behavior without realizing it. Frequent ambiguities in the rules or facts provide additional room for rationalization to occur and may permit attorneys to act unethically without sacrificing their positive self-image.

Third, while we tend to predict we will act ethically, expecting to behave as our "ideal" selves, real-world pressures such as time constraints, financial pressures, the prospect of suffering a loss, and fatigue can impact our decision-making in the moment. This disconnect between predictions and practicalities can make it hard to regulate our conduct because we fail to recognize the power of immediate concerns to distort our ethical perceptions.

Finally, a host of social factors can influence negotiator ethics. Attorneys are affected by their perceptions of how ethically their peers negotiate. Pressures exercised by billing partners can be strong. And negotiating as an agent on behalf of a client can impact ethics, as people tend to be more likely to act unethically when the unethical behavior can benefit another person. It is also easier to endorse an unethical suggestion made by another, making it more likely that either attorney or client will accede to an unethical course of action suggested by the other.

Action Plan—What You Can Do Differently Tomorrow

One important way attorneys can protect themselves from inadvertent missteps is to become well versed in the psychology of ethics. Those attorney negotiators who understand, for example, that they are more likely to overstep ethical bounds when losses loom large, when they are feeling tired, when they believe an adversary is likely to take advantage, or when they are acting on behalf of someone else, may be less likely to slide down the slippery slope of ethical misconduct.

As well as gaining this knowledge, attorneys can take some specific affirmative steps to protect themselves. First, they can make ethics more salient, finding ways to remind themselves of ethical obligations and to put greater emphasis on ethical aspects of their decisions by deliberately instructing themselves to make ethics part of the analysis. Second, they can be deliberately self-critical regarding their own ethics, examining their rationalizations and consulting others who may provide insight. Yet it is also important to be humble about one's ability to assess one's own ethics, as those who are too confident about their own ethics are more likely to overstep bounds.

Third, attorney negotiators should try to anticipate ethical issues that will arise and plan how to handle them in an appropriate fashion. It is predictable that a seller will not want to reveal certain negative information about a product, property, or service, and it is predictable that a buyer may not want to reveal her complete business plan.

Negotiators should think ahead about how to handle these and other dilemmas so that they will more likely be governed by their ideal selves than by pressures of the moment.

Fourth, when attorneys are part of an organization (law firm, company, or government agency) they should be prepared to recognize and confront others' unethical negotiation conduct. We can only resist social psychological phenomena if we are willing and able to call out our colleagues, clients, and even supervisors on potential ethical errors. It is possible to alert others diplomatically to such issues rather than engaging in nasty confrontations. For example, one might ask a coworker or a boss whether they are sure it is acceptable not to disclose certain information, or one might raise a question as to whether a client, negotiation counterpart, or regulator might take issue with a particular statement.

Finally, remember that the framing of issues and the language used in communicating with clients, colleagues, and adversaries are important. Refer directly to the requirements of relevant rules or statutes. One is more likely to make ethical decisions when it is clear that issues have ethical dimensions. It can be equally important to focus on colleagues' and counterparts' language. One must be careful, for example, not to let a colleague's euphemisms or a counterpart's self-serving language cause one to slide down an ethical slippery slope.

When attorney negotiators work within organizations, including businesses, government agencies, and law firms, these organizations can have a big impact on negotiators' ethicality, both for the better and for the worse. The ethical culture of an organization has an important impact on how ethically members of that group behave. But the ethical culture of the entity depends not only on its expressed ethical policies, but also more broadly on its systems and practices. Thus, legal organizations that want to promote ethical negotiation behavior should promote discussions of negotiation ethics, including by their respected leaders. The organizations should encourage attorneys to negotiate ethically, not primarily for instrumental reasons (for example, not getting caught), but out of concern for others, shared values, or a sense of broader justice. Setting out these more positive goals has been shown to be more effective in encouraging ethical behavior.

Legal organizations should also take action to encourage ethical negotiation. First, they should educate their attorneys about ethics, and particularly about the psychological factors that inform decision-making. Second, such organizations should encourage their attorneys to learn from their mistakes. Those who approach mistakes with a growth mindset rather than a fixed mindset are more likely to learn and improve. Third, organizations need to take what steps they can to protect their attorneys from cognitive, temporal, and financial stresses. If a legal organization can ensure its attorneys are better rested, better fed, and less stressed, it will be less likely to suffer the consequences of unethical negotiation. Fourth, legal organizations should try to reward ethical negotiation behavior. The attorney who shares information appropriately should be praised rather than vilified. Finally, such organizations should monitor their negotiators' ethics and encourage ethical reporting by attorneys themselves and by others who interact with them. It is virtually inevitable that attorney negotiators will sometimes cross ethical lines, but if organizations take balanced steps to monitor behavior and discourage misconduct, they are more likely to ensure that their negotiators behave ethically.

Conclusion

Psychological forces inevitably put attorney negotiators on an ethical precipice—always in danger of crossing lines and violating rules and standards. But if attorneys familiarize themselves with these pressures, they can act individually and through their firms, businesses, and government agencies to protect themselves against inadvertent missteps. It is important to plan in advance, before major mistakes are made that may lead to serious negative consequences for attorneys and their clients and organizations.

This Ties in With:

Schneider et al., Ch. 24, Reputation; Hinshaw, Ch. 25, Ethics; Welsh, Ch. 26, Fairness

41

Lawyers, Clients, and Informed Consent

Jacqueline Nolan-Haley[1]

Introduction

How can you, the negotiator, ensure that your client is really onboard? How can a client ensure that her lawyer serves her interests at the bargaining table? How can she prevent exploitation or guarantee that a durable agreement is reached? Lawyers will not only better serve their clients but reach better, more lasting agreements by paying more attention to informed consent before and again at intervals during negotiation, and then taking care to reaffirm consent as the process reaches agreement. The purpose of this chapter is to sketch a framework for informed consent between lawyers and clients that is based on a deliberative counseling process. It is based on J. NOLAN-HALEY, *Agents and Informed Consent: After the 2008 Financial Crisis,* in

1. **Jacqueline Nolan-Haley** is a Professor at Fordham University School of Law, where she directs the Conflict Resolution and ADR Program. She teaches courses in alternative dispute resolution (ADR), mediation, international and interethnic conflict resolution, and Catholic perspectives on conflict at Fordham Law School and in its Queen's University Belfast and University Dublin Summer Program. Her scholarship focuses on ethical and justice issues related to ADR. Her books include *International Conflict Resolution: Consensual ADR Processes* (coauthor), *Alternative Dispute Resolution in a Nutshell*, 4th ed., and *Global Issues in Mediation* (coauthor, forthcoming). She consults on several public policy projects and is former chair of the Alternative Dispute Resolution Section of the Association of American Law Schools and the New York State Bar Association Dispute Resolution Committee.

2 The Negotiator's Desk Reference 431–438 (Honeyman & Schneider eds, 2017). The full references in that chapter can be found at www.ndrweb.com/chapter-80--public.html.

Why This Concept Might Change Your Thinking

When lawyers negotiate for their clients, informed consent matters. It is the foundational moral and ethical principle that promotes respect for individual self-determination and honors human dignity. In representative negotiations, the principle of informed consent is not an end in itself, but is a means of achieving the fundamental goal of fairness. Fairness requires that clients know what they are doing when they authorize lawyers to negotiate for them, that they understand the decision-making process, including their right to withdraw consent and discontinue negotiations, and that they understand the outcome reached in negotiation. Toward this end, the principle of informed consent protects the psychological and legal interests associated with the values of autonomy, human dignity, and efficiency.

Beyond these aspirational goals, the principle of informed consent has enormous practical significance. Consent is critical to the long-term durability of agreements that lawyers negotiate on behalf of clients. When a court finds that valid consent is suspect or missing from a negotiated agreement, its life span is short-lived. Informed consent also has potential to address principal-agent tensions in negotiation, which, if not managed, may present a barrier to settlement.

Action Plan—What You Can Do Differently Tomorrow

How do lawyers gain their clients' informed consent in representative negotiations? The short answer is, through a *robust deliberative counseling process* with their clients.

As a matter of general principle, informed consent is an operative rule in legal negotiations. The "law of negotiation" provides remedies and imposes penalties where consent is obtained improperly in negotiation, whether through fraud, coercion, duress, or the like. But the question of *how* informed consent operates in representative negotiation settings is an empirical issue about which we know very little. How is disclosure provided? What counts as consent?

The foundational analysis of an informed consent principle in the lawyer-client relationship is rooted in the lawyer's professional obligation to inform clients of relevant information and in the client's autonomy interest in participatory decision-making.

The informed consent obligations of lawyers acting as agents for clients in negotiations are found in the professional responsibility rules for the legal profession. While the rules provide some conceptual support for the principle of informed consent, they offer little practical guidance to lawyers on how informed consent should operate. The informational requirements for lawyers in Model Rule 1.4, though not as extensive as those imposed upon physicians under tort law, demonstrate a clear mandate for disclosure. Lawyers are required to "explain a matter to the extent reasonably necessary to permit the client to make informed decisions regarding the representation." Regulation of client "consent" rights, on the other hand, is somewhat murky. Model Rule 1.2(a), which governs the allocation of decision-making power in the attorney-client relationship, establishes in effect an "ends/means" approach, in which the client decides the "ends" of a given problem, i.e., whether to accept a particular settlement offer, and the attorney decides the "means." The inherent complexity of determining what constitutes real ends and means has made it difficult to integrate this distinction in legal practice.

In a world of perfect informed consent practice, the transfer of authority from the client to the lawyer would be a relatively straightforward matter. Clients would understand their positions and the underlying interests that support them as well as the opposing party's underlying interests. They would also understand the range of possible agreements and their best alternative to a negotiated agreement (BATNA). Likewise, lawyers would understand their own interests and where they might not be aligned with those of their clients. They would inform clients of their divergent interests, clarify the extent of their authority, and determine whether there were any nonnegotiable issues. Clients and lawyers would then discuss all these issues, clients would grant authority to lawyers, and negotiations would proceed.

In the real world, the informed consent process is a much more complicated project. Enter the human factor—the emotions, psychological biases, and different behavioral orientations that affect clients *and* lawyers, and influence the agendas of both. Mere discussion between clients and lawyers will be unlikely to create an understanding of the client and the lawyer's respective divergent interests.

Much more deliberation is required for the kind of understanding between clients and lawyers that will result in integrative agreements that truly satisfy a client's interests.

Deliberation honors the reasoning power of clients and lawyers. In the give and take of argument and debate, lawyers and clients gain a better understanding of each other's views. The deliberative process calls for careful calculation and reasoned dialogue. It is a reflective activity that requires active participation by client and lawyer. The heart of the deliberative process is the exchange of ideas and debate between client and lawyer about ends and means, goals and strategies.

Too often, representative negotiations are not preceded by any meaningful deliberation between lawyers and clients. Lawyers do not truly listen to their clients, but often *presume* to know their goals. The methodology of deliberation can improve representative negotiations and foster mutual respect between lawyers and clients. Frank discussions between lawyer and client about the relative merits of courses of action can go a long way toward achieving participatory and educated client decision-making, the hallmarks of the informed consent doctrine. Imagine the good that might have been accomplished if Wall Street and major bank lawyers had engaged in a deliberative counseling process when negotiating for their clients before the global financial crisis in 2008.

Modifiers, Caveats, and No-Go Areas—When This Advice Just Won't Apply

There are two contexts where future research is necessary to determine the relevance of this advice: multiparty negotiations and culture. First, given how little we know about the operational aspects of informed consent in bilateral, representative negotiations, we know even less about how it functions in multiparty negotiations, where the presence of coalitions and shifting nature of BATNAs add layers of complexity to the negotiation process. Whether the framework for a deliberative informed consent process that I have sketched has any traction in the multiparty setting is an empirical question that must take into account two separate issues: (1) the process of identifying the stakeholders whose consent must be obtained, and (2) the process that occurs in the shadow or back-table negotiations that authorize and give legitimacy to representative agents.

The second context that requires further research relates to culture. In considering the state of our knowledge about informed consent practice in representative negotiations, we need to learn more about its cultural content. What are the functional equivalents of informed consent, if any, in other cultures, and how do they operate? Norms and expectations about informed consent are not universal. We know that as a general matter, not all cultures share the West's reverence for the principle of informed consent or the values that it honors. What implications does this have on representative negotiations in the international arena?

Conclusion

I have suggested that a deliberative informed consent process is an asset in representative negotiations, particularly when lawyers negotiate as agents for clients. The values honored by informed consent, as well as its practical benefits, can be helpful in managing principal-agent tensions that can act as barriers to the negotiated resolution of disputes. The exchange of ideas and debate between lawyers and clients about ends and means, goals and strategies, enhances understanding of each other's interests and contributes to integrative agreements. The extent to which the deliberative informed consent model would work in other contexts, including multiparty negotiations and different cultural settings, raises empirical questions waiting for answers.

This Ties in With:

Wade, Ch. 42, Limited Authority

42

Limited Authority to Settle

John Wade[1]

Introduction

It is rare for an individual present at a negotiation or mediation to have unlimited authority to settle or make decisions. Even the most rugged individualist usually has someone looking over his or her shoulder. People in the background, sometimes in the shadows, can be described as supporters, influencers, bosses, stakeholders, or constituents. Here, "the tribe" will often be used. This chapter is based on J. WADE, *Shadow of the Tribe,* in 2 THE NEGOTIATOR'S DESK REFERENCE 397–411 (Honeyman & Schneider eds, 2017). The full references in that chapter can be found at www.ndrweb.com/chapter-78--public.html.

Why This Concept Might Change Your Thinking

There are three forms of authority to agree: legal, persuasive, and "reasonable outcome" authority. Most negotiators have authority

1. **John Wade** is an emeritus professor of law of Bond University, Queensland, Australia. He practiced as a lawyer in Australia between 1987 and 2012, and also had an active mediation practice in organizational, family, and commercial conflicts during those years. He has taught over 300 mediation and negotiation courses in Hong Kong, New Zealand, London, Canada, the U.S., and Australia. John has published over 100 books and articles. His teaching awards include best law teacher at Sydney University (1989); at Bond University (1990); and in Australia (1998). John now lives in Vancouver, Canada, with his growing family, and he teaches intensive negotiation courses there.

and willingness to settle as long as the agreement provides a good or a reasonable outcome that will placate the various members and factions in their tribe. But if any outcome is emerging or imminent outside those vague criteria, then their legal authority, moral willingness, and nerve tends to wobble or fade away. Thus for most negotiators, the accurate answer to the question "Do you have the authority to settle this dispute?" is "yes and no"; or "it depends"; or "I do have authority, but I will tell you later if I have willingness."

Distinguishing between these types can alert you to impending trouble: First, with *legal* authority, someone can "bind" others because she has signing rights for a club, a partnership, or a corporation, or for some other group. Or an individual may have *persuasive* authority—the ability, demonstrated by history and moral courage, to convince the various factions within a tribe to comply and cooperate.

Action Plan—What You Can Do Differently Tomorrow

Two vital tasks for any negotiator are to identify who the influential outsiders/constituents/tribal members are behind each visible negotiator and how these influential outsiders can be managed/included/excluded. Standard questions during preparation documentation, telephone calls, and private meetings with each of the parties—including her own client—can reveal key tribal members. Such questions include:

- "If you reach an agreement that is less favorable than you hoped for, is there anyone in the background who might be critical of you?"
- "Are there any important people in the shadows to whom you will need to sell the outcome of the mediation?"
- "Do either of you have armchair critics or constituents who are looking over your shoulders?"

Despite such tactful investigation, a negotiator may not be told until the fateful request to make a phone call at the end of the negotiation. Likewise, many parties who have assured everyone that they have full authority to settle have taken the negotiated agreement back to their constituent organizations and been torn to shreds by bitterly disappointed hawks.

When key tribal members are identified (or suspected), set out below are 13 standard responses. All have advantages and disadvantages.

1. Refuse to Negotiate

You might refuse to negotiate or mediate. This may lead to further conflicts or litigation, or subsequent lying about authority to settle. Yet it can also cause emergence of the influencers from the shadows.

2. Adjourn Until Authority Figures Are Present

One or more disputants may refuse to negotiate or mediate on major questions unless and until key authority figures are "present" (in person or on the phone.) In many conflicts, such brinkmanship is futile, as those with persuasive or legal power are too many, too distant, too expensive or too busy to appear. Nevertheless, many mediations and negotiations are organized creatively to enable:

- an auditorium of constituents and families to be present, witness, speak, and vote;
- a CEO from overseas to be present via teleconferencing or telephone; and
- travel of key family or board members to an all-day (and sometimes all-night) meeting in a convenient central location.

3. Carry On Regardless

The third response to absence of complete authority to settle is to say nothing and continue. The risk is that many negotiations stumble and fail due to the influence of hovering armchair critics.

4. Normalize

The mediator or negotiator can give "normalizing" speeches. The aim is to convince one of the disputants that the need for outside ratification is culturally normal; is not devious; is not normally part of a good cop/bad cop negotiation tactic (though it could be that!); that competent negotiators do not fuss over this procedural step; and that progress can be made despite the need for outside approval.

5. Ask Ritualistic "Authority" Question

The negotiator can ask ritualistically, "do you have authority to settle this dispute?"—in advance writings or at a meeting. A mumbled "yes" may suggest a lie or more complex motives. A more correct answer could be, "Yes, I have complete authority to settle this dispute so long as the outcome is fair/reasonable/in the range. . ."

But in certain cultural groups, the influence of community opinion is very strong. For example, extensive consultation is normally necessary when negotiating with most Malaysian, Arab, Aboriginal, and Japanese organizations. In such cultures, the question "Do you have authority to settle?" is itself an absurdity and an embarrassing sign of the questioner's ignorance.

6. Insist on Written Authority to Settle within Subjective Range or Objective Range of "Fairness"

A negotiator may insist that disputants produce a written (and irrevocable) authority to settle. This step may appear to provide more certainty. In reality, those who draft such written authorities know that they provide little certainty.

7. Agree to Use Best Efforts

You could negotiate for the agent to use her best endeavors to sell the outcome to the constituents. This option may seem weak. However, the writer and other colleagues have used it successfully on a variety of occasions. The negotiators can usually be persuaded to agree orally or in writing as follows: "If we reach an agreement after working hard through a range of possibilities, we will unanimously report back to *X* about the issues and options and will unanimously and enthusiastically recommend the outcome we reach as satisfactory, workable, and the best option available. We will endeavor to 'sell' the outcome to our constituents."

8. Opinion from an Evaluative Mediator or Expert

Hiring an evaluative mediator respected in the relevant field, and/or bringing an expert as an observer and commentator, also have their moments. At the end of the mediation or negotiation, the expert and/or evaluative mediator then writes a note on her letterhead for the middle managers or agents to take back to head office or to their constituents.

9. Consult with the Outside Authority or Influence before the Negotiation

Consulting with an influential outsider *before* the joint sessions begin is an approach the writer has used as a mediator for over a decade, in many disputes. The process now has a routine, described in the above-noted chapter in *The Negotiator's Desk Reference*, but not here for space reasons.

10. Consult with Outside Influences before the Negotiation and Arrange Decision-Making Process

You might insist upon and organize a decision rule within each group of constituents. Groups can decide to make decisions by majority of members, majority of a class, weighted voting based on seniority, etc. During preparation for mediation *between* parties, you might facilitate discussions *within* each of the parties' tribes on the key question—"By what process will the group make a decision?"

You can also offer to help each group develop its answer, offering a range of ways used elsewhere. And writing down and publicizing the resulting rule for each group helps discourage later reneging. It also encourages negotiators, who can see that the decision-rules may be a way of controlling hawks on their own team, or on the opposition's team. Without a visible decision rule in place, a skilled hawk can exploit the inevitable post-recommendation or post-settlement regrets within a group and organize rejection of almost any negotiated or recommended agreement.

11. Explain Settlement and Progress to Outside Authorities before Anyone Else

This can complement the previous two responses. After each session, the mediator or *designated negotiator* strives to report to the influential constituents *before* (or at the same time as) their own representative negotiators do so. This enables the representatives to build upon the designated negotiator's report and reduces the representative's onus of reporting, disappointing, defending, and blaming.

12. Warn of Dangers of Reneging—"What If . . . ?"

Negotiators usually have a range of phrases to exhort disputants to perform their agreements, despite pressures from outsiders to renege. These can help prepare the disputants for such pressures and give them a practiced repertoire of language when placed under such pressures to renege.

13. Throw Tantrum

This high-risk option involves a negotiator expressing strong and theatrical disapproval when one party suddenly suggests that he needs to consult with an influential outsider. This confrontation would normally take place in a private meeting. The brow-beating mediator or lead negotiator has the goal of pressuring the wavering negotiator into signing immediately rather than passing responsibility to outsiders.

Conclusion

Obviously, each response above has advantages and disadvantages. But together they can help a lawyer add value to negotiations. First, question strategically in order to identify any influential outsiders; second, pose a neutral problem-solving question (for example, "how to respond to influential outsiders?"); and third, be aware of and, if possible practiced in, the thirteen responses to this question.

This Ties in With:

Borbély & Caputo, Ch. 44, Organizations; Amsler, Ch. 45, DSD

43

What Lawyers Should Know about the Friendly Interpreter

Sanda Kaufman[1]

Introduction

Language is the currency of negotiations. The many prescriptions for ensuring mutual understanding indicate its centrality. Lawyers don't have to go abroad to encounter clients with weak or no English skills. Having interpreted in various contexts including courts, the author describes how interpreters ply their trade. They are effectively interveners with a broad berth, since parties don't fully understand each other's language (or they would not need interpreters). The better they are, the more innocuous their presence. Lawyers should be aware of interpreters' impact in specific situations, to avoid loss of control in the relationship with their clients and with opponents. This chapter is based on S. KAUFMAN *The Interpreter as Intervener*, in 2 THE NEGOTIATOR'S DESK REFERENCE 725–742 (Honeyman &

1. **Sanda Kaufman** is Professor of Planning, Public Policy, and Administration at Cleveland State University's Levin College of Urban Affairs. Her research spans negotiations and intervention in environmental and other public conflicts; social-environmental systems resilience; decision analysis; program evaluation; and negotiation pedagogy. Her articles have appeared in *Journal of Conflict Resolution*, *Negotiation Journal*, *Conflict Resolution Quarterly*, *International Journal for Conflict Management*, *Negotiation and Conflict Management Research*, *Revue Négociations*, and others. B.Arch. and M.S. in Planning, Technion; Ph.D. in Public Policy Analysis, Carnegie Mellon University.

Schneider eds, 2017). The full references in that chapter can be found at www.ndrweb.com/chapter-100--public.html.

Why This Concept Might Change Your Thinking

The chapter discusses two client-interpreter arrangements: a mediator-like role, with one interpreter for all, and an agent-like role, with one interpreter for each party. Neither analogy is perfect. Some key similarities and differences: interpreters have no control over, formal responsibility for, or input in the negotiation process; they do have some power over the content. Like mediators, interpreters are expected to be neutral. Like agents, they may have indirect input in the content of negotiations; however, their fiduciary relationship is partial, as is recognition of this relationship. Unlike agents, clients have weak control over interpreters and little ability to evaluate their work.

When only one (English-language) interpreter is present, his or her native tongue may be English (with the second language learned) or vice versa. With two interpreters, each usually translates into his or her native language, in which speaking skills and vocabulary tend to be stronger.

These observations address direct negotiations among disputants. But lawyers may need interpretation to work with their own clients, as well as to negotiate with someone else's lawyer. In the first instance, interpreters tend to act mediator-like, ensuring understanding between lawyer and client who are on the same team. In the second instance, each lawyer may/should bring their own—agent-like—interpreter. The interpreters may check each other's accuracy, and warn their clients if they believe the sense of their words got distorted through translation, whether intentionally or not. Still, mistakes can happen.

All the cautions regarding work with counterparts from different cultures than one's own apply to situations necessitating interpretation. In fact, at times the interpreters help others understand the other culture, including nonverbal communication. Nevertheless, it's possible that the interpreter might wish to help one of the parties by selectively translating or altering the meaning of communications, especially in situations where that party might incur serious consequences (e.g., jail time or high monetary penalties). There is no general cure for this risk. Thorough preparation, including some independently acquired understanding of the other party's culture, may partially mitigate it.

When negotiating electronically, texts can be translated more or less accurately, with the advantage of asynchronous exchanges. However, difficulties derive from the very nature of electronic communications (lacking visual and auditory clues), exacerbated by the possibility that translations miss nuances a native speaker gleans from original texts. Such mishaps have happened in the distant and recent past with serious consequences, when communicating through (translated) letters.

And at this point we cannot yet dispense with interpreters. The computer translators have yet to reach the quality and precision necessary for negotiations.

Action Plan—What You Can Do Differently Tomorrow

Interpreters work with our words, the very vehicle through which we negotiate. Therefore, they affect the dynamics and outcomes of cross-language negotiations. Whether intentionally for their own purposes or inadvertently, they can alter nuances, tone, emotions, and even the content of arguments. They can add to, or subtract from, offers, threats, and promises, in ways that hinge on skill, values, identities, and sometimes interests. Moreover, negotiators can exert only limited control over interpreters, who tend to be more responsive to their professional peers' evaluations, philosophies, and ethics codes than to the parties. What is a lawyer to do?

To begin, understanding the nature of interpretation, what we can and cannot expect from it, and some dangers inherent in the activity helps mitigate some of the risks. For example, avoid seeing interpreters as akin to a neutral, mechanical service; recognize instead their centrality to negotiations. This calls for investing scrutiny in the selection of interpreters commensurate with their potential impact on process and outcomes. Can you trust the interpreter in either the mediator-like or agent-like role? An existing working relationship, a trusted recommendation, or a reputable firm offering the service helps increase our level of confidence.

Next, lawyers should seek to enhance the level of control they can have on the quality and neutrality of interpreters. This can be achieved in several ways. For example, when stakes are high, having bilingual observers present or securing an extra, machine-translated version of what is being said—however limited in quality—can provide a measure of control and even increased accuracy, given interpreters' sensitivity to peer opinions.

Preparation is routinely recommended for negotiation, and this applies here, too. Lawyers needing interpreters may want to prepare by meeting with them before the negotiations begin, to discuss expectations, process, ways of enhancing precision and reducing ambiguities, and any concerns with the agency aspects of the relationship. For example, lawyers and their interpreters need to agree on the length of time anyone can speak before stopping for the interpreter to translate, unless the service is provided simultaneously through headphones. Lawyers and interpreters should also agree on signals to be used when the interpreter is unsure of the meaning of an important word, or when he or she needs a break for any other reason; interpreting, especially in high-stakes situations, can be very taxing. And when each lawyer brings her own interpreter—as in many international negotiations—this can further exacerbate the management challenges.

Depending on their trust level, lawyers may or may not disclose to interpreters whether they understand the others' language or to what extent. Simultaneous translations have some downsides in this respect: not only do they leave no room for fixing errors in real time, resist oversight by the means mentioned, and distract from watching the counterparts' nonverbal cues; they also reduce the possibility for those who understand the other language to use the slack time to think about how to respond. For repeated encounters, lawyers and their interpreters should debrief each session, to fine-tune the process and check for any misunderstandings that could not be ironed out in real time. If uncomfortable with service quality or unable to develop a relationship of trust in their agency, lawyers should not hesitate to seek other interpreters, even midstream.

It is important to know that anyone with a level of familiarity with the second language has an advantage: the interpreter can be checked and will not know to what extent the lawyer actually understands the communications without his or her help. Even in such situations, interpretation services are useful to ensure the precision necessary in court or in the shadow of the law. They also secure more strategizing time in the moment (while the interpreter translates words already understood). Note that this advantage usually belongs to the non-English speakers: many foreigners are quite able to understand English, while native English speakers are more seldom conversant in other languages.

Modifiers, Caveats, and No-Go Areas—When This Advice Just Won't Apply

In language interpretation, factors including gender, race, or other personal traits important in social interactions (such as negotiations) play little role because interpreters, especially good ones, are almost invisible to the negotiating parties. They quickly become voices difficult to distinguish from the parties on whose behalf they speak. And their service is better delivered when their personal traits are not salient to negotiators. In fact, interpreters needn't be in the negotiation room at all; their voices can come through headphones. Much like mediators, interpreters are valued most when they work with subtlety.

Computer software is the ultimate unobtrusive, unbiased means of translating documents and conversations. However, despite all the precautions necessary when using interpreters, for the moment, it remains more perilous to use machine translations. Words missing from the data bank (and therefore not translated) might make a real difference in negotiations. Colloquialisms are increasingly but still insufficiently incorporated in software, giving rise to text that would be comical were it not for the perils it poses for negotiations. (We have all attempted—and failed—to understand machine-translated user instructions for various devices, while Facebook's English translations from other languages are sometimes as opaque to the reader as the original language.) Although it has advanced considerably and continues to make progress, machine translation remains helpful mostly to those with a *good* existing grasp of both languages involved. They can identify misinterpreted terms (especially when part of an expression that means something else than its components), colloquialisms, and the strength and double meaning of some words, which differs between languages. Translation software still has some way to go to equal even an average human interpreter.

Conclusion

Words have both power and weaknesses as vehicles for mutual understanding, and as barriers to it. People doggedly pursue their own interests rather than the words that represent them, so no unifying words can bridge real and persistent differences. Interpreters can only do so much.

This Ties in With:

Nolan-Haley, Ch. 41, Agents; Mayer, Ch. 48, Allies

Section IX

Groups and Third Parties

Section IX expands the number of people we must consider as part of the negotiation. Chapter 44 addresses how organizations can improve their overall negotiation performance by managing it strategically, with consistent training, incentives, communication, and support. Chapter 45 analyzes the larger, systematic context in which a negotiation takes place, and shows why lawyers must remain alert to the potential for systemic injustice to be perpetuated by their actions. Chapters 46 and 47 focus on mediation: A general overview of mediation's uses is followed by a chapter analyzing why one mediator is frequently so different from another, and what you might need to watch out for. Mediators, however, are not the only outside people who might become useful in a difficult conflict. Chapter 48 analyzes a whole series of non-neutral (and yet, not classically "agent") roles, under the general heading of *allies* who might be usefully invoked by a party.

44

Organizational Factors in Negotiation

Adrian Borbély[1] *and Andrea Caputo*[2]

Introduction

Lawyers do not negotiate in a vacuum. This is even truer when their clients, especially public or private organizations, are repeat players in contracts and/or disputes. In these situations, the negotiator is embedded in a context that includes other, parallel negotiations, as well as the organizational landscape at both management and strategic levels. The negotiator cannot be truly effective if these

1. **Adrian Borbély** is a mediator, negotiation consultant, and teacher in France. He was previously Assistant Professor in International Negotiation at IESEG School of Management in Paris. A litigation lawyer by training, he also holds a master's degree in public affairs from Indiana University and a Ph.D. in management from ESSEC Business School. His interests include the promotion of negotiated dispute resolution within organizations, lawyer-client relationships, and the interplay between negotiation, management, and corporate strategy. He also pursues the development of innovative teaching tools, such as real-life negotiation cases and a problem-based approach of negotiation teaching.
2. **Andrea Caputo** is a Reader in Strategy & Entrepreneurship at the Lincoln International Business School in the United Kingdom. After earning his Ph.D. in management at the Tor Vergata School of Economics in Rome, Italy, he served as Assistant Professor of Business Administration at Princess Sumaya University of Technology in Amman, Jordan. He is a visiting professor at the University of Alicante and at the University of Malta. His research relates to negotiation, decision-making, entrepreneurship, and strategic management. In 2018, he co-founded with other academics the UNESCO Chair in Responsible Foresight for Sustainable Development and the Lincoln Innovation in Family Enterprises Observatory at the University of Lincoln. He is also an active management consultant and negotiator.

factors go unconsidered. We propose to approach negotiation from an organizational engineering perspective and through a four-lens framework, with varying focal distances, to cast light on the full complexity of negotiation. This chapter is based on A. Borbély & A. Caputo, *The Organization as Negotiator*, in 2 The Negotiator's Desk Reference 227–238 (Honeyman & Schneider eds, 2017). The full references in that chapter can be found at www.ndrweb.com/chapter-67--public.html.

Why This Concept Might Change Your Thinking

When one considers negotiation, one generally thinks of what happens at the table between two or more parties (lens 1). For the negotiation strategist, this is at best a partial perspective. Three additional perspectives can be added, in growing order of focal distance.

First, separate negotiations may influence one another through "linkages" (lens 2), a concept borrowed from Larry Crump. For example, how a lawyer gets along with her client necessarily impacts her ability to negotiate the dispute's resolution with her counterpart. Or when concurrently negotiating with two possible suppliers, each *negotiation* may serve as the best alternative (read: benchmark) to the other one. So, to harvest all value, we should not look only at one negotiation at a time, but at the entire field of negotiations: a "control tower" view, capturing all relevant movements at once, is advisable.

Furthermore, within an organization (the client or the law firm), negotiation activities can be subjected to some form of management (lens 3). Some organizations provide negotiators with structures to share their experience among peers or with their hierarchy. Management control of negotiation activities may be stringent. There may also be *processes* to ensure that operational managers brief lawyers in good time (before negotiation efforts become useless) and feed them with all necessary information to make informed decisions at the negotiation table. In other words, there exist management mechanisms to foster negotiators' efficiency as well as hinder it.

Managing negotiation is one thing; aligning negotiation efforts with the organization's strategy is another (lens 4). This is true within both law firms and their clients. When given a negotiation assignment, the negotiator (corporate counsel or independent attorney) may not be fully aware of the strategic ramifications of her task.

These may not be discussed explicitly. Lawyers may want to check with their clients that the negotiation strategy they are about to put into motion truly fits with the client's strategic objectives.

When thinking about negotiation, such a wider perspective may increase situational awareness and efficiency at various negotiation tables. Most importantly, it casts "management" as a key addition in a negotiation (management as the function, not the persons). In other words, negotiation is not solely a negotiator's task; it can and should be *engineered* from an organizational perspective. As a general counsel or a managing partner at a law firm, you have levers to help your people negotiate better.

Action Plan—What You Can Do Differently Tomorrow

Here we suggest moving away from advising negotiators to focus our advice on the "negotiation engineer," the person charged with ensuring that the organization's negotiators are *all* put in the best possible position to achieve their objectives. This may be the general counsel, leading the legal team, or a senior partner in a law firm, or even the client organization's CEO. Suggested efforts at managing negotiation go along four separate lines: training, incentives alignment, support structures, and communication.

For people to be able to take a collective approach to a problem, a good first step is to train the whole group on the issue. It enables them to share the same vocabulary and conceptual frameworks on the topic, so that they can share ideas, exchange news about difficulties, and hypothesize possible remedies. This is true of every art and science, and it applies to negotiation, as well. We therefore support in-house, tailor-made negotiation training efforts that include enough time to discuss the trainees' own cases and some form of collective coaching effort on negotiation.

Incentives have long been a question of interest in sales and purchasing, but much less for other negotiators, notably legal counsel. Here, we are talking about how to encourage lawyers, through rewards, to negotiate toward their client or boss's objectives. An organization that promotes negotiation should reward *and promote* its best negotiators—so that they deal with the most important cases.

Incentives raise two separate issues. First, what performance indicators to use. Do we solely focus on the negotiation's immediate result (e.g., the sum at the bottom of the document)? Conversely, factoring in less tangible elements, such as the quality of the parties' relationship, or of the lawyer-client relationship (read: client satisfaction), or the smoothness of the negotiation process, may lead negotiators to adapt their behavior in ways that may end up mattering even more than the supposedly sacrosanct "bottom line." Incentives need to be aligned with the goals set by the client. For example, should the client be better off without a settlement, why should legal counsel be negatively perceived for breaking off negotiations?

The second issue with incentives has to do with how to implement control. Most negotiations take place behind closed doors; hence, there is no direct control mechanism, and observers must rely on self-assessment reports, which may prove misleading. However, the simple idea that management control of some sort *will* be applied breaks the negotiator's isolation and invites productive discussions on the topic.

Management of negotiation activities is not only about control, it is foremost about support. When in charge of a case, it is important that lawyers feel they can get assistance from their peers, for example through periodic experience-sharing meetings and/or mentoring programs, using senior lawyers to coach more junior ones. This requires a work culture that supports curiosity and exchange (asking for external advice should not be perceived as weakness or incompetence). Collaboration among negotiators may lead to the creation of tailor-made negotiation tools, such as an in-house preparation checklist or case analysis framework.

Knowledge management may also serve to document past cases that can be used as reference for current negotiation efforts. We have, in the past, offered in our in-house trainings the possibility for participants to draft their own negotiation simulation based on past cases they have experienced. This has proven very useful in promoting knowledge exchange among members of the same legal team.

Finally, there lies the issue of communication. In order to ensure that negotiators do a good job, they need to hear about the overall strategy their actions are part of. This requires one-on-one discussions with their principal, where information flows freely. When a lawyer is simply being tossed a case in a folder, she cannot develop a full-fledged negotiation strategy. This also requires open discussions, within the client organization, to fully understand and be able to implement the organizational strategy. The client needs to *communicate* its full strategy and ensure (feedback loop) that the negotiator fully understands her mission.

In brief, negotiation may be managed, much like many other professional activities, and there exist many tools available to be tested internally or commissioned from external consultants. The objective is first to create a culture of negotiation within legal services and law firms where negotiators feel free to share and reflect together on their cases. Second, such a group may be piloted by being offered the right resources and appropriate leadership. The necessary changes may not be easy at first. But the long-term benefits can be substantial.

Modifiers, Caveats, and No-Go Areas—When This Advice Just Won't Apply

All this advice admittedly competes with the traditional idea that all negotiations are different. We reject the argument that since negotiations are not comparable, they cannot be subject to any form of management. Conversely, we believe that negotiation, like any other activity in a large organization, should be observed, controlled, and appropriately supported.

This is not to say, however, that negotiation should be standardized along strict lines: a negotiator is no robot, and should not be turned into one. Her discernment will remain a key success factor, and she needs to keep enough autonomy to address the unique factors in the situation at play.

Conclusion

Many otherwise successful organizations "leave money on the table" by failing to take fairly obvious precautions that would help ensure that their negotiations are not ad hoc, but instead take account of the organization's full strengths, background knowledge, and overall strategy. Ensuring consistent success at all the organization's negotiation is not a one-case-at-a-time matter. It should be a continuous and central aspect of *management*.

This Ties in With:

Wade, Ch. 42, Limited Authority; Amsler, Ch. 45, DSD

45

Negotiating Justice and Accountability in Dispute System Design

Lisa Blomgren Amsler[1]

Introduction

Negotiators, particularly *lawyers* as negotiators, have a unique responsibility to call attention to issues of justice and accountability arising out of the context within which they negotiate. To fulfill this responsibility, they need to understand the institutional context within which they work. Analyzing these contexts involves the field of dispute system design (DSD). Negotiators have an opportunity to take a system apart, critique it, and make the system more accountable. The Vatican and leaders of the Roman Catholic Church had systems in place to respond to claims that priests sexually abused

1. **Lisa Blomgren Amsler** (formerly Bingham) is Keller-Runden Professor of Public Service at Indiana University's O'Neill School of Public and Environmental Affairs, Bloomington, and Saltman Senior Scholar at the William S. Boyd School of Law, University of Nevada, Las Vegas. An elected fellow of the National Academy of Public Administration, Amsler received awards for empirical and doctrinal legal research from the American Bar Association (ABA) Section of Dispute Resolution, Association for Conflict Resolution, International Association for Conflict Management, American Society for Public Administration, and Labor and Employment Relations Association. Her research addresses dispute resolution, collaborative governance, public engagement, and dispute system design.

parishioners; but their systems suppressed claims and transferred offending priests from one parish to another. For years, lawyers negotiating for claimants accepted settlements that preserved those systems. Yet around the globe, other people have forced the Church to disclose those systems, proving that it can be done.

Lawyers as negotiators can incorporate performance measurement into DSD to provide accountability. Specifically, lawyers need to build in measures and transparency that will allow us to determine whether and how a system delivers some form of justice to those who participate in it. Accountability means this is a lawyer's job, regardless of role as negotiator, advocate, designer, or neutral, to determine when a system is structured and operates so as to produce injustice. This chapter is based on L. AMSLER, *The Negotiator's Role within a Dispute System Design: Justice and Accountability*, in 2 THE NEGOTIATOR'S DESK REFERENCE 249–264 (Honeyman & Schneider eds, 2017). The full references from that chapter can be found at www.ndrweb.com/chapter-69--public.html.

Why This Concept Might Change Your Thinking

Negotiators need to understand their context, whether they are working toward a particular policy through a city council's draft ordinance on which there is public engagement, or helping agencies, churches, and nongovernmental organizations (NGOs) negotiate their relative roles and jurisdictions in emergency management after a hurricane, or collaborating with local, state, and federal actors in negotiation over a terrorist hostage situation. Negotiators operate across the policy continuum: with government as a whole in its legislative, executive, or judicial role, or with individual agencies in their quasi-legislative, executive, or quasi-judicial capacities. Whether a lawyer represents a client as a lobbyist, or is an employee of an organization and acting as its agent in a network of other organizations, that context is part of a *system* for addressing conflict.

To analyze that system, lawyers need an analytic framework. The Analytic Framework for DSD, published in 2009 by Stephanie Smith and Janet Martinez and then expanded with me in 2015, asks you to consider these system elements: 1) goals, 2) stakeholders, 3) context and culture, 4) processes and structures, 5) resources, and 6) success and accountability. This concept may change your thinking about your responsibility and accountability to the broader public as you participate as a negotiator in our contractual, legal, judicial, and dispute resolution systems. As members of the bar, lawyers are responsible for moral professional conduct and compliance with the code of ethics. However, what if the code of ethics does not encompass justice in a negotiating context? Two elements of the Analytic Framework for DSD provide a lens for thinking about justice: goals and accountability. First, designers may set goals that encompass concepts of justice. Second, designers make themselves and the system accountable by evaluating its performance; for example, they have used measures of procedural and distributive justice to assess system performance.

Action Plan—What You Can Do Differently Tomorrow

People who design and manage DSDs should be accountable to the people who are participants in these conflict management systems. The capacity to analyze a DSD and judge its accountability to participants empowers a negotiator to broaden the nature of a principled negotiation by surfacing interests in the justice of the system. It also provides a new set of principles and norms related to procedural and distributive justice to bring to bear on resolving impasse.

Goals

As to goals, what form of *justice* does the system provide? The Catholic Church's Boston Archdiocese developed a system to intervene in an alleged case of sexual assault of a child by a priest as soon as parents reported it to the police, to negotiate a settlement with a confidentiality clause, and to suppress public knowledge of the event. It did not deliver retributive justice. Lawyers who participated in this system felt obliged to maintain confidentiality due to attorney-client privilege. This helped keep the system secret and not accountable.

Accountability

Accountability means the obligation or willingness to be responsible for one's actions; it means being called to account for one's actions to carry out the public will and the values it embodies. It is an instrument for a higher authority to exert control. There are three key elements: 1) information provided by the accountable party, 2) discussion between the accountable party and the oversight body, and 3) the consequences for the accountable party.

Justice as to Goals and Accountability

There are many definitions of justice, both in terms of process and outcome or means and ends. An oversimplified grouping of definitions includes justice related to outcomes, procedures, organizations, and communities. Justice related to outcomes includes distributive, substantive, utilitarian, and social justice. The field of dispute resolution has considered distributive justice in its dialogue about whether alternative dispute resolution (ADR) is "second-class justice." Distributive justice looks at who gets what as the outcome of a system. Differing distributive justice theories might contrast equal shares with equitable shares of a good, such as wealth. Distributive justice might provide ways to examine the pattern of outcomes or ends a DSD produces. For example, the U.S. Department of Justice's ADR program collected data on the use of ADR in litigation conducted by the Assistant U.S. Attorneys (AUSA) in their representation of federal agencies. Since the AUSAs represent the public and taxpayers, this raises a question of accountability. Is ADR second-class justice? One study compared samples of cases in which AUSAs used ADR to those using traditional litigation without ADR; researchers matched cases based on claim, subject matter, and district. They found no statistically significant difference in outcomes (awards as a proportion of the claim), suggesting ADR was not second-class justice.

Justice related to voice and control over processes includes procedural and organizational justice, reflected by one's ability to participate in a DSD, respectful and dignified treatment, and information. Procedural justice provides a way to examine how DSD produces its ends or outcomes, and to measure a system's performance. In the field of dispute resolution, researchers and program evaluators have used win-loss rates, outcome as a proportion of demand, satisfaction with process and outcome (procedural and distributive justice), time to disposition, interpersonal transformation, or willingness to use a system again or recommend it to others. While useful and practical performance measures, one might question whether they represent sufficient accountability to those who participate in the system.

Thinking about a system's accountability for justice can help a negotiator challenge the assumptions and rules that frame any negotiation. What about a DSD that produces systemic racism, as did governance in Ferguson, Missouri? The U.S. Department of Justice found Ferguson's police department disproportionately arrested people of color and lower income; Ferguson's municipal court then put those people in jail for contempt when they defaulted on paying a fine they could not afford. The pieces of the system together produced governance that violated the Fourteenth Amendment. A lawyer armed with that information can negotiate for a jailed client on entirely new terms, by challenging the legitimacy of the system in jailing their client in the first place.

In another example, a housing court of limited jurisdiction, negotiators can focus in on analyzing what happens in the courtroom as an action arena by examining participation, party roles, process or outcome function, outcomes, party control, transparency, and costs. Examining landlords' and tenants' relative power using these criteria can help a negotiator clarify what elements of the DSD to challenge based on justice and accountability. Can tenants collectively challenge the landlord? If there is an adhesive arbitration clause in the lease, they may not be able to. The arbitration clause may effectively privatize justice and oust the court of jurisdiction, deprive the individual litigant of choice of housing court over arbitration as an outcome function, and change the costs and benefits of challenging the landlord. If all the similarly situated tenants abandon their claims in fear of the costs of individual arbitrations, what does this mean about that system's justice? (Still, some lawyers have used the tactic of multiple individual arbitration cases to pressure the single respondent to negotiate, for example, representing many Uber drivers with similar claims.)

For a negotiator, such measures provide ways to quantify how the system functions. Lawyers have used quantitative studies of system patterns in discrimination cases, for example, in DSDs for grievances over employee discipline and evaluation. If the data reveal a race-based or gender-based pattern, this provides evidence; negotiators can use it to support a demand for the system to provide more accountability. This is leverage that changes the nature of the assumptions underlying the negotiation.

Modifiers, Caveats, and No-Go Areas— When This Advice Just Won't Apply

Analyzing a DSD and how it functions in relation to justice is a way of changing the subject of a negotiation and demanding accountability.

However, the DSD may be a product of a culture, or intentionally related to gender, or part of a self-defined community of faith or voluntary association. For example, criminal allegations that cross jurisdictional boundaries between a state and a sovereign Native American nation may be addressed using traditional justice systems within tribal boundaries. A sexual harassment claim might be subject to an employer's special complaint policy specifically adopted for these cases as a defense against condoning sexual harassment. Faith-based organizations may develop their own systems for domestic relations or business deals. Negotiators should analyze a DSD to determine whether or not to raise questions of justice and accountability given the underlying assumptions of these systems in the negotiation.

Conclusion

Lawyers negotiate not only in the shadow of the law, but also in the shadow of their client's best alternative to a negotiated agreement (BATNA), which may be court or arbitration or some other DSD. Lawyers as negotiators have both an important responsibility and unique capacity to call attention to issues of justice and accountability arising out of the context within which they negotiate.

This Ties in With:

Welsh, Ch. 26, Fairness; Zartman, Ch. 33, Process & Stages; Wade, Ch. 42, Limited Authority; Borbély & Caputo, Ch. 44, Organizations

46

Using Mediation for Advantage

Lela Love[1] *and Joseph Stulberg*[2]

Introduction

Using mediation well involves thoughtful analysis. You must know the client's interests; analyze the particular mediator's goals and practices; and match the client's objective to a suitable mediator. You must also devise negotiation strategies appropriate to your client's needs. Mediation is not a cookie-cutter process, but rather one with a range of possible goals, involving multiple mediator approaches. This chapter is based on L.P. LOVE & J.B. STULBERG, *The Uses of Mediation*, in 2 THE NEGOTIATOR'S DESK REFERENCE 671–681 (Honeyman &

1. **Lela Porter Love** is a professor of law and director of Cardozo Law School's (NYC) conflict resolution program. She is past chair of the American Bar Association (ABA) Section of Dispute Resolution, where she initiated the first International Mediation Leadership Summit in The Hague. In addition to numerous articles, her writing on mediation includes law school textbooks (coauthored with Carrie Menkel-Meadow and Andrea Schneider); *The Middle Voice: Mediating Conflict Successfully* (coauthored with Joseph Stulberg); *Stories Mediators Tell* (coedited with Eric Galton); and *Stories Mediators Tell—World Edition* (coedited with Glen Parker). She is an active mediator and trainer of mediators in the U.S. and abroad.

2. **Joseph B. ("Josh") Stulberg** is the Michael E. Moritz Chair in Alternative Dispute Resolution at Ohio State University Moritz College of Law. A former vice president of the American Arbitration Association in charge of its Community Dispute Services, Josh has mediated disputes of national significance, including Native American land claims, police-community group confrontations, and state budget negotiations; trained people to serve in court, agency-based, or community-based dispute resolution mediation programs; and published fifteen books and manuals and more than sixty-five articles on conflict resolution topics. He served as reporter for the Model Standards of Conduct for Mediators (2005).

Schneider eds, 2017). The full references in that chapter can be found at www.ndrweb.com/chapter-96--public.html.

Why This Concept Might Change Your Thinking

To choose the right sort of mediation, first understand the client's interests. What is the client's ideal outcome? In a landlord-tenant situation, does the tenant want to remain in her apartment? Then a good relationship between the parties might be a common interest—along with getting the appliances fixed. A mediator whose goals target understanding and problem-solving, as well as agreement, might be a good choice—i.e., a facilitative mediator. In an employment context, does the employee want to quit but maximize the dollars he receives? Then a mediator who's prepared to evaluate might serve better—an evaluative mediator.

Facilitative mediators can help broaden parties' thinking beyond the legal issues and help them work together toward consensus. For example, in a trust and estate matter, if your client wanted to resolve the dispute but also keep the family intact, you would want a mediator who facilitates discussion, so the parties might uncover all points of family tension, and one who sparks consensus building, to address all the issues raised. Such a mediation might be conducted in a joint session with active client participation—and attorneys assuming a counselor role. By contrast, in a situation involving sexual misconduct, where your client is not comfortable being in the same room with the perpetrator of her distress, you might want a mediator who primarily uses separate meetings and who might affirmatively suggest settlement terms—i.e., an evaluative mediator.

So, you need to find the right mediator. Moreover, your own attitude and skills required might differ in various types of mediation. In facilitative mediation, you need to help your client positively connect and influence the other side, since the party across the table, along with your client, is a decision-maker. In evaluative mediation, in addition to forging positive synergy with the other side, you must portray the story convincingly supported with sound legal analysis, since the mediator may make a persuasive recommendation toward the end of the mediation.

Action Plan—What You Can Do Differently Tomorrow

Client Interests

How do you uncover your client's interests? First, *talk* to your client, and not just about "the merits." What is their ideal resolution of the matter? What financial, religious, moral, or emotional considerations come into play? What relationship do they want with the other side?

Interests are the powerful movers behind what people want (their positions). Common interests include: recognition, reputation, survival, connection/affiliation, family, financial stability, control, freedom, fun. Positions constitute concrete ways to strengthen or advance one's interests. Commonly stated demands include, for example: "I want money (a specific amount)." "I want the person to apologize." "I want the person out of my life." Positions can be changed and still be acceptable so long as they secure or advance a client's interests.

Mediator Choice

Once you know your client's interests, the negotiating issues, and your client's range of acceptable proposals, you can pick a mediator.

You can start by asking lawyers you know what mediators they recommend and why. What made those mediators successful: Getting the deal done? Helping the parties to a better understanding? Eliciting a creative outcome? Have different "go-to" mediators, depending on their particular strengths and on what your client needs in the particular situation.

When narrowing your choices, you will study their background (usually it's on their website) and then interview (by telephone) your top choices. Some questions you might ask include:

- What training have you had? Was it in a "transformative" setting—where the goal of mediation is party empowerment and recognition? A facilitative school—where the goal of mediation is understanding, problem-solving, and agreement? An evaluative training—where the goal emphasizes a monetary settlement?
- What mediation experience do you have? Some mediators are former judges. Others have experience mediating community disputes (for example, landlord-tenant), commercial disputes (e.g., business-to-business, or B2B), or serving on a mediation

panel of a particular court (personal injury claims). Their experience may enable you to predict their orientation.

- How would you describe your approach? Variables often include: Does the mediator frame the issues broadly (addressing every concern the parties raise) or narrowly (restricting discussion to the legal cause of action)? Is the mediator facilitative (helping parties make their own decisions) or evaluative (supplying recommendations and opinions)?
- And multiple questions targeted at process dynamics: Does the mediator primarily address parties or the lawyers? Make an opening statement explaining her process and then ask the parties and their representatives to make opening statements in turn? Urge the attorneys to present their legal case or focus on bargaining issues? Work mostly in joint session with all parties present, or more in caucuses, where the mediator goes back and forth between parties located in separate rooms?

Once you know the answer to such questions, you can effectively discuss with your client who might be the best mediator and help the client make an informed choice.

Your Negotiation Strategy

For lawyers and other advocates in mediation, what should your own negotiating approach be?

As with any negotiation, your goal is to persuade the other side. A combative approach tends to be counterproductive. Differentiate your role as an advocate in an adversarial process and in a consensus-building process. In a consensus-building process, you need to be persuasive to the other side—i.e., convince *them,* either directly in a joint session, or indirectly via a mediator who uses caucuses, to adopt mutually agreeable settlement terms. Stated differently, you must use your strong advocacy skills in a way that invites your counterparts' engagement and doesn't turn them off.

Here is a list of desirable advocate traits and tasks that promote that goal:

- *The right attitude.* Display courtesy. A respectful tone and good listening skills generate trust and collaboration. Attacks and threats, by contrast, polarize participants and prompt a defensive, less creative posture.

- ***An articulate presentation.*** Crisply identify your client's interests, clarify the negotiating issues, and explain your proposals; summarize those of the other side so that they are confident that you understand them. Highlight common interests. Your client should be prepared to tell a moving and clear story. Use charts and visuals if that will help tell it.
- ***A good listener.*** Listen to your own client, reframing their comments where necessary to help all participants understand. Display the same skill set when summarizing the statements of other participants.
- ***Know Your BATNA (best alternative to a negotiated agreement).*** Be prepared to explore the BATNA of your own side and the other side: How long might a litigation take? How much would it cost? What sort of suffering is involved if the matter stays unresolved?
- ***Support your ideas and proposals.*** Use objective criteria and reasons to support the options you propose. Be prepared to give examples.
- ***Look for a "win-win" outcome.*** Where possible, if you can make an outcome that is a "win" for you into a "win" for both sides, you will move quickly to resolution.
- ***Use the mediator to help build understanding, problem-solving, and agreement.*** Mediators are there to help negotiating parties. Use the mediator to record interests, issues, and proposals on a flip chart—so that goals, challenges, and opportunities stay visible to all. Use the mediator to share private information that might shape the direction of the outcome. Ask for the mediator's advice regarding constructive bargaining moves. Use the mediator to conduct a brainstorming process to get more ideas on the table.

Modifiers, Caveats, and No-Go Areas— When This Advice Won't Apply

There may be limits to your choice of mediators. What if the other side very much wants a particular mediator? In such a case, you might simply go with that mediator to make your counterpart comfortable.

What if you want a facilitative mediator and the other side wants a mediator who provides evaluative input? Propose that if and when one party wants a mediator evaluation, both sides must agree that using such a process would be helpful, and, presuming such agreement, jointly request it.

Or, what if free mediation services are connected with a particular court and you are *assigned* a mediator? If possible, research your mediator and, where appropriate, talk with that person before the mediation starts, so that you and your client can be properly oriented and, perhaps, share with the mediator your suggestions regarding the approach that you and your client would find most helpful.

Conclusion

Make sure you are clear about your client's objectives and creative about pathways to achieve them. Adapt your negotiation style to the particular type of mediation you have chosen. Then, seize the moment: mediation offers tremendous opportunity to those who have chosen the mediator carefully and are prepared to grasp its benefits.

This Ties in With:

Honeyman, Ch. 47, Using Mediators; Mayer, Ch. 48, Allies

47

The Mediator and You

Chris Honeyman[1]

Introduction

To take a case to mediation, once rare, is now a common experience for lawyers. Mediators can be highly skilled and claims of neutrality as well as quality of service are universal. Yet both the qualitative and neutrality claims warrant a closer look. This chapter summarizes decades of thinking about how mediation works, and about its practical limitations in both areas. It is based on C. Honeyman, *Working with Mediators,* in 2 The Negotiator's Desk Reference 683–696 (Honeyman & Schneider eds, 2017). The full references in that chapter can be found at www.ndrweb.com/chapter-97--public.html.

Why This Concept Might Change Your Thinking

More than thirty years ago, the author, then a full-time mediator-arbitrator, repeatedly encountered some troubling phenomena.

1. **Chris Honeyman** is managing partner of Convenor Conflict Management, a consulting firm based in Washington, DC. He is coeditor of *Negotiation Essentials for Lawyers*, *The Negotiator's Desk Reference*, and five other books, and author of over 100 published articles, book chapters, and monographs. He has directed a thirty-year series of research-and-development programs in conflict management (see www.convenor.com/projects). Chris has also served as a consultant to numerous academic and practical conflict resolution programs, held a variety of advisory roles with the American Bar Association (ABA), International Mediation Institute (IMI), and other organizations, and served as a mediator, arbitrator, and in other neutral capacities in more than 2,000 disputes.

In one, some parties, or more often, factions within parties, seemed ever-ready to leap to an accusation of bias whenever presented with unwelcome suggestions by a mediator—while many fellow mediators seemed ever-ready to claim blanket neutrality on behalf of all of their actions. A first effort to analyze sources of bias within mediation revealed *nine different kinds,* some of which a mediator could not avoid. At the same time, the analysis suggested that for the most part, these biases were far from conclusive as to their likely result in practice and that some of them might even cancel each other out. Certainly, parties and lawyers should know this.

A concurrent issue was presented by a stark difference in mediators' results and reputations within a single work group. This led to an analysis of how a mediator actually works, which in turn revealed a set of skills that parties and lawyers might intelligently look for in a mediator, at least in the given setting. Subsequent studies have shown that exactly how the skills should be defined and prioritized varies according to the disputing culture involved in the particular case. So an understanding of how the skills of mediation actually apply to your particular matter may affect how skillfully you can select the right mediator.

Action Plan—What You Can Do Differently Tomorrow

When deciding on a mediator or your strategy for a mediation, it's best to keep in mind three factors that influence how the mediator will behave: (1) skill differences, which tend to be large in a largely unregulated profession; (2) policies and philosophies, which are generally overt and therefore predictable; and (3) biases, which are often unrecognized by the mediator.

Skills

Some "mainstream" mediation programs operating in the US have used mediator skill definitions along these lines:

1. *Manage the Startup:* Effectively begin a productive relationship with the parties.
2. *Gather and Comprehend Facts:* Effectively identify and seek out factual information relevant to the case, and sift and organize information that has been gathered.

3. ***Understand Underlying Positions and Interests:*** Draw out and understand the parties' essential concerns and needs, whether or not they are articulated in factual information.

4A. ***Express Empathy Verbally:*** Be consciously aware and considerate of the needs and values of others.

4B. ***Express Empathy Nonverbally:*** Be aware and considerate of the needs and values of others, in body language and other ways not captured by Scale 4 A.

5. ***Convey Impartiality:*** Convey a sense of neutrality to the parties.

6. ***Manage the Personalities:*** Effectively cope with strong personalities and conflicts between clients and professional representatives.

7A. ***Assist Parties in Generating Options:*** Pursue collaborative solutions, and assist parties in generating ideas and proposals consistent with the facts and workable for opposing parties.

7B. ***Generate Options:*** Generate ideas and proposals consistent with the facts and workable for opposing parties.

8A. ***Assist Parties in Generating Agreements:*** Effectively help the parties move toward finality.

8B. ***Generate Agreements:*** Effectively move the parties toward finality and "close" an agreement.

9. ***Move the Parties Toward an Improved Relationship:*** Effectively help the parties move toward better relationships with each other and third parties.

10. ***Manage the Interaction and Conclusion:*** Effectively manage the concluding process.

Policies

In practical use, such definitions often come with detailed criteria for each, varying by culture and omitted here for space reasons. But even as shown here, it should be obvious that at least at a high level, each of these characteristics represents an aspirational ideal for a mediator, not what's expected of a typical mediator. (One of the top mediators in the US once reviewed such a list and declared that he thought he could hit the top note on two or three of the scales—on a good day.)

Thus a good mediator will show real strength in one or a few of these areas and be adequate in the rest. But since different mediators have different areas of strength, and intend to *use* their talents, you should expect them to act quite differently. And they do.

The (a) and (b) variants of criteria 7 and 8 above, meanwhile, reflect differences in mediators' (and entire programs') *intent*. In these variations, mediators who see their role as helping parties settle a given dispute might look to the (a) definitions. But mediators who believe their purpose is to help empower parties and help them handle disputes better in future will stress the (b) definitions. Moreover, relative strengths on criteria such as these may well influence what kind of mediation a given professional gravitates toward in the first place. For example, someone with unusual skill in both varieties of criterion 4 might gravitate toward family mediation; high-level public policy mediators, from personal observation, seem to be unusually strong in criteria 6 and 10; mediators of high-dollar commercial disputes are likely to show particular strength in criteria 7B and 8B. Outside mainstream US mediation culture, the differences in intent are certainly larger.

Bias

Equally influential in the subtle actions of a mediator are potential or actual biases. Among these, the bias most people think of most, a preference for one party over the other, may be the *easiest* to guard against—and therefore the least problematic. But even a brief rendition of possible biases in mediation has to include the following:

- Apparent (as opposed to actual) personal bias.
- Biases resulting from the mediator's source of appointment (e.g., an international mediator appointed by the secretary-general of the UN is unlikely to suggest solutions that tend to disadvantage the UN itself).
- The tendency for mediation to encourage discourse based on interests and rights rather than raw power—inevitably helping weaker parties more than stronger ones.
- The tendency, in disputes involving groups, for mediation's focus on dialogue to favor moderate factions within each party, at the expense of radicals.
- The risk, for similar reasons, that minority interests within a group will get less play in mediation.

- The possibility that an agent (such as your opposing counsel; perish the thought that it might be you) might use the confidentiality of mediation, and the ability to communicate with the mediator away from the principals, to explore deals that favor the agent's interests over those of her principals.
- The pressure to "produce" a deal on a timely basis, which may lead a mediator to press for the *first* mutually acceptable outcome at the possible expense of the *best* mutually possible outcome.
- The possibility that a "bad actor" could use confidentiality, plus the mediator's need to maintain acceptability, to cloak proposals made in bad faith.

Yet all *other* processes raise their own bias and skill concerns too, of course. The bottom line is that these aspects of mediation, in the real world, should be taken into account in selecting and working with a mediator—but should not be overblown. And indeed, sophisticated parties and lawyers have known all of this for a long time and have used mediators successfully on countless occasions. None of the issues noted here outweighs the value that a skilled mediator can bring to the parties.

Modifiers, Caveats, and No-Go Areas—When This Advice Just Won't Apply

The examples given above, particularly with respect to skills, derive from Western, particularly US, culture. And within that, they derive primarily from kinds of mediation that can be defined as a "case." For mediators operating in other cultures, particularly collectivist ones, or mediators who operate as a continuing presence in the parties' lives, adaptations are necessary both as to which definitions of skill should be applied and as to what constitutes a bias worthy of consideration.

Conclusion

Both biases and differences in talents are facts of life. Those described here should be no more alarming than such legal biases as the presumption of innocence or the burden of proof. The growing use of mediation, and its frequent success, show that the effects of bias are limited, that the talents available are considerable, and that parties can learn to live with imperfection.

The fact that the biases not only exist but apply in different ways to mediators with different balances of skills, different personal histories, and different sources of appointment, adds to the differing policy choices among even rather competent mediators to produce a remarkable variety of possible conduct. A lawyer should not in any way be put off mediation by this analysis. She should, however, consider all these elements when choosing a mediator.

This Ties in With:
Love & Stulberg, Ch. 46, Mediation

48

The Lawyer as Ally and Coach

Bernard Mayer[1]

Introduction

As professional negotiators, we try to do all we can, using the most powerful tools at our disposal, to advocate for our clients. This often means taking over a negotiation from our clients and keeping them in the background or away from the negotiating table entirely. But assuming the primary responsibility often disempowers clients, fails to recognize the important role they can play as direct participants, and neglects the impossible situation this creates for the many clients who cannot afford the high costs of legal representation. If instead of viewing our primary role as that of an advocate, we take the broader perspective of being an ally, a powerful new set of roles, tools, and strategies becomes accessible. This chapter is based on B. MAYER, *Allies in Negotiation*, in 2 THE NEGOTIATOR'S DESK REFERENCE 707–724 (Honeyman &

1. **Bernard Mayer**, Ph.D., is Professor of Dispute Resolution in the Negotiation and Conflict Resolution program at Creighton University's Department of Interdisciplinary Studies and a founding partner of CDR Associates. Bernie has provided conflict intervention for families, communities, NGOs, unions, corporations, and governmental agencies throughout North America and internationally for over thirty-five years. Bernie's latest book (2015) is *The Conflict Paradox: Seven Dilemmas at the Core of Disputes*. Earlier books include *The Dynamics of Conflict*; *Beyond Neutrality*; and *Staying with Conflict*. Bernie received the 2015 John Haynes Distinguished Mediator Award presented by the Association for Conflict Resolution and the 2013 President's Award presented by the Association of Family and Conciliation Courts.

Schneider eds, 2017). The full references in that chapter can be found at www.ndrweb.com/chapter-99--public.html.

Why This Concept Might Change Your Thinking

When we view ourselves primarily as allies, we readily see that direct advocacy is only one of a wide range of roles potentially useful to our clients, including consultant, coach, strategist, spokesperson, and counselor. But the most profound difference is in how we see our relationship to our clients. As an advocate, we tend to see ourselves as in charge of the negotiation. We create documents, formulate offers or responses to offers, manage the process, conduct the face-to-face interactions, instruct our clients on how to handle direct interactions they may have with other parties or their representatives, and draw up any agreements reached.

This is a role that many clients want and need, but there are two major problems with this model of the professional-client relationship. One is that many clients cannot afford the costs of this labor-intensive approach. Perhaps the most significant challenge that justice systems across the common law world (and elsewhere) face is the tension between providing genuine access to justice, in a system premised on the availability of legal representation, and the reality that fewer and fewer people can afford full representation. That is the major reason why upward of 50 percent of clients in civil and family cases are self-represented. One response to this has been the increasing use of limited-scope retainers, sometimes referred to as unbundled legal services, which allow lawyers to function as an advisor without taking on the responsibility for an entire case. An attorney using a limited scope agreement might choose to play a variety of roles. For example, they may offer an initial legal assessment, review documents or agreements, prepare clients for a deposition, or advise them on how to handle a direct negotiation. This approach has long been available to lawyers but its use is still very limited.

These are all legitimate ally roles, and lawyers have often functioned in this manner, but these roles may not address the second problem. They do not change the nature of the relationship from one in which the lawyer provides expert advice to one in which the lawyer genuinely empowers clients to negotiate on their own behalf. Only when we truly understand the power that clients can bring as their own best representatives can we maximize the client's effectiveness. When negotiation professionals embrace the value of acting as supporters, coaches, and consultants, rather than defaulting to being case managers and lead negotiators, we are best able to address the constraints that drive so many to represent themselves.

Action Plan—What You Can Do Differently Tomorrow

Perhaps the best manifestation of this in practice is the emerging role of the negotiation coach. Everywhere we turn, it seems, we find new incarnations of the professional coach. We see executive coaches, personal coaches, lifestyle coaches, divorce coaches, legal coaches, and conflict coaches. Some of this is, of course, a fad. But it also reflects something important about the role of the coach, drawn from the world of sports. What is appealing about coaching, I believe, is that at its best it is about helping someone develop their own capacities through teaching, practice, feedback, encouragement, and planning. Coaches do not take over the task from clients. Instead, they focus on the development of their capacity and execution.

Coaching is just one ally role, but an important and powerful one, particularly but not only for clients obligated to act on their own behalf. So I will focus on this particular role here. To be effective as an ally-coach requires a set of attitudes and skills that are often obvious, but always challenging:

Clients Are Powerful (and Competent)

To be effective allies, we have to believe that our clients have the capacity to be effective negotiators. This does not mean that they can suddenly understand the intricacies of the legal system, but that they can articulate their concerns, understand their choices, and make sound decisions. This requires:

- Taking their ideas, concerns, suggestions, and insights seriously. In other words, we need to focus on what they have to say and treat it as valuable input, rather than just on the message we want to deliver and the information we have to impart.
- Recognizing and building on their power. Not all clients will be skilled negotiators, but all have strengths that they bring to the table that we can build on.

- Appreciating the importance of emotions and values in negotiation. Clients are often particularly effective at speaking to the emotional and moral dimensions of the issues involved in a negotiation. Far from being a distraction, these are often the key to finding common ground, to moving a process forward, and changing unproductive power dynamics. This means listening for the emotional message and helping clients express this in an effective way.
- Accepting clients' decisions even when we disagree with them. Even better, unless a decision is illegal or unconscionable, we should not assume we know better.

One Size Does Not Fit All

Clients are different, with different strengths, weaknesses, life experiences, and needs—even if their legal, financial, or substantive concerns are very similar. Unless we develop the capacity to assess our clients' needs and capacities and to modify our intervention accordingly, we are not likely to be effective allies. This means:

- Developing our ability to assess not only our clients' negotiating position, but also the strengths and liabilities they bring as direct negotiators.
- Crafting our intervention based on those strengths. For example:
    - If they are well versed on the facts but have a difficult time separating the essential from the nonessential, then we should help them prioritize what is most important, what will make the most impact on others, and how to present these.
    - If they are likely to shut down, become either overly aggressive or inhibited when faced with a forceful argument or rebuttal, or if they are so conflict-avoidant that they may agree to the first offer they are presented, we may want to work with them on slowing down their response, taking time-outs, or insisting that they be given the time they need to consider any tentative agreements before finalizing a deal.
- Identifying the "one thing" that clients should particularly focus on. Effective coaches do not leave their clients with the

35 most important things for them to work on. They may conduct a wide-ranging discussion about what is important but, in the end, they should emphasize one or two things that will make the most difference. None of us can handle more than that in the midst of an intense activity—whether it is skiing or negotiation.

- Consider how far we can push our clients. Finding that sweet spot where we can push clients beyond their comfort zone but not beyond their capacity is often the key to effective coaching.

Good Listening Is Key—and Harder than It Looks

- Good listening requires that we genuinely believe that our clients have something important to say, that we don't already know what they are trying to communicate, and that we have to work together to make sure we are communicating effectively.
- We often give lip service to this, and almost all of us think we are great listeners, but unless we are working hard at communicating, we are probably not doing it well.
- Helping our *clients* learn to listen in negotiations, even in the face of some pretty unpleasant messages from others at the table, is often the most important contribution we can make. And we need to start by doing it ourselves.

Conclusion

We are all allies and coaches at times, and we all have those who function in this role with us. This is a natural part of life. We need allies and so do our clients. But when we work with clients who will be negotiating for themselves, we often forget the most important element of being an effective coach—believing in their capacity to be effective and committing ourselves to maximize this capacity. The assistance that we all need in preparing for negotiations is not only or even mainly about substance, but about process, communication, and attitude.

This Ties in With:

Love & Stulberg, Ch. 46, Mediation; Reynolds, Ch. 51, Activism

Section X

Getting It Done

The final section of the book addresses the strategies that we need to close that deal. Chapter 49 is about ambiguity and how a bit of ambiguity just might be the grease that gets the deal done. Or, one could think about how, for any resolution to be possible, many disputes and other negotiations require a lawyer to adopt more than one kind of role. Chapter 50 explains the dual role of Doberman/Diplomat.

But sometimes, what a situation needs is somebody who will really shake things up. Chapter 51 assesses the possibility that an activist might not (always) create conflict, and instead might sometimes be essential in resolving it. Of course, if the matter is to be truly *resolved*, you'll want the agreement to hold. So, Chapter 52 addresses how to make sure that when you and your counterparts finally do "sign on the dotted line," the results stick.

Finally, we close with Chapter 53, which gives examples of how dispute *prevention* can work—and maybe even reduce the need for many of the strategies discussed in the book—when lawyers actually think about all of this in advance!

49

The Discreet Charm of Ambiguity

Chris Honeyman[1]

Introduction

Lawyers are trained to dislike ambiguity. Yet ambiguities abound in contracts. When interests are strong or parties are motivated by principle, either calculated or innocent ambiguity can supply the lubrication necessary for the gears to move—and it can be not only useful, but a morally defensible act, under the right circumstances. This chapter is based on C. HONEYMAN, *The Uses of Ambiguity*, in 2 THE NEGOTIATOR'S DESK REFERENCE 609–617 (Honeyman & Schneider eds, 2017). The full references in that chapter can be found at www.ndrweb.com/chapter-91--public.html.

1. **Chris Honeyman** is managing partner of Convenor Conflict Management, a consulting firm based in Washington, DC. He is coeditor of *Negotiation Essentials for Lawyers*, *The Negotiator's Desk Reference*, and five other books, and author of over 100 published articles, book chapters, and monographs. He has directed a thirty-year series of research-and-development programs in conflict management (see www.convenor.com/projects). Chris has also served as a consultant to numerous academic and practical conflict resolution programs, held a variety of advisory roles with the American Bar Association (ABA), International Mediation Institute (IMI), and other organizations, and served as a mediator, arbitrator, and in other neutral capacities in more than 2,000 disputes.

Why This Concept Might Change Your Thinking

Under quite common circumstances, ambiguity can reasonably be used to moderate otherwise unacceptable risks. Of course, an agreement that is clear, easy to administer, and durable is best. But lawyers represent principals who must live in an imperfect world. They may contend with disagreements, within their own party, almost as serious as those with its nominal opponent; factions within a labor union that must negotiate as a bloc with an employer are a classic example. Especially in these circumstances, the more radical members of your side may see clarity of language as a weapon in their internal battle with moderates—and if they prevail, an overall agreement becomes much less likely. An ambiguity here or there may allow the moderates to keep control of the negotiation and thus allow a deal to be made. The key in using (or tolerating) an ambiguity is to understand how the ambiguity will be applied in practice. *If* the agreed-on enforcement mechanism is appropriate to this end, leaving ambiguities can imply that the disposition of subsidiary disputes will be fact-driven and moderate in overall effect.

Action Plan—What You Can Do Differently Tomorrow

Ambiguity is often thought to imply either an unconsidered point or a deliberate failure to come to grips with the problem. These interpretations suggest that where there is ambiguity there is no agreement. But if push comes to shove, an arbitrator is often called in for a final interpretation—and a standard piece of advice to arbitrators has long been that agreements are to be read as a whole. Parties have impliedly anticipated that agreement-readers will strive to do so.

I believe the interpretation of an ambiguity depends largely on the enforcement mechanism specified in the agreement. Suppose you are negotiating different matters with two parties at the same time. Each party sends you a draft agreement. In the event of a later dispute over its interpretation, one proposed contract calls for mediation, followed by arbitration, if necessary. The other draft contract specifies good-faith negotiations but provides for either party to sue in the courts of Singapore for enforcement. By chance, in another section, both drafts also contain the exact same clause—a rather ambiguous one. Will that clause, in practice, mean the same thing in both contracts?

Every agreement contains at least one express or implied means of securing compliance with its terms. But when exposed to ambiguity, *different mechanisms of enforcement generate different results.* So an agreement, read as a whole, can in fact provide a functional interpretation to the ambiguity.

The choice of negotiation, mediation, arbitration, litigation, or unilateral action implies something about the balance of power within each party as well as that between the parties. Negotiation, for instance, inherently preserves to the parties the power to create something new; but it always requires a backup process, since settlement cannot be guaranteed. Mediation is similar. But both processes imply more. They anticipate some give-and-take, suggesting that parties specifying these processes are willing to settle for a moderated result in a given case, one that is likely to draw as much from the exigencies of circumstance as from principle. Compared with the rights-only implication of specifying litigation, or the raw power-display of unilateral action (such as, in a labor context, the right to strike over grievances) that expectation of give-and-take is likely to result in significant differences in the practical interpretation of ambiguous language.

Litigation as the "bottom line" mechanism, meanwhile, also implies that the parties jointly accept high expense and also a complainant's burden of proof. So the contract example specifying the courts of Singapore as final arbiter is imposing a significant cost on a party that later wants to challenge some action under the contract. That suggests in turn that when an ambiguous clause is later at issue, a larger sphere of unilateral discretion flows to the "acting party," and correspondingly less to the "responding party." And so on. Thus which process, or combination of processes, the parties choose can be an index to the interpretation of other parts of the agreement.

Labor agreements provide an excellent illustration, because they have a long history of using negotiation, mediation, and arbitration, often as steps in the same dispute—and labor and management are also no strangers to litigation or unilateral action. Arbitration, in this context, is particularly revealing. Unlike other domains of alternative dispute resolution (ADR), the history is thoroughly documented, with thousands of labor arbitration awards published and codified, and with many prior grievance settlements discussed in those awards.

Also, arbitration alone combines the terminating force of an imposed decision with a value system theoretically drawn from the agreement itself. If in fact ambiguity implied the absence of an agreement, the thousands of reported pronouncements of labor arbitrators on ambiguous clauses should reflect that. The fact that they typically do not is instructive. Finally, labor arbitration's principles come as close to pure reliance on the perceived intent of the parties as decision-making systems get. It is significant, therefore, that labor arbitration awards concerned with ambiguous contract language, in effect, tend to apply a general rule that *ambiguity implies moderation.*

For example, the common clause in labor contracts providing that an employee may be discharged (or disciplined) for "just cause" is clearly vague. So why do so many parties use it, even though contracts which lay out specific grounds for discharge do exist, and provide a clearer alternative? Well . . . the company agrees to "just cause" because it is hard to maintain a claim that it should have the right to discharge employees for unjust reasons or no reason at all. The union agrees to it because it is hard to maintain that employees who by definition are getting what they deserve should be kept on the job. Even a cursory review of the vast profusion of cases decided under this standard shows that the awards are generally moderate in tone and fact-driven. And while the parties routinely complain about the result, they rarely change the underlying standard.

The long line of subcontracting (or in more recent parlance, "outsourcing") cases supplies a second illustration (detailed in the underlying chapter in the *Negotiator's Desk Reference*), which draws from a different kind of ambiguity. But the principle is the same. In either example, the negotiators who constructed the agreement and the arbitrator who interprets it all show their relationship to the moderate and radical elements on both sides by the practical and predictable result of their actions. The arbitrator in particular—a creature of the agreement and, one hopes, uniquely sensitive to its nuances—serves the moderates' goals by distinguishing between tolerable and intolerable incursions into each party's "principles." The arbitrator couches her decision in terms of the agreement, and strains to avoid using the term "equity" in order to escape the accusation of the radicals on the losing side that the award does not "draw its essence" from the agreement. And in turn, the courts refrain from second-guessing the arbitrator. At the same time, the "bargaining in the shadow of the arbitrator" that takes place in the earlier stages of grievance processes ensures that the vast majority of grievances are resolved at relatively low transaction costs, preserving to both parties the financial ability to contest a grievance to the point of arbitration when they feel they must. From the point of view of the moderate on either side who desired a workable if not ideal agreement, *the various processes of dispute resolution thus form an intricate ecology, in which each process depends on the others for the success of the whole.*

The result for negotiators is that ambiguity can be employed as a tool in achieving an adequate, if imperfect, settlement of a dispute. This enables the moderates in either party to avoid reliance on rhetoric and ideology, and to compel discourse on terms acceptable to them.

Modifiers, Caveats, and No-Go Areas—When This Advice Just Won't Apply

One critical element is the negotiator's careful analysis of whether any subsidiary disputes seem likely to be manageable. If the negotiator suspects that a proposed ambiguity will *not* be interpreted according to the kinds of standards applied above, but instead be subject to unilateral action, this is a strong danger signal. Under these circumstances, fostering an ambiguity means taking on a technically difficult and morally problematic calculation of the "mutual best interest" of the conflicting parties. While ambiguity is usable, no one has said ambiguity is easy to use.

Conclusion

Where a "moderating" system is likely to be applied for the disposition of subsidiary disputes, gracefully admitting the impossibility of a complete meeting of the minds may be nothing more than a recognition of reality. Under those circumstances, to allow an ambiguity to pass into the agreement is just another way to get the agreement done.

This Ties in With:

Wade, Ch. 42, Limited Authority; Wade & Honeyman, Ch. 52, Enduring Agreement

50

Being Both a Doberman and a Diplomat: How to Reopen Deadlocked Negotiations

John Wade[1]

Introduction

This chapter sets out seventeen common strategies used by skilled problem solvers, including lawyers, to reopen negotiations between deadlocked disputants. As at least 95 percent of client claims eventually settle, lawyers (or their teams) are schizophrenic: they are steadily building diplomatic bridges ready for the settlement, while at the same time they are growling Dobermans on the surface. This chapter is based on J. WADE, *Dobermans and Diplomats: Reopening Deadlocked Negotiations,* in 2 THE NEGOTIATOR'S DESK REFERENCE 639–653 (Honeyman & Schneider eds, 2017). The full references in

1. **John Wade** is an emeritus professor of law of Bond University, Queensland, Australia. He practiced as a lawyer in Australia between 1987 and 2012 and also had an active mediation practice in organizational, family, and commercial conflicts during those years. He has taught over 300 mediation and negotiation courses in Hong Kong, New Zealand, London, Canada, the US, and Australia. John has published over 100 books and articles (see epublications@bond.edu.au). His teaching awards include best law teacher at Sydney University (1989); at Bond University (1990); and in Australia (1998). John now lives in Vancouver, Canada, with his growing family; he teaches intensive negotiation courses there.

that chapter can be found at www.ndrweb.com/chapter-94--public.html.

Why This Concept Might Change Your Thinking

Opening jammed negotiations is difficult, because people in long-term conflict usually do not want to be perceived as weak. The negotiator wants to give out *double* messages of aggression and peace-making. For example, lawyers commonly say on the telephone, "Before our clients start up World War III again, should they talk first?" Words are important. Experienced lawyers do *not* usually say "My client would like to avoid World War III, can we talk?" At a high level, this requires uncommon skills and character. Yet I have found *seventeen* methods that have been used successfully.

Action Plan—What You Can Do Differently Tomorrow

Most clients respect their lawyers more if they can set out options beyond the predictable alleyways of stalemate. A lawyer can routinely assist a client, at the right moment, by illustrating some of the seventeen reopening options. These are organized by actions we can take ourselves, actions with the other side, and then actions using a third-party process.

1. Conciliatory Signals

A conciliatory signal is a small, often subtle, comment or action that indicates a willingness to be helpful, even cooperative. It may amount to a minor act of politeness or kindness amidst a long-term battle. One function of these signals is that it may create cognitive dissonance for both the sender and receiver, helping both to recognize that things could yet be different.

2. Superordinate Goals

It is common during a stalemate for a disputant to announce to the media, or to one of the parties on the other side, that "despite our differences, we do have a number of things in common." These speeches, letters, or diagrams may need to be repeated at strategic moments by key parties on all sides.

3. Expressing Willingness to Discuss Procedure (Negotiating about Negotiating)

Moderate members from each side can often reopen negotiations on *procedural* topics. A request for better negotiation procedural rules is not usually interpreted as weakness. The implication can be preserved that "we will still be tough when and if the *substantive* negotiations resume." Possible topics might include finding a neutral location; setting a formal agenda; changing key negotiators or representatives; setting time limits; or setting procedural rules, such as who may speak or how records of the meeting will be kept.

4. Vigorous "No Surrender" on Interests

This strategy consists of one or both parties making public or discreet statements that whatever solution is reached, it *must* incorporate certain vital interests. The speaker has thereby communicated that she is willing to move off an initially preferred solution—as long as any suggested alternative embraces her interests and goals.

5. Flexibility on Specific Solutions

This is a signal given by one or both of the disputants that there may be several acceptable solutions, not just the single historical entrenched demand. This is often coupled with a restating of the client's general goals.

6. No Unilateral Concessions

This is a powerful face-saving strategy for the person who has backed oneself into a corner by insisting over years that there is only *one* possible solution—mine. The message of tit for tat could be "If *X* is going to move off her historic offer, she must be given something in exchange" or something similar.

7. Clearly Reject Unacceptable Past Solutions

Insisting that a *particular* past solution is totally unacceptable can placate hawks on one's own negotiating team, warn about potential exasperation caused by recycling rejected solutions—and yet indicate some flexibility.

8. Prioritize Interests

This involves acknowledging the deadlock but nevertheless agreeing to list issues from most important to least important from one's team's perspective. Disputants then agree to return to the negotiating table with their respective lists of priorities, as possible trade-offs may be thus revealed.

9. Back-Channel Contacts

While the official and public negotiators are posturing, unofficial meetings can take place. The back-channel personnel may be friends, relatives, or technicians (for example, accountants in family feuds). They have no authority to settle and they speak as individuals, *not* for the organizations or tribes. The back-channel meeting may have a real or feigned secretiveness.

10. Keep Communication Open

Often associated with back-channel contacts, this may appear platitudinous where disputants have been in a long-term deadlock. However, the suggestion has subtle and powerful applications. Knowing that the standard dynamics of pushing to the extreme *will* occur, a wise conflict manager will preserve a line of communication with some key person, ready for the eventual settlement.

11. Reward Others for Helpful Initiatives

Whenever a member of the opposition does anything helpful, an effort is made to express thanks or be helpful in return. This act encourages repetition of a cooperative cycle and undermines dehumanized and demonized stereotypes of the opposition.

12. Mild Threats or Consequences

One or both disputants can make a mild threat such as "If we both continue to come up with no solution, then—!!"

This strategy is dangerous, as it appears to be a tired repetition of the past history of threats and counter threats. The subtle differences are that the tone is not hostile, there is often an element of *mutual* harm, and the consequences are presented not as cataclysmic, but still painful. The threatened consequences are presented as systemically inevitable (distraction from work; alienation of relatives; investigation by tax officers).

13. Identify Division between Hawks and Doves

One disputant communicates to the other that "It's not my fault that I'm being so unreasonable and entrenched. I'm trying to satisfy a whole team, some of whom are hawks. But others are willing at least to explore possible solutions."

14. Acknowledge the Other's Interests

Often in the "fog of war," entrenched negotiators cannot accurately articulate what is important to the other side. Obviously, a fundamental negotiation skill is to listen, and then to demonstrate to the other person that she has been heard, by attempting to restate what has been said.

15. Use of Intermediaries

The intermediary may act on his or her own initiative, actual or feigned. Or she may insert personal interests as an added form of authority—"If you each fail to make some constructive offers in the next month, I will withdraw my vote/subsidy/weapons supply/testamentary provision, etc., from you." Or she may be approached by one party, as a person perceived to have moral authority, neutrality, and wisdom by the other disputant(s).

16. Assemble an Expert Problem-Solving Team

One or both disputants announce publicly that a team of experts has been or will be assembled to study the problem and come up with a range of alternatives and recommendations. This shows the problem is being taken seriously; creates time for passions to cool; removes problem individuals from direct negotiations; reserves power to the disputants to reject the team report; gives disputants some time to attend to other business; raises the possibility that the expert team will discover creative solutions; and raises the possibility that the team may find possible systems for *future* conflicts.

17. Make a Formal Claim

Commonly used by lawyers, this strategy is intended not to invoke a third-party *decision*, but rather to invoke some incidental procedures attached to filing. Both the pluses and minuses should be communicated to clients. On the plus side, a formal claim provides:

1. A series of sanctioned deadlines and mandatory processes for the exchange of information.
2. A series of official forms, with deadlines, that may create a degree of sworn clarity about positions and supporting evidence.
3. Usually, additional pressure to settle due to added costs and work.
4. Some time, ritual, and orderly process whereby passions may cool.
5. An ultimate deadline (trial date), to terminate procrastination.
6. A code of ethics during conflict.
7. Potential involvement of an expert or mediator with new perspective on "how these conflicts normally are settled."
8. The settlement in a consent order rather than in a "mere" contract, allowing ready supervision later by a court if need be.

However, The Potential Disadvantages Are Also Many, Including:

1. A formal claim may be interpreted as confrontational.
2. More courts now have aggressive case management practices. The disputants lose control of the *timing* of negotiations and may be pushed quickly toward an actual hearing.
3. The disputants may similarly be pushed quickly into procedural appearances.
4. In some cultures (particularly, certain Asian cultures), filing a formal claim is considered to be a form of public insult, necessarily adding a layer of offence to existing dysfunctional communications.

Modifiers, Caveats, and No-Go Areas—When This Advice Just Won't Apply

Beware of being too eager for agreement by relying too heavily on any one or more of these strategies. At the same time, working steadily on *realistic* alternatives can pay dividends.

Conclusion

This chapter has set out seventeen standard strategies in a negotiator's repertoire for recommencing communications where a deadlock has occurred. These strategies are essential to the daily work of litigation and transaction lawyers, managers, politicians, and diplomats—otherwise known as "conflict managers."

This Ties in With:

Craver, Ch. 4, Classic Techniques

51

Thinking of Activism as ADR

Jennifer W. Reynolds[1]

Introduction

Is activism part of alternative dispute resolution (ADR), or is activism the opposite of ADR? At first blush, one might conclude that activism—often characterized by partisan agendas and an unwillingness to compromise—is incommensurate with the principles and skills associated with negotiation, mediation, dispute systems design, and other foundational processes of ADR. Yet thinking of activism this way ignores the history of ADR and unnecessarily curtails the potential breadth of alternative methods. By exploring how activism and resistance fit into ADR practices—in other words, how the "alternative" of ADR may include "activism"—we may enrich our dispute resolution practice. This chapter is based on J.W. Reynolds, *The A Is for Activism*, 2 The Negotiator's Desk Reference 743–758 (Honeyman & Schneider eds, 2017). The full references for that chapter can be found at www.ndrweb.com/chapter-101--public.html.

1. **Jennifer Reynolds** is an Associate Professor at the University of Oregon School of Law. She teaches civil procedure, conflict of laws, negotiation, and mediation. Her research interests include dispute systems design, problem-solving in multiparty scenarios, and cultural influences and implications of alternative processes. She serves as the faculty director of the nationally ranked, award-winning Oregon ADR Center, and is the co-chair of the Legal Education Policy Committee for the American Bar Association (ABA) Section on Dispute Resolution. Before law school, Reynolds worked as a systems analyst and associate director for information technology at the University of Texas at Austin.

Why This Concept Might Change Your Thinking

Many dispute resolution professionals focus on process. We seek to build containers for conflict (e.g., mediation sessions, town halls, settlement talks, dispute management systems) that allow people to speak their truths, share information, vent emotions, explore options, and perhaps find agreement and closure. Within these containers, we move toward interests and away from partisan positions, because we know that entrenched positions make it impossible to handle conflicts effectively. We also attempt to model active listening, empathy, and other communication skills that improve understanding and relationship among everyone involved. We do not push for one particular resolution, or in fact for any resolution; instead, we strive to create the conditions in which the parties are able to work together on how to move forward.

Given these process commitments, it is not easy to see whether and how activism might ever be an effective response to conflict. Activism, after all, often features values-saturated, highly positional rhetoric and hardline tactics that tend to delegitimize other people and perspectives. Activists often reject overtures to negotiate and refuse to engage in dialogue with opponents. They are suspicious of the containers and processes we build, and in fact may try to dismantle them. With this in mind, it is easy for dispute resolution professionals to think of activism as an obstacle and to develop strategies that reduce or eliminate activist approaches in conflict management.

But shutting out activism may situate ADR in the uncomfortable position (uncomfortable because ADR is supposed to be neutral) of preserving the status quo and thus fortifying the stronghold of powerful, entrenched interests. This is ironic, considering that the modern ADR movement itself has activist roots. Early ADR pioneers sought to transform institutionalized systems of justice by creating dispute resolution processes that addressed disputes holistically and situated the parties as decision makers. These pioneers disrupted settled procedures and upended social norms, making it possible to reimagine and reengineer conflict resolution. Given this history, we should be careful about being too fastidious about our own processes.

Action Plan—What You Can Do Differently Tomorrow

You may find that the default ADR responses (negotiation, mediation, facilitation, and so on) are not always workable in a particular situation or for particular clients. If the only thing we can offer clients dealing with conflict is interest-based negotiation or mediation, then they may be unable to take steps toward resolving their conflict depending on the context of the dispute, the substance of the disagreement, or the willingness of others involved to participate. This may be true, for example, when clients are seeking large-scale political change that may not be suited to litigation, or when they are defending values that, for them, are nonnegotiable. Just as we may consider litigation as one possible avenue for people in conflict, we may want to consider activist approaches as another.

With this in mind, instead of thinking of activism as the opposite of negotiation, try thinking of activism as a special type of negotiation—a negotiation in which values are of high importance and the available methods include what we might consider "hard bargaining." On this view, activism is a complex form of negotiation that exists in an open system, often with indeterminate participants and loose, shifting leverage; it does not conform to the dyadic contained structure that we teach students and attempt to manage as practitioners. Even so, like all negotiations, activism can be analyzed as a matter of parties and relationships, interests and values, power, strategy, and process. Paying more attention to how activism works will open you to a different set of tools for conflict and expand your ability to advise clients around the potential for engaging in or responding to activism.

Moreover, taking activism seriously may allow dispute resolution professionals to better reflect on the larger structure in which we work. How do traditional mediation and negotiation tend to preserve or disrupt the status quo? Where are the limits of neutrality, consent, and self-determination in particular conflicts? Interrogating the relationship between process, institutional violence, and structural oppression is exactly the kind of analysis that early ADR pioneers engaged in when they set out to transform the dispute resolution culture. Today, many of us are ideologically invested in the principles of our field (neutrality, civility, peace), which in turn can make us suspicious of activism, since activism is long on advocacy and sometimes threatens violence. But to the extent that we are invested in those principles, we need to be aware of how they may be used to promote or preserve agendas that may not match up with our intentions.

With this in mind, you can immediately improve your thinking around the connections between activism and dispute resolution by doing two things: external analysis and internal reflection.

First, consider refining your analytical perspective on activism. Every day we see reports on people mobilizing around particular issues. As an expert in conflict and dispute management, you are accustomed to thinking about what works well and what should be done differently when it comes to negotiating thorny issues. With this in mind, examine whether and how a particular movement might be gaining or losing traction. What moves are the leaders making, and what rhetoric appears to work? How durable are the impacts that the activists are making? What additional moves, such as building alliances or raising publicity, might lead to better outcomes—and how would "better" be defined? How does context (setting, timing, etc.) affect activist choices and effectiveness? Analyzing activism in this way is admittedly an armchair exercise, but one that nonetheless can have significant impact on your thinking about what moves are possible or desirable in particular situations.

Second, take some time to reflect on your own ADR practice. What drew you to the field? What keeps you in the field? How do you think dispute resolution should intersect with activism and politically charged issues? Is anything outside the bounds of traditional dispute resolution processes? Because many of us are trained mediators, we may find ourselves at a crossroads whenever we encounter a politically charged conversation. Is it our primary responsibility to facilitate the discussion, which often means putting our opinions aside, or can we decide to engage as an advocate? And if we do engage as an advocate, have we lost our ability to facilitate? Is it possible to be a facilitative advocate? These questions are not easy but may be useful inroads to thinking more deeply about the professional and personal tensions in our field.

These two moves—analyzing current activism and reflecting on our own philosophical and practical commitments—help remind us that we exist within a historical moment, within our own experience and biases, and must therefore always be examining what we are doing and why. When it comes to causes that we or our clients care about, we need to be thoughtful about how to draw lines around what can or cannot be talked about; or whether giving equal time to all disputants creates an unacceptable false equivalency; or when we personally can or should take a stand.

Finally, for those wanting to take this exercise further, consider offering support to activists. We can learn from their campaigns (which are a form of negotiation) while providing expertise and insight on how they might think through particular interactions or challenges, inside and outside the activist group. After all, ADR is not just for court-connected conference rooms, corporate offices, mediation centers, guidance counselor offices, and other institutional spaces; moreover, ADR is not just for private interpersonal conflicts and one-on-one difficult conversations. Let's see what comes of pushing the boundaries of alternative practice.

Modifiers, Caveats, and No-Go Areas—When This Advice Just Won't Apply

Some environments are legally or organizationally constrained, such that professionals working within those environments may feel that they lack discretion to apply the suggestions here. That said, if you perceive that your role dictates that you participate in an ongoing injustice, then there may be no option (that is *both* moral and practical) other than to withdraw from providing service.

Conclusion

Exploring how activism operates as an alternative approach to working through conflict and (perhaps) working toward agreements will refine our ability to handle conflict appropriately and authentically. In addition, such an exploration has the potential to improve the quality of activist efforts themselves. Activism is hard—it's hard to get people involved, hard to keep people involved, hard to make a lasting impact. If negotiation and conflict experts study activism and advise activists on their strategies and communications, activists may be able to extend their influence and effectiveness as they work for lasting change and a true resolution of the tensions underlying the "presenting" dispute.

This Ties in With:

Welsh, Ch. 26, Fairness; Amsler, Ch. 45, DSD; Mayer, Ch. 48, Allies

52

Creating an Enduring Agreement

John H. Wade[1] *and Chris Honeyman*[2]

Introduction

What percentage of negotiated agreements in various types of transactions or types of conflict, or in various cultures, are actually performed as written or promised? For how long do agreements in these varieties or areas endure or stick? And is there anything you can do that will improve the odds of your agreement surviving?

1. **John H. Wade** is an emeritus professor of law of Bond University, Queensland, Australia. He practiced as a lawyer in Australia between 1987 and 2012 and also had an active mediation practice in organizational, family, and commercial conflicts during those years. He has taught over 300 mediation and negotiation courses in Hong Kong, New Zealand, London, Canada, the US, and Australia. John has published over 100 books and articles (see epublications@bond.edu.au). His teaching awards include best law teacher at Sydney University (1989); at Bond University (1990); and in Australia (1998). John now lives in Vancouver, Canada, with his growing family; he teaches intensive negotiation courses there.

2. **Chris Honeyman** is managing partner of Convenor Conflict Management, a consulting firm based in Washington, DC. He is coeditor of *Negotiation Essentials for Lawyers*, *The Negotiator's Desk Reference*, and five other books, and author of over 100 published articles, book chapters, and monographs. He has directed a thirty-year series of research-and-development programs in conflict management (see www.convenor.com/projects). Chris has also served as a consultant to numerous academic and practical conflict resolution programs, held a variety of advisory roles with the American Bar Association (ABA), International Mediation Institute (IMI), and other organizations, and served as a mediator, arbitrator, and in other neutral capacities in more than 2,000 disputes.

For example, low rates of durability (only 10-20 percent lasting more than twelve months) may attach to child visitation agreements in certain categories of families. Conversely, high rates of vendor-purchaser durability (85-90 percent lasting indefinitely) seem to attach to house purchases in Australia or America. Purchaser or bank mortgage contracts may also have high rates of performance amongst the middle class—until recession and job losses escalate.

Many of the factors that hinder *initial* commitment to reaching an agreement also contribute to undermining *ongoing* commitment to performance. Briefly noted below are some of the anecdotal reasons why negotiated agreements may not be durable; we then discuss tactics that can help. This chapter is based on J. WADE & C. HONEYMAN, *An Agreement that Lasts*, in 2 THE NEGOTIATOR'S DESK REFERENCE 655–669 (Honeyman & Schneider eds, 2017). The full references in that chapter can be found at www.ndrweb.com/chapter-95--public.html.

Why This Concept Might Change Your Thinking

Lawyers interested in reaching a deal may not always think through whether the deal will hold. But a long list of factors can interfere. Cultural expectations of flexibility (in many cultures) are just one reason why a deal may not be as final as the paperwork seems to imply. Others include complex ongoing obligations (the more complex the terms of any negotiated agreement, the higher the likelihood that some obligations will break down over time); "shallow peace"; buyer's remorse; changed circumstances; legal rules that allow setting aside an agreement based on—for example—innocent or negligent, let alone fraudulent, misrepresentation; *lack* of consistent legal rules due—for example—to expense, delay, uncertainty, or corruption; lack of informed consent; loopholes in contract drafting; deferral of important points to later fine-tuning; conditional agreements subject to others' ratification; and great wealth of one party, creating an unequal ability to tolerate years of legal fees in case of a breach. For most of these threats, however, there are techniques that can help to avert them.

Action Plan—What You Can Do Differently Tomorrow

If the above is a catalog of possible reasons for agreements being breached, or being less than durable, how then to make negotiated agreements more durable?

In simplistic terms, as with the original perceived incentives to *enter* the agreement, *performance* can also be made attractive, and nonperformance made unattractive, via economics, emotion, various versions of morality, reputation, legal rules, and accessible, affordable, and honest legal enforcement mechanisms.

If some of the durability or stickability elements cannot be added to the dynamics of the agreement, then expectations should be lowered. The parties may have achieved one success criterion, namely a (signed) agreement. But they may only have a low or moderate chance of another measure of success, namely performance. Many risk-taking negotiators are willing to buy the chance of performance and then experience the rollercoaster of performance and breach, as the predicted ratio of performed to non-performed agreements is still considered to be a worthwhile investment.

The chances of performance of an agreement are enhanced by the following:

- Try to enter contracts with people, groups, or nations with whom there are strong long-term relationships. This provides a layer of incentives to perform promises rather than alienate friends and future business.
- When negotiating with cultural groups that perceive an agreement as mainly the beginning of a relationship, be prepared for a lengthy series of rounds of negotiation in exchange for the promise of a long-term relationship.
- Attempt to clarify across cultures whether "yes" means "maybe" or even "no," and whether signed and detailed documents are considered to be binding, morally, legally, and/or in reputation—or just amount to the declaration that a working relationship now exists, with the actual commitments subject to continuous renegotiation.
- Include a serious discussion and contractual clauses (more than boilerplate) on how future misunderstandings and problems will be addressed procedurally and emotionally by skilled people (dispute resolution clauses).
- Tactfully negotiate and agree early that if problems occur later with performance, then these will ultimately be resolved at a specified court or arbitration venue. Such a specified venue should ideally be, first, not corrupt, second, governed by stable

and clear legal precedents, and third, governed by legal precedents that have minimal scope for varying or setting aside the particular type of agreement.

- Where possible, convert a negotiated dispute settlement into a court order so that any breach of the agreement immediately opens additional enforcement mechanisms.
- Draft the agreement in detail, if possible, in accordance with standard industry practices.
- Contract with stable countries and people, cultivate back-up suppliers, and take out insurance as risk management for non-performance or currency fluctuations.
- Include carefully planned procedures for managing hawks and armchair critics in the background.
- Lower expectations, where there is long-term escalated conflict with some of the emotional and structural changes attached to such entrenched conflict. This particularly applies to tribal conflicts in Ireland, the Balkans, Israel, and parts of Africa, but also within many families and businesses. The first year, decade, or century of agreements will undoubtedly not be durable with such dynamics in the background.
- Attempt to enter agreements that recognize the procedural, emotional, and substantive needs of all parties. An aggrieved negotiator at any of those levels will probably be looking for payback or exit at a strategic moment.
- Where a negotiator is on an emotional rollercoaster, try to include his or her long-term friends, doves, moderates, associates, allies, or business partners in the negotiations. For years after the initial agreement is signed, they will exert pressure (ongoing negotiations) on the wavering party to honor his or her commitments, or risk losing their friendship.
- Do not walk close to the line on any of the legal rules, such as duress, deceit, vague terminology, or illegality, any of which gives other parties opportunity to allege a loophole to finality.
- Lawyers should use a range of standard clauses that attempt to negate duress, misrepresentation, and/or illegality, and which make specific allowances for future contingencies.
- Try to avoid complex agreements with multiple long-term obligations of performance; try to create clean-break obligations

where one performance is swapped for another (for example, a bank check upon delivery of goods); try to include self-enforcing clauses so that the transaction costs of enforcement are reduced (for example, interest rate of 12 percent runs on payments in default; security is held by a bank or by one party until performance occurs; payments are released upon progressive certification by an architect; liquidated damages; 1 percent extra for each day early; 1 percent less for each day late, etc.).

- Discover and perform an appropriate ritual of commitment—in some places, it is eye contact and a handshake. In others, it may be an alcoholic celebration or a vow in the presence of a holy book or priest.
- Attempt to reduce buyer's remorse by making congratulatory speeches about the benefits of the agreement, mentioning the list of risks that would follow no agreement; by never agreeing quickly to any clauses; by theatrical displays of anguish and pained speeches about the tough terms, special deal, or hard bargain that is being imposed; and by adding post-agreement gifts and bonuses (corner office, luggage racks, set of steak knives, 12 months' free warranty).
- Publicize the deal by mutual agreement. Then a wider audience places an expectation on all parties that they should perform or lose face and credibility in future arrangements. Most people have a strong desire to act consistently with their own clear commitments. Thus, a media announcement of a treaty, a takeover, or a trade agreement is more than a celebration; it is aimed at moving at least the visible parties from agreement to a deeper level of commitment.

Modifiers, Caveats, and No-Go Areas—When This Advice Just Won't Apply

All of the above options are potentially helpful to add degrees of legal, structural and emotional stability to a negotiated contract. However, clients should be warned with local statistics or stories that there are many common methods to default effectively on contractual obligations. These include declaring bankruptcy; fleeing overseas; dying; inflicting attrition by attack, lies and litigious processes; social and business isolation for the aggrieved complainer; refusing to perform the contract and offering instead some "damages"; promising future business opportunities to an aggrieved party; using corrupt, biased or incompetent judges or arbitrators; lobbying for legislation to override a class of contracts, and so on. Experienced lawyers are well aware of all of these loopholes and more, especially in cross-cultural contracts.

Conclusion

Most negotiators want more than an agreement. They want commitment and performance. It is helpful for negotiators, first, to be aware of the smorgasbord of factors that present warning signs of impending breaches; and second, to be aware of and skilled at working on those factors that increase the likelihood of commitment and performance.

This Ties in With:

Lewicki, Ch. 22, Trust; Groton et al., Ch. 53, Thinking Ahead

53

Pre-Dispute and Pre-Escalation Techniques to Improve New Business Relationships

James Groton,[1] Chris Honeyman,[2] and Andrea Kupfer Schneider[3]

1. **James P. Groton** is a retired partner in the Atlanta law firm of Sutherland, Asbill and Brennan (since 2016, part of Eversheds Sutherland), where he headed its Construction and Dispute Prevention and Resolution practice groups. Groton has conducted research and written extensively on processes used in the construction industry and other relationship-based businesses to prevent and de-escalate disputes (see www.jimgroton.com). In his work for the Global Pound Conference he advocates for broader use of these processes. He holds degrees from Princeton University and the University of Virginia Law School.
2. **Chris Honeyman** is managing partner of Convenor Conflict Management, a consulting firm based in Washington, DC. He is coeditor of *Negotiation Essentials for Lawyers*, *The Negotiator's Desk Reference*, and five other books, and author of over 100 published articles, book chapters, and monographs. He has directed a thirty-year series of research-and-development programs in conflict management (see www.convenor.com/projects). Chris has also served as a consultant to numerous academic and practical conflict resolution programs, held a variety of advisory roles with the American Bar Association (ABA), International Mediation Institute (IMI), and other organizations, and served as a mediator, arbitrator, and in other neutral capacities in more than 2,000 disputes.
3. **Andrea Kupfer Schneider** is a Professor of Law at Marquette University Law School, where she teaches dispute resolution, negotiation, ethics, and international conflict resolution and is the director of Marquette's nationally ranked dispute resolution program. Andrea has written numerous books, book chapters, and articles on negotiation skills and styles, dispute system design, international conflict, and gender and negotiation. She was given the American Bar Association (ABA) Section of Dispute Resolution Award for Outstanding Scholarly Work for 2017. Andrea received her A.B. *cum laude* from the Woodrow Wilson School of Public & International Affairs at Princeton University and her J.D. *cum laude* from Harvard Law School.

Introduction

In several domains of conflict—construction, international relations, and US labor relations—there are by now highly sophisticated and widely adopted techniques for reducing future conflict. These techniques cannot ensure outright that there will be only few such conflicts. But they make it more likely that the conflicts that inevitably follow the formation of a new relationship will be handled with a minimum of time, cost, and stress to all involved. For the most part, the evidence is that these systems work. Surprisingly, however, most other industries and domains have yet to adopt anything comparable. This chapter argues for broader adoption of these tools, and is based on J. Groton, C. Honeyman, & A.K. Schneider, *Thinking Ahead*, in 2 The Negotiator's Desk Reference 265–281 (Honeyman & Schneider eds, 2017). The full references in that chapter can be found at www.ndrweb.com/chapter-70--public.html.

Why This Concept Might Change Your Thinking

Smart companies, particularly in the construction industry, have been using with great success sophisticated tools for improving business relationships. These not only prevent and de-escalate problems and potential disputes, but sometimes achieve almost instantaneous resolution of them. The same tools also improve efficiency and business processes.

Through use of techniques such as these in any commercial relationship context, it is entirely possible to have a business relationship which strengthens over time, which fixes problems instead of fixing blame, and which never experiences a formal mediation, let alone an arbitration or litigation.

The availability and advantages of these "thinking ahead" techniques should by now have come to the attention of competent transactional lawyers who advise clients about commercial relationships. And it should be expected that those transactional lawyers would customarily make them known to their clients and advise them about such techniques.

Furthermore, "thinking ahead" advice is by now well enough known that in future it could be argued that a transactional lawyer's failure to provide such advice to a client who is about to enter into a commercial relationship would be a breach of the lawyer's duty to the client.

Action Plan—What You Can Do Differently Tomorrow

When discussing the formation of a new business relationship, the parties should anticipate that the business will experience future conflict. Representatives charged with negotiating an initial agreement should have the parties agree in advance to deal with each other in future in an organized and collaborative way, setting up a dispute control system that uses *problem-prevention* tools, *problem-solving* tools, and *dispute de-escalation and "real-time" resolution* tools to deal with future problems.

After the dispute control system has been incorporated into the contract that sets up the business relationship, the individuals who handled the negotiations for dealing with future problems should *continue to monitor* the collaborative problem-solving and conflict-mitigation process, to make sure that these processes and tools are implemented whenever a problem arises.

Among the specific thinking-ahead and problem-prevention tools that the parties' representatives could consider when establishing the dispute control system are the following:

Problem-Prevention Tools

- Good, open communications
- Realistic allocation of risks to the party best able to manage, control, or insure against particular risks
- Joint initial analysis of the potential for disputes during the course of the relationship
- Consideration of incentives that could enhance cooperation between the parties
- Establishing a "partnering" cooperative relationship

Problem-Solving Tools

- Notice and cure agreements
- Covenant of good faith and fair dealing
- Agreements that encourage rational behavior
- Internal tools in each organization that encourage problem solving

Dispute De-escalation and "Real-Time" Resolution Tools

- Negotiations and step negotiations
- Selection of an expert, trusted person to be a "standing neutral" (who can be readily available to provide impartial advice if the parties cannot immediately resolve a problem)

How these strategic practice tools work together both to reduce and to handle serious disagreements is graphically illustrated in the following flowchart. It contrasts the strategic approach with the

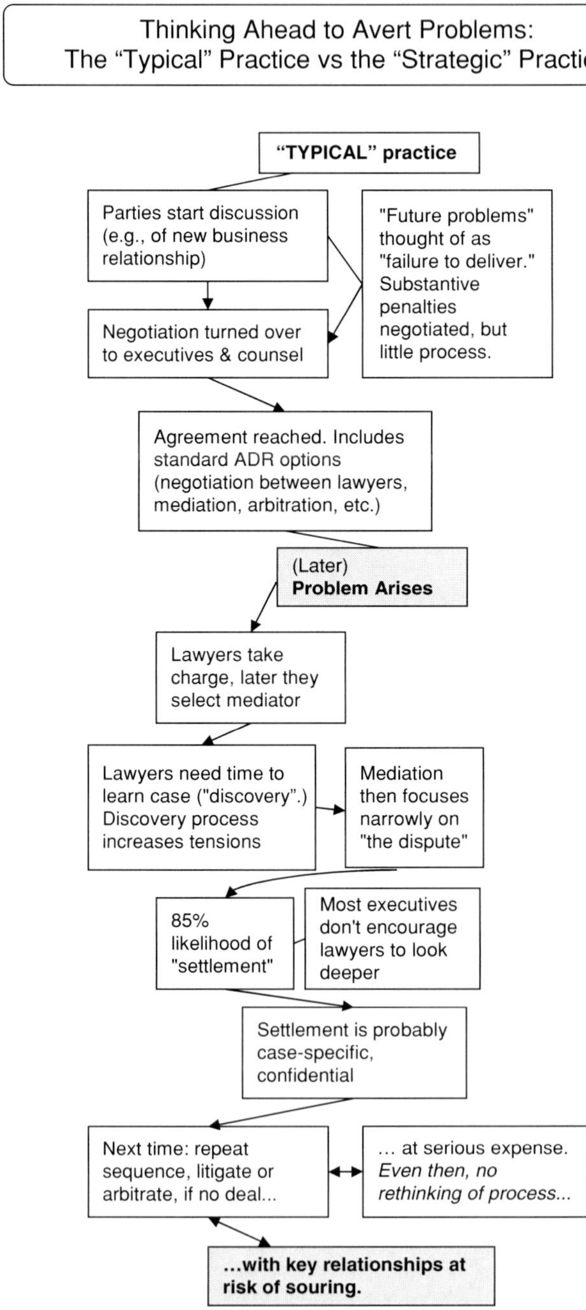

typical or "business as usual" approach that, unfortunately, obtains in most business relationships:

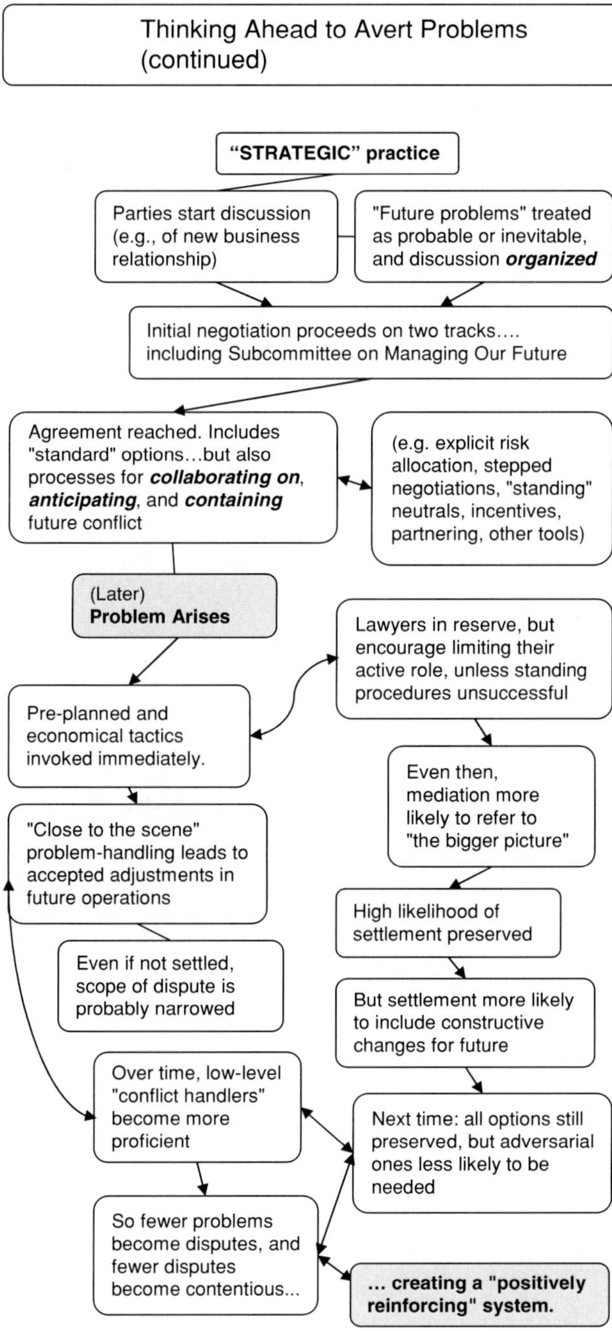

Modifiers, Caveats, and No-Go Areas—When This Advice Just Won't Apply

This does not apply, of course, to truly one-time transactions. That may appear to be a very large category. Note, however, that many relationships start with a single transaction that on its surface looks to be one-time. The parties may be well-served by erring on the side of expecting more interaction in future, in which case this chapter applies, after all. In fact, with this kind of planning, future interactions are more likely.

Conclusion

Using the proactive "up-front" techniques and principles that are outlined here and more fully described in our chapter in *The Negotiator's Desk Reference* is just as important for relationship-building and success-building as it is for avoiding, de-escalating, and preventing disputes. This is increasingly recognized: at the worldwide Global Pound Conferences on the future of dispute resolution (2016–2017), voting overwhelmingly favored prioritizing the use of "pre-dispute or pre-escalation processes to prevent disputes" over all other dispute resolution processes.

This Ties in With:

Borbély & Caputo, Ch. 44, Organizations; Amsler, Ch. 45, DSD; Love & Stulberg, Ch. 46, Mediation

A search engine replaces the index. And we have a special offer:

This book draws on the Canon of Negotiation Initiative's larger stream of publications. Instead of a fixed index, we have therefore provided a customized search engine. For example, searching for an author's name will not only identify all references that the author is relying on here, it will also show related chapters in the larger *Negotiator's Desk Reference* (NDR)—including the NDR's updates in volume 3. The search facility is at www.ndrweb.com/search and does not require purchase of the NDR.

Want more on negotiation?

By special agreement among them, the ABA, DRI Press, and NDR Books are pleased to offer a 20% discount on the Web edition of the full *Negotiator's Desk Reference* (C. Honeyman and A.K. Schneider eds, DRI Press and NDR Books, 2017). This discount is valid for any purchaser* of *Negotiation Essentials for Lawyers* and reduces the price of the full Web edition, including updates, to just $24.

The *Negotiator's Desk Reference* is, simply, the most comprehensive treatment of negotiation available. It has the background of each chapter here—and it also addresses *over fifty additional topics* that are important to a thorough understanding of negotiation, with more to be added in future in the NDR's updates volume (#3.) See www.ndrweb.com/about-the-ndr

If you prefer hard copy, the NDR is also available from Amazon and other booksellers everywhere.

*To take advantage of this offer, just send an email to wantmore@ndrweb.com and attach a copy of your receipt (PDF or photo). Instructions for using the discount will be returned promptly.